Death Row Saved My Life and Other Stories

Death Row Saved My Life and Other Stories

Finding Meaning in a Harsh World

Clifford Williams

RESOURCE *Publications* • Eugene, Oregon

DEATH ROW SAVED MY LIFE AND OTHER STORIES
Finding Meaning in a Harsh World

Copyright © 2026 Clifford Williams. All rights reserved. Except for brief quotations in critical publications or reviews, no part of this book may be reproduced in any manner without prior written permission from the publisher. Write: Permissions, Wipf and Stock Publishers, 199 W. 8th Ave., Suite 3, Eugene, OR 97401.

Resource Publications
An Imprint of Wipf and Stock Publishers
199 W. 8th Ave., Suite 3
Eugene, OR 97401

www.wipfandstock.com

PAPERBACK ISBN: 979-8-3852-6399-8
HARDCOVER ISBN: 979-8-3852-6400-1
EBOOK ISBN: 979-8-3852-6401-8

VERSION NUMBER 01/16/26

"poetry be lifez konversayshun with death" Copyright © 2018 by kétuoladuwa

"Found Dead" Copyright © 2026 by Ellen Palmer

Contents

Introduction | vii

Jesse: Invited to Tragedy | 1

1 Death

Kétu: Death Row Saved My Life | 9
"Evelyn": Burned in a Flash Fire | 17
Ellen: Found Dead | 23
Shirley: Death of My Infant Son | 36
"Tessa Mae": Swept Up Into the Clouds | 42
Saved from Suicide | 49
    "Annette": The Letter | 49
    "Naomi": Coloring in a Professor's Office | 53
    "Caleb": A Long Hug | 54
    "Caroline": Moral Beauty | 54

2 Family

"Sara": Betrayed by My Husband | 59
"Bella": Extricating Myself from Domestic Violence | 70
"Stephanie": A Schizophrenic Mother and an Abusive Father | 76

Lora: Homeless as a Child | 83
Katie: Finding My Birth Family | 90
Falling in Love | 102
    Ruby and David | 102
    Denise and Jon | 109

3 Hurdles

"Alliyah": A Black Woman's Journey Through Academia | 117
Jenni: Escaping My Heroin Addiction | 126
"Robyn": Fighting Anorexia | 138
"Ariana": Confronting My ADHD | 146
Michael: Recovering from a Stroke | 154
Rebecca: Surviving the Suicide Disease | 161

4 Transitions

Michelle: Transitioning to a Woman | 171
Amy: From a Refugee Camp to the United States | 181
Jonas: Growing Up Amish | 188
Bobby: Am I Really Gay? | 198
Kendall: The Audacity of Speaking Out | 208
Andrew: The Making of an American Rock Musician | 216
"Claudia": A Month and a Half in a Cult | 224
"Matthew": Disillusioned with Teaching | 231

Bibliography | 239

Introduction

Everyone has a story. And that story almost always involves some kind of trauma. The trauma might have been short-lived or have lasted for years. It might have come from a disaster or a disease, from a physical injury or an emotional wound. It is often difficult to defeat, with its effects becoming a major part of one's life.

Everyone also loves to hear a story in which trauma is overcome. The hero gets past a seemingly impossible barrier. The besieged victim rises above adversity. Suffering does not win in the end.

This book contains just such stories, nearly all of them involving major adversity. Though Ellen found her husband dead on the floor of their bedroom after being away for a week, she did not wither away. "Bella" extricated herself from domestic violence. Kétu did not let death row kill him.

I got these stories from my friends and acquaintances and also from their friends, plus occasionally from the friends of their friends. In everyday conversations, my ears perked up when I heard something that sounded as though there was a something behind it. I asked whether I could listen to that something. I also asked nearly everyone I talked to whether they knew anyone who had a good story. They knew what I was looking for, and some did know.

I was often astonished at what I heard. I had no idea that "Ariana's" life had been upended with ADHD. I never suspected that Michelle, whom I had known as male presenting, had been struggling with her gender identity all her life. And until I knew these about them, I realized I didn't know

INTRODUCTION

them very well at all. For these were at the core of who they really were, embracing their self-identity.

I was also astonished at the variety of stories I heard. "Evelyn" almost died in a flash fire. "Annette's" suicidal impulses began to dissolve with the arrival of a letter from someone she had never met. One Sunday morning, Jonas walked away from the Amish community he had grown up in. Bobby was not able to admit that he was gay until his midthirties.

I interviewed each person via video call, then edited the transcription of each interview for readability. The edited stories were approved by each person. I used their real names except for some who wanted pseudonyms, which are enclosed in quotation marks.

If everyone has a story, then I do too. My wife of nearly fifty-seven years died three years ago. She had begun to deteriorate due to Lewy Body dementia, gradually losing her ability to walk, talk, or eat. Even though I had that time to prepare for her death, it was more painful than I ever imagined it would be. When I discovered that she was no longer breathing first thing one morning, the image of her lying completely motionless, with her eyes shut and her mouth open, instantly began to haunt me.

During the coming weeks I had tortuous fits of sobbing. Though they did not last long, they were excruciating.

I could scarcely get up in the morning. Although I sensed that life could be good again whenever I talked with someone, that sense left as soon as the call ended or we parted. I felt paralyzed—I could not do the things I had previously loved.

At times I wondered why there is such a thing as death. Actually, it was less wondering and more a piercing resentment at death's having taken my Linda.

Mostly, I simply went through the motions of staying alive.

There was no precise moment when things began to change. I kept doing numerous video calls. I saw people, sometimes on the front porch and sometimes for walks. They listened and gave warm affection. I started going to lectures and musical events at a nearby college, occasionally running into people I knew. I gradually increased the length and speed of my walking.

Doing these functioned as a rescue operation. The people I encountered eased me from constant, incapacitating sorrow. I felt that I could love life all over again. The gratitude I had for those with whom I spent time itself felt life-giving. I moved beyond the interlude I had been in.

INTRODUCTION

The stories in this book begin with Jesse's "Invited to Tragedy," which invites us to become acquainted with tragedy—actually, more than that: to feel tragedy acutely. To use Jesse's words, we are invited "to grasp painful human experience more sharply."

It is painful to feel another's pain. But our pain can be replaced with delight when we learn how tragedy and trauma have been overcome.

Pain can also be replaced with illumination: "So that is what my friend experienced."

And with identification: "That is just what I went through."

Along with satisfaction that comes from having fulfilled one of life's great ends: to feel keenly both the tragedy and the magnificence of human existence.

Doing this book was not just an impersonal academic project. My eyes teared up as I was writing Katie's account of meeting her birth mother. I was elated when I learned that "Ariana's" life was transformed after being treated for ADHD. I felt a deep connection with each person as they let me into the secret recesses of their hearts, the places they don't let just anyone.

In Jesse's words from an informal conversation, I found it fulfilling when the people I interviewed "revealed their raw emotions" to me. They made themselves vulnerable, and I felt a contented satisfaction when "they opened up their true selves."

Sometimes I felt like a counselor, one who listens without judgment and whose listening helps heal. On occasion, I stared out the window and wondered, "What is this thing called life with its suffering and anguish?" I asked myself, "Do I myself have to go through severe trauma to know how to live?"

I found myself admiring the arduous work the people I talked to had done to overcome emotional pain. I felt gratitude for coming to know an important strand of their life stories.

Jesse: Invited to Tragedy

"Looking into the faces of victims causes me to grasp painful human experience more sharply. I see people for who they are."

After graduating from college, Jesse became an interpreter for Spanish-speaking patients in health care settings while serving in El Salvador in the Peace Corps. His interpreting both there and in the United States brought him into contact with numerous people who were experiencing severe trauma. He himself had to deal with the trauma of witnessing that trauma. That witnessing prompted him to feel "the rawness and reality of life along with intimacy" with those people. Jesse was twenty-five when we talked.

The Blind Woman

The first interpreting Jesse did was for El Salvadorians who were seeing eye doctors. "A woman who had been blind for ten years came in. She couldn't even see her own hands waving in front of her. Typically that would mean that she had a very dense cataract or something more serious. The ophthalmologist examined her and found that she didn't have a cataract. She had myopia, he thought, a bending, or a squishing, of some part of the eyeball, which could be corrected with a lens. She would be able to regain 100% of her eyesight.

"I was elated to tell her this. The woman, who was in her forties or early fifties, wasn't expressive facially, but I could hear in her voice what it would mean for her to be able to see again. She was quiet, but there was a sense of excitement between her and the doctor and me."

What happened next, Jesse said, was that the doctor measured the degree to which the woman's eyes were deformed and estimated the strength of the lens she would need to correct her vision. "That was stronger than any lens the doctor had, but he thought he could use a slightly weaker lens, which he did have, to restore part of her sight until he could get a stronger lens. We were expecting that the woman would be able to see with the lens the doctor had.

"She was not.

"The doctor then used a different machine to look into the back of her eyes and discovered that she had retinal scarring. This meant that she would be permanently and incurably blind.

"I had to tell her that. I felt that I was taking away something we had given her, almost like breaking a promise.

"I had a profound sadness. The simple thing that we believed would help this woman see again was taken away in an instant.

"I held her hand. I often held the hands of the eye doctor's patients I interpreted for, because they could not see well. I led them to a chair and sat down with them. Particularly for the older women, touch was part of their interaction. I especially remember holding this particular woman's hand.

"The woman's reaction to hearing that she was not in fact going to be able to regain her sight was not pronounced, but it was definitely a deflation. She had gotten up her hopes but then had to resign herself to not getting her sight back. Despite this, she was very gracious. She didn't blame me or the doctor. In her words she communicated, 'Oh, well. I thought I'd come in case you could do something. And you haven't been able to, so that's okay.'"

Jesse led the woman out of the room and through the hallways of the cathedral in which the health clinic had been set up, holding both of her hands while he walked backwards and she walked forwards so that she could negotiate steps. They went back to a pew in the cathedral, where she waited for someone from her family.

"I have come back to this experience a number of times," Jesse said. "We three were ecstatic when we believed the woman would get her sight back. And then we became sad and disappointed, and lost all hope, when I communicated to her that she would not get it back."

Vicarious Experience

"There's something about interpreting that lets me vicariously experience other people's emotions," Jesse said. "I am going through some difficult or traumatic or scary situation with them. My own daily life does not typically have the fear or disappointment or even the anger that I witness when I interpret. This is good, because it means that my life is not constantly filled with trauma and disaster. But I like feeling the emotions of people who are in scary or vulnerable positions.

"Maybe 'like' isn't quite the right word. A better way to put it is to say that there is something satisfying about experiencing the emotions of people who are in the midst of trauma or disaster. There is the satisfaction of knowing that I am meeting someone's need to communicate. There is also the satisfaction of having access to emotions that make me feel alive. I feel impactful things, serious things, raw things."

Jesse does not have that satisfaction every time he interprets. "But I definitely had it with the woman in El Salvador. I felt something very human, very basic. I felt the rawness and the reality of life along with intimacy with another person. All these combined to make me feel acutely alive."

Emergency Rooms

In the States, Jesse has interpreted in the emergency rooms of hospitals. On one occasion, he interpreted for a man who had been stabbed in the back with a four-inch kitchen knife. It was hard for the man to speak, because the knife had punctured one of his lungs and his lung had collapsed.

"I told him things like, 'The doctor is putting in an IV now. You're going to get a shot. You'll feel this, you'll feel that.' It was extremely harsh for me to watch. Seeing someone who had been stabbed, seeing huge quantities of blood all over the bed and dripping onto the floor—it was a reminder of human mortality.

"It is one thing to see that on television, but when it happens in reality, it's a whole other thing. To see a victim of violence who was vulnerable and weak was a totally new experience for me.

"I don't know what happened to the man in the emergency room after he was taken away. He had asked me a few times whether he was going to be okay, whether he was going to die. I said that to the doctor, who said, 'No, he probably won't die,' which I communicated to the man. He was very

Stoic, did not have much emotion, didn't cry at all. It was painful for him to breathe. I don't remember my last words to him—probably something along the lines of, 'You're going to feel a pinch in your arm.'"

Psychology Clinic

Jesse has also done interpreting at a psychology clinic, where he interpreted for clients who were seeing a psychologist or psychiatrist. The repeated, one-hour appointments provided long, sustained opportunities to be "let into the secret regions of their lives."

"One of the persons I interpreted for was a sixty-year-old man who was schizophrenic and in a difficult situation at home. He lived with his daughter, who did not want him there, which she had made clear. He had not had work in ten years. He had been in jail in Cuba, had lived on the streets in the U.S. for a long time, had been marginalized at school. I had enough interaction with him over several months so that I was able to see him more holistically than I imagine other people do. I heard things about him that I am guessing few people knew.

"Although it was disturbing to interpret for this man, it was much more disturbing to interpret for a four-year-old girl who had been sexually abused at a daycare center. I got called into a children's hospital and interpreted for the girl and her mom. The girl was very explicit about what had happened to her. She talked about a big boy at daycare taking her into a room by herself and taking her pants off and touching her. I felt intense distress and sadness. Her mom was crying throughout the entire forty-minute consultation. The girl cried when the doctor, who was a woman, tried to examine her. She recoiled at any touch of the doctor. To witness the anguish that the sexual abuse had created in the mom and the discomfort in the little girl made sexual abuse very personal to me."

Connecting to Others

"That," Jesse declared, "is one of the meaningful things about interpreting. Even though it is very upsetting to hear what some of the people I interpret for say, I learn about reality in an intimate way. I perceive it more clearly. Looking into the faces of victims causes me to grasp painful human experience more sharply. I see people for who they are."

Sometimes Jesse is able to talk to people outside an office or the emergency room at a hospital. "Recently I interpreted for a woman who had moved to the U.S. from Mexico three months earlier. Her daughter had gotten a respiratory virus and had been in the hospital for four days. I had a chance to talk to the woman for a little bit in a waiting room. We talked about her move from Mexico and about how cold it was here. She told me what it was like to live in a country not knowing the language.

"There was nothing in our conversation that was much different from a lot of other conversations. The rewarding thing about it was simply that we connected. And that was true of my other experiences of interpreting."

1 Death

Kétu: Death Row Saved My Life

"From that point on, my every thought, my every inclination, was that if the state of Massachusetts was going to kill me, I was going to know who I was."

Kétu was arrested in 1966 and convicted for murder. Up until the time the judge pronounced him guilty, he believed he was going to be released but instead spent five years on death row. Kétu was in his late seventies when we talked. Italicized passages are from his poem, "poetry be lifez konversayshun with death." © 2018 by kétuoladuwa. His website is at www.rootfolks.com.

Before Death Row

From birth to about nine years old, Kétu's life was idyllic. "I was raised in a village twenty miles north of New York City in a foster home where I was loved and cared for. Our house was on High Street: *the oldhouse alive with luv, sound & feeling.*

"I remember sitting with my back to an old oak tree, my feet in the stream that ran past it, watching the wildlife, the pheasants, and the foxes.

"The dirt street we lived on was tarred during the summer to keep down the dust. I liked to chew on that tar: *an impishboy chewing sweetblakktar/dug frum highstreet.*

"I roughhoused with Michael. One day, we set fire to the dry weeds in a vacant lot. When we could not stomp it out, I ran home and hid in the bathtub, which I filled with warm water as the fire engines sirens wailed. It was my first real fear: *twoboyz—wunblack, wunwhite/in thetall grass with matchez./laffing at theirown mischief.* Then: *a burning lot, flamez & fumez/& thenasty nayscent tuch uv firstfear.*

"I climbed trees. I played war. I dreamed of grandeur. *Life waz good. theboy karedfor/luvd, cherished in wayz fosterkidz didnt muster.*

"When I was nine or ten, I ventured beyond my immediate neighborhood. Outside of High Street's safety there were unfamiliar people and situations that scared me. Within that fear, I developed a personality that relied on violence to keep people away from me. My protective armor became my willingness to do violence.

"That became my reputation. I didn't have any trouble. I didn't have any problems. People understood that I would go to war.

"I chased things that young Black men on the street chase, all the things that are written about in the press. Though I didn't get involved in drugs, I did do alcohol, marijuana, and theft. These were my rites of passage.

"I had some run-ins with the law and got an ultimatum from a neighborhood cop, who said that the next time he caught me doing something I shouldn't be doing, I would go upstate. That meant prison. The fear drove me into the service at seventeen. I stayed until I was twenty."

The Murder

The murder occurred a year later. "I went to Springfield, Massachusetts, where I had been in the service. I was going to go to the Newport Jazz Festival in Rhode Island with some friends whom I'd served with in the Air Force. At a party my former roommate threw on the Saturday before the 4th of July, there was a young woman named Carolyn Willis. She was the fiancé of one of the guys I'd been with in the service. That party was the last place Carolyn was seen alive.

"A week or so later, my former roommate, his brother, and Carolyn's fiancé were arrested and detained in the Springfield County Jail. I and other guys from the base were out in the community trying to find out who had killed Carolyn.

"The police questioned me on the Wednesday or Thursday after the body had been found and after my friends had been jailed. I was at the station for about twelve hours before they let me go. I went back into the neighborhood for the weekend trying to find information that would get my three friends out of jail.

"The following Monday or Tuesday morning, the police called me back down to the police station. This time they kept me there for forty-eight hours. About hour thirty-six, I told them that I would tell them anything they wanted to know if they would just let me get some sleep. I had been surviving on coffee and candy and was running on adrenaline. The police were harassing me. At hour forty-eight, I caved and signed a dictated confession.

"My thinking was that when they investigated the case, it would become evidently clear to them that I was the wrong person and that I didn't have anything to do with the crime.

"That calculation was obviously wrong. The police had no intention of investigating anything. They had a body that they could fill a slot with. And I was it.

"I didn't have any support, because I wasn't from that community. My community was back in New York. Nobody there knew what was happening to me, and there wasn't anyone to advise me. I was advising myself. Given my political unsophistication and my social naïveté, I was easy pickings. Plus, there was an election the coming fall. The district attorney, who was the prosecutor, was up for reelection and needed the Black vote. The case was gory and spectacular, which gave him a media spotlight and name recognition in the Black community to get reelected.

"I had been arrested in July of 1966, and by October of that year I was on death row. Even back then, that time frame was unprecedented—just three months from arrest to conviction.[1]

"The whole time I was in jail and throughout the trial, I believed I was going to go home. There was no evidence except the confession I had given to the police under duress. There was no physical evidence. There were no supporting witnesses. There was nothing else. My attorney tried to have my confession thrown out, but the judge wouldn't allow it.

"Up until the time I was sitting in the dock, chained, waiting for the verdict, I was convinced I was going home. But when I heard the judge say, 'You have been convicted, and may God have mercy on your soul,' I woke up. It was not until then that the reality of the situation I was in came into focus."

---

1. Kerrigan, "Ronald Fisher sentenced October 4, 1966, for the killing of a 15-year old girl."

DEATH

Into Prison

"I vividly remember being taken to the entrance of Walpole State Prison by the state police.[2] They handed me over to the prison guards who took me through an iron gate that slammed behind me. Life got real then. The guards walked me to the back entrance of the cell block and then past the electric chair. They made sure to stop there to let me see the place I was going to leave the world.

"For the first couple of weeks, I told everyone I talked to that I didn't have any business being there. I wasn't guilty. Then I had a conversation with Pete, who was also on death row. He stopped by my cell and told me, 'Listen. Don't you know that everybody here is innocent?' It became clear then that I was going to have to change my mindset.

"My mother visited me four or five weeks later, during Thanksgiving. She asked me whether I had killed the person. I told her no, and she told me that I would be there for five years, two months, and some days. Mama's prophecy missed the mark by only a month."

A New Focus

"From that point on," Kétu said, "my every thought, my every inclination, was that if the state of Massachusetts was going to kill me, I was going to know who I was. Why was I in the position I was in? I needed to understand that. It became my whole focus.

"I began to read, and read and read and read, between five to six hundred books during the whole time I was in prison. Every book filled one of the empty spaces in me.

"I read Tao Te Ching, the Bible, and the Koran, plus histories of Afrika, the Americas, and Europe. I read magazines ranging from *Popular Mechanics* to *Ebony*. I read *The Souls of Black Folks* by W. E. B. Du Bois, *The Autobiography of an Ex-Coloured Man* by James Weldon Johnson, *Soul on Ice* by Eldridge Cleaver, *Malcolm X Speaks* edited by George Breitman, *Seize the Time: The Story of the Black Panther Party and Huey P. Newton* by Bobby Seale, *Black Power: The Politics of Liberation* by Kwame Ture and Charles V. Hamilton. I read James Baldwin, Charles W. Chesnutt, Zora Neale Hurston, Langston Hughes, and contemporary poets, including

---

2. Now called Cedar Junction. "Massachusetts Correctional Institution."

Amiri Baraka, Haki R. Madhubuti, Gwendolyn Brooks, Margaret Walker, Sonia Sanchez, and Nikki Giovanni.

"I watched the nightly news on a television that was sitting directly in front of the cell I occupied. That was the time of the Great Black Rebellion in the U.S., and from 1964 until 1968 or 1969 America was on fire every summer. I kept up with all that was happening.

"I also watched programs about the Black experience on WNET, New York City's public television station. There were programs on the changes that were taking place among people of Afrikan descent, changes in their understanding of who they were and of their identity. We Black people had moved from being colored and Negro in the forties and fifties to being Black in the sixties.

"When I was growing up, I had accepted the White version of my history. But now the new framing of Black history that was happening in the U.S. was also happening in me. I came to a new understanding of political and cultural history. I adopted a new notion of the idea and practice of race in America and how I fit into that picture."

Feeling Free

Kétu felt liberated. "Being in prison was the best thing that ever happened to me, because it gave me the opportunity to free myself from the idea of what America was supposed to be. That idea is what put me on death row. It is the idea that you're innocent until proven guilty, the police are there to protect and help you, and they do their job.

"I came smack up against these ideas and saw the lies in them. What I learned from reading transformed my thinking and my idea of myself. By 1968, two years after I was convicted and sent to prison, I was liberated. Though I was in prison, I was free. That sense of freedom became a political practice and a new identity."

The Politics of Power

In 1968, Kétu and two others on death row bum-rushed the deputy superintendent's office.[3] "It was Palm Sunday, and we told them that we wanted

---

3. Bum-rush: to attack or seize with an overpowering rush. https://www.merriam-webster.com/dictionary/bum-rush.

to go to church. Our intention was never to go to church but was to take hostages in the deputy superintendent's office. And that is what we did—the deputy superintendent and four guards. Our purpose was to demand that we be treated like human beings.

"We got to shower maybe twice a week. Food was given to us in metal trays that were slid on the floor underneath the cell doors. There was no recreation, because we were not allowed outside. And there was no air conditioning. We were locked in our cells twenty-three and a half hours a day. All that became intolerable, so we did something about it.

"Twelve hours later, the prison superintendent agreed to hear our demands, and we allowed the hostages to go free. A month later, all of the men on death row had time in the yard and access to a shower every day—except for me and the two others. We three got six months on lockdown, because we had violated the rules of the institution. That meant we were in our six-by-nine cells twenty-four hours a day and were allowed out for half an hour a week to take a shower. After six months, we finally got to go outside. That was three years after I had gone to prison. The first day I went out, it rained. I went out anyway and rolled in the mud.

"That whole event brought politics clearly into focus for me. Political movements have to be collective. They are not individual. It's not about one-person-one vote and other nonsense. It has nothing to do with that. It has everything to do with the individual understanding herself or himself as part of a collective."

Death Row Saved My Life

Kétu did not read any law books while in prison. "I never did any case readings. I didn't do anything to try to get off death row. All my effort was to find out who I was and why I was in the position I was in before the state of Massachusetts killed me. That was my whole purpose.

"My lawyer was not a criminal defense attorney. He was a corporate lawyer who had defended me in an assault case that came up after a football game when I was in the ninth or tenth grade. My mother went to him, and he agreed to take me on pro bono, because we didn't have any money. He got my conviction overturned on the basis of the Miranda and Escobedo court cases that require police officers to inform suspects of their right to remain silent and to obtain an attorney during interrogations while in police custody. The police had not read me my rights. They had not told me I had a right to an attorney. They had not given me access to a phone call.[4]

"In October of 1971, I walked off death row.[5]

"I had become totally transformed. I was no longer the person who went in. Before I went in, I did not understand anything about myself or about the contexts I lived in. I had no understanding of what gave my life meaning. When I came off death row, I understood all that.

"Before I went in, I did not understand that life was about power. I was merely drifting along on the tide of expectations of how young Black men should live. But the power I thought I had on the street was taken from me. When I got out of prison, I recognized that I had the ability to do what I wanted to do when I wanted to do it. I had the ability to make a new life for myself. That recognition came first as a feeling. As I read more and more, I was able to articulate that feeling and put it into focus.

"Before I went in, I had no understanding of what it meant to be Black in America. I knew that the color of my skin was different from the color of some other people's skin. But I had no grasp of the political weight of that or of the social or economic weight of it. When I came out, I was fully conscious of being Black. In prison, I found my Afrikan identity. I gave up being an American and changed my name.

"When I came out, I understood that despite the rise of my people from enslavement to citizenship and voting rights and all the other Johnson-era reforms, we were still enslaved mentally. In prison, I escaped that mental enslavement.

"When I stepped off the bus in Boston, there was a reporter from Boston University Radio—WBUR. He asked me whether I was bitter. I think he was surprised when I told him no, I had no bitterness in me. Death row

---

4. The two cases governing informing a suspect of their rights are Miranda v. Arizona, 384 U.S. 436 (June 13, 1966) and Escobedo v. Illinois, 378 U.S. 478 (1964). Miranda is summarized at https://www.oyez.org/cases/1965/759, and Escobedo is summarized at https://www.oyez.org/cases/1963/615.

The double jeopardy that is prohibited by the Fifth Amendment to the U.S. Constitution does not prohibit someone whose conviction has been overturned due to Miranda or Escobedo violations from being retried, but evidence that was obtained by means of the Miranda and Escobedo violations in the first trial cannot be used in a retrial. Kétu was not retried.

5. *The Boston Globe,* October 10, 1971, 18. "The total of men under death sentence was dropped from 17 several weeks ago when Ronald Fisher was freed on grounds he was not properly advised of his constitutional rights when he was arrested in the killing of a 15-year-old Springfield girl."

had saved my life. From that point to now, that's the clearest way to say what happened to me. Had it not been for death row, I'd have been dead a long time ago. That was the track I was on before I went to prison.

"My ancestors saw more in me than I was able to see in myself. I got smacked and received a time out. Those five years on death row were a time out to see if I deserved the life I'd been given.

"On death row, I gained the ability to think clearly. I came to understand the context I lived in. And I realized I had the ability to make my world. That is what I have done with my life."[6]

---

6. For readers interested in law, below are two court cases in which Kétu was involved.

(1) COMMONWEALTH vs. RONALD FISHER. 354 Mass. 549 (March 4, 1968 – June 26, 1968) http://masscases.com/cases/sjc/354/354mass549.html. An appeal of the 1966 trial on grounds of Miranda and Escobedo violations. Relief was denied. The original conviction was upheld.

(2) Ronald Fisher v. Palmer C. Scafati, Etc., 439 F.2d 307 (1st Cir. 1971). United States Court of Appeals, First Circuit, March 4, 1971. An appeal of the 1968 case, COMMONWEALTH vs. RONALD FISHER, granting relief, that is, overturning the 1968 denial of relief and the 1966 conviction. *Court Listener:* https://www.courtlistener.com/opinion/295263/ronald-fisher-v-palmer-c-scafati-etc/?q=&court_mass=on&order_by=dateFiled+desc.

"Evelyn": Burned in a Flash Fire

"I never had a moment when I thought death was imminent or even a possibility. However, the care team told my parents once I was stable that when I first came in they weren't sure I would survive."

Evelyn was caught in a sudden and unexpected fire that instantly swept over her. She could do nothing to protect herself from it, but was, fortunately, rescued by a passerby. She was in her early forties when we talked.

Fire!

The fire occurred fifteen years ago, in May of 2009, on the sailboat of Evelyn's future husband, "Ryan," who later became her ex-husband. "He and I and his nine-year-old daughter plus his dog had spent the night on the boat, which was at a dock. In the morning, we got up and went for a walk around the town we were near. It was cold and damp, a drizzly, rainy morning. So when we got back to the boat, we decided to make some tea to warm us up.

"The stove was a portable camping stove that burned highly flammable alcohol. When Ryan went to light it, he found that it was out of fuel, as we had used the stove earlier that morning. The place where you pour fuel into the stove is also the place where the flame comes out. When Ryan poured fuel into that place, the residual heat from earlier ignited the fuel he was pouring. The whole stove went up in flames.

"We were on the lower level of the sailboat at the end of the companionway, the stairway that comes down from the upper deck. I was next to the stove, facing Ryan, and the wind was coming down the companionway. It swept the flame in my direction. That meant I got the brunt of it.

"I had a polyester-cotton hoodie on, which is very flammable. It caught right away. I quickly covered my face with my hands. I could still see through my fingers, and I saw the dog lying on the bed at the front end of the sailboat. It was looking back at me.

"I remembered from grade school that the thing to do when you caught fire was to stop, drop, and roll. The sailboat was only twenty-seven feet long, and the place where the stove was, the galley, was very tight. Plus, a table was there, so there was no room to roll.

"My sweatshirt was engulfed in flames. I dropped to the floor, with my hands still on my face, and tried to smother the flames as much as I could. Ryan was fumbling around for the fire extinguisher or a towel or something he could use to smother the fire. At the time, though, I wasn't aware of what he was doing."

Rescue

"Four miracles saved us," Evelyn continued. "The first was that Ryan happened to have put on a new, flame-retardant jacket right before we tried to make tea. So he wasn't injured very badly. He was able to see what was going on with me instead of being incapacitated by the fire. He ended up being in the hospital for only a few days.

"The second was that his daughter was not in the galley with us. She was not on the boat at all. She lagged behind Ryan and me while we were out walking. And when he and I went onto the boat, she sat on a bench in a nearby park.

"The third miracle was that because it was the start of the boating season, there was a young, college-age guy working at the marina for the summer who happened to be walking by. He grabbed a fire extinguisher that was on the pier and came and put out the fire. From the time the fire started to the time he put it out, it was probably under a minute, though I don't really know.

"Last, the harbor master was driving around in the parking lot, which was near the sailboat. He had a radio that had direct access to life-flight helicopters. He called 911 and then for a helicopter. An ambulance arrived first—two actually, one for Ryan and one for me.

"By this time, I had somehow launched myself through the companionway up onto the deck of the sailboat. I had grabbed a towel from someplace and had put it on my face. I was lying face down.

"The paramedics who came with the ambulances weren't sure how they could get me off the boat. My arms were burned, and they were afraid of damaging me more. I said, 'I can get up and walk.' They said, 'What do you mean you can get up and walk?!' But my legs weren't hurt at all.

"I stood up and walked off the boat. The paramedics put me on a stretcher and took me to one of the ambulances. Then they cut off my jeans. I was in my late twenties, still getting on my feet financially, and my first thought was, 'I just got those jeans, and they weren't cheap.' My second thought was, 'Did the fire hit the jeans?' Later I realized that the fastest way to check a person was to cut their clothes off. That was just their standard procedure.

"I'm not too sure what else the paramedics were doing to me, but it wasn't too long before the helicopter got there. Ryan and I were taken from our separate ambulances and put into it. I asked Ryan whether my face was still intact, because my arms had made a chimney that the fire could climb up when I put my hands on my face. I had seen people in a television show whose faces had been severely disfigured because of bad burns. Ryan said, 'You're okay. You're okay.'

"I don't remember much after that, though I was told later that I was put on morphine. I didn't have any pain before then, maybe because of the adrenaline. I do remember the chaos and the helicopter landing.

"We were flown to the nearest hospital. I was there for five weeks."

In the Hospital

Evelyn's head enlarged significantly because of the fluids that had built up after her burns. "They call it a 'pumpkin head.'

"For sixteen days, I was intubated, plus for a day or two in between surgeries—a tube that breathed for me was put down my throat. For twenty-five days, I was fed intravenously. Before I was allowed to eat or drink, they had me do swallow tests to make sure I could swallow okay.

"During the time I was intubated, I couldn't talk with anyone. My mom, though, made a letter board so that I could spell out words.

"I had four surgeries. The fire had burned the skin off my hands, arms, and neck, so the doctors had to transplant skin from my legs to those places. That created scars on my legs, which are still visible. And there are scars where the burns were.

"Fortunately, I didn't lose much hair, because I had it in a ponytail at the time of the fire. My ears were pretty severely burned, though, so the hospital nurses trimmed my hair around my ears so it wouldn't stick to the ointments on my ears.

"I didn't lose my eyebrows, either, maybe because I had my hands on them. But I did lose my eyelashes. They grew back fast, though. And when they got to the right length, they stopped. My mom found it pretty amazing that they did that.

"It never occurred to me that I could die. I never had a moment when I thought death was imminent or even a possibility. However, the care team told my parents once I was stable that when I first came in they weren't sure I would survive.

"One of the hardest things I had to deal with was the hallucinations I had. I sometimes could not tell the difference between a hallucination and reality. My family had to tell me that what I had experienced in a hallucination had not happened.

"Before I left the hospital, I had to do physical therapy to relearn how to walk, because I had been in bed for so long. After I got out of the hospital, I had to go to physical therapy twice a week to stretch the new skin on my neck and fingers. I couldn't bend them because there was no extra skin at the knuckles or neck.

"I am sure that my being in the hospital for so long was harder for everyone else than it was for me, especially when I was sedated during the first two weeks. Plus, I was occupied with different things. I needed to have this done and that done. The nurses took me into a shower room and scrubbed my wounds. But my family and friends could only sit around and wait.

"My care team told me that my hospital stay should have been longer but that the support of others helped me heal faster. My parents visited every day for the five weeks I was there, driving two hours each way. My room was plastered with cards, pictures, and posters. And my friends came to visit me. I have to believe that all that was part of why I healed as well as I did.

"As hard as it was to be in the hospital, it was also a precious time for me. I don't think many people get to feel that much outpouring of love from those around them. That often happens only at your funeral. But I got to experience it way before then. I still have all the cards. Every few years I look through them, and I still feel loved because of them."

Reactions

The fire affected Evelyn's life in a number of ways. "The scars on my hands and arms were especially visible during the first few years after they had been burned. When I met new people, I didn't know whether to tell them about the fire. If I didn't tell them, they would be uncomfortable wondering about the scars. If I did, that usually shut the conversation down. They didn't know what to say. So I was in a balancing act of figuring out when to explain my scars and when not. And there were also times when I didn't feel like talking about the fire.

"Now, fifteen years later, the scars are not as visible. I don't have to deal with that balancing act or talk about something I don't want to talk about as much.

"When the fire occurred, Ryan and I had been dating for only two months. In the hospital, I said to him, 'You didn't sign up for this. I have a lot of family and friends to support me. You don't need to feel obligated to stay with me.' But he did stay, and we formed a trauma bond. Three years later we married.

"Eight months after we married, we separated. After our wedding, he had slept with one of my bridesmaids, who was a close friend of mine, as well as with another woman.

"That is the biggest emotional scar from the fire. Earlier, he had helped me through the trauma of having been badly burned. He had been trustworthy. But then he turned and wasn't. The one person who was in the fire with me and who knew what I had experienced is the one who left me. That hurt. Besides baggage from the fire, I had baggage from a divorce.

"I then had to deal with trusting people because of that infidelity, especially in new relationships. And I had even more of a balancing act to perform. It was hard to hide the scars, so I often told new acquaintances about the fire. But now I also had to figure out how to tell them about my short-lived marriage.

"I've never had any flashbacks because of the fire. I still go sailing, and I still enjoy sitting around a campfire. The first time I got back on the boat, I went down below where the fire happened and I had a conversation with the boat. I said, 'You know, boat, this wasn't your fault. You were a victim in this too, because your skin, the carpet that was here then, burned and had to be replaced.'

"People said to me, 'How can you get back on that boat!?' But it was actually a comfort for me to get back together with it. I don't, however, like lighting my propane grill, because it reminds me of the fire. So if someone else is nearby, I ask them to do it. At the same time, I don't mind at all building a fire out of wood.

"Sometimes people said, 'There's a purpose for this,' or 'It will be amazing to see what you do with your experiences,' or 'God uses these types of things for good.' But I had the mindset of, 'What if I don't want to do anything with what happened? What if I just want to recover and go back to the life I loved?'

"It felt as though they were putting additional expectations on me that I didn't want. I just wanted to focus on getting better, not changing my career and becoming an inspirational speaker who wanted to change the world.

"Sometimes the well-intentioned things people said were not helpful."

Ellen: Found Dead

"When you love someone deeply and widely, they become your home. And losing home makes refugees of us all."

What is it like to find your spouse dead on the floor when you were fully expecting to see them up and alive? In this dramatic and moving piece, written by Ellen, we find out. Ellen wrote this when she was in her early sixties, four years after the death of her husband, Tim, who was sixty-eight when he died, in 2019.

Turn for the Worse

It was days before my vacation. After thirty wonderful and recently terrible years of married life, I would be spending a week in Scotland visiting my best girlfriend. Alone. My husband didn't want me to go.

"If you go, you'll see how much better your life is without me and you won't come back," he said.

"Going is how I stay," I came back.

My husband—veteran philosophy and psychology professor, wearer of gym shoes, inveterate extrovert, relentlessly perceptive, unfailingly persistent and unwaveringly kind—had, with the support of a good therapist, struggled with lifelong post-traumatic stress disorder from a brutal childhood. Early in our relationship, he told me, with his earmark bulldog determination, that he refused to pass on the abuse, and with typical tenacity, he did not. But at sixty, all hell broke loose.

Years after the dust settled, I came to believe it was Parkinson's disease that served as the catalyst. Whatever it was, seemingly overnight, my husband—a man who taught so long and was so beloved that former students would see him from afar in foreign countries and come running to embrace him—became a paranoid recluse with tormenting obsessive compulsive disorder.

In a short time, endless iterations of locks requiring complex, repeated maneuvers to secure appeared on doors and windows. "Checking" closets and the smallest hidey holes for potential killers who might emerge as we slept became a redundant routine. I recall feeling deep relief at the fact that he never registered the existence of a transom over the back door in our old vintage apartment, an oversight for which I was grateful.

After the first few shocked months waiting for the tide to turn and "helping" with his security routines, it became clear that this was a permanent, degenerative state, one that indulgence only perpetuated. I spent the next eight years bearing witness while my favorite person in life descended into occasionally lucid madness. I split my nonwork time between tending to his physically, socially, mentally and cognitively deteriorating state while feverishly searching the internet for potential answers, solutions, and treatments. I tried mightily to maintain my own boundaries.

Those first few months lasted a lifetime. Simply refusing to participate in his OCD proved to be an emotionally draining second job. The shock of suddenly finding myself the solitary breadwinner in a recently two-income family was, under the circumstances, petrifying. Managing finances, including the long, circuitous process of applying for his disability, was tricky, given that he was in denial of the fact that he was now unable to write checks for the bills he had been paying.

Realizing we would need to move—with all its implications of finding somewhere feasible to live, packing, making all the pre and post arrangements, overseeing the logistics of the event, and getting us settled in—was daunting, particularly when he couldn't help and vowed he wouldn't go.

On the healthcare front, eventually and with cruel clarity, I realized there would be no answers. And anyway if there had been, he would likely be too resistant and paralyzed by terror to make use of them.

His descent continued.

Like repetitions of background scenery in bad anime, excruciating moments arose and re-arose: him sobbing at the table, head in hands, pleading, "What's happening to me?" or me in Wylie Coyote form, way past my limit and finding myself scrambling in thin air with the cliff edge long behind me, panicking and thinking, "I have to get out."

On my doctor's advice, I turned a walk-in closet into my sanctuary. I decorated it with care and hung a sign on the door saying, "Please wait." I went over the rules with him: He could not enter without my permission and was not to talk to me if I went in. It was the only way I could stay in my possessed home and escape the insanity. And it was our best possible shot at me not having to abandon ship, a choice we both knew would almost certainly leave him homeless. For eight years, we were able, by the grace of God, friends, and our own deep love to stay that course.

Eventually, though, I needed a break.

Seven days away from him. It was going to be just five days plus two to travel.

Getting Ready to Leave

I packed, checked my passport, itinerary, etc., all the things you do before traveling to the other side of the world. We talked about his care. I wanted to ask my friend, a woman he'd met once and liked, to look in on him. She was a nurse, and the fact that he himself hadn't directly known her "in his past life" meant he'd feel less ashamed about his stunning change. But he wouldn't hear of it.

I had long decided to pick my battles and concluded that if all I could do was offer him a protected place in which to slay his dragons safely (even if he didn't think it was) then, so help me God, that's what I would do. I took extra pains to arrange things so that he could tend to his most basic needs himself and the rest could wait until I returned. I thought I had all the bases covered.

I was wrong.

A few days before I was supposed to leave, I repeated to him that I was going in order to take care of myself, to restore myself so that I could return revitalized and able to stay. I told him I loved him and that that was what I wanted more than anything in the world. He told me he loved me too. He told me he was afraid to let me go.

Then without knowing I was going to say it, I told him I refused to leave with things between us the way they were. I insisted he give me a blessing. The idea struck both of us as somehow important. He said he wanted one from me too, and we both decided to take the day to consider what we'd offer each other.

At the end of it, he said, "I hope you have a good time with Penny. I hope you get to relax and have fun and enjoy yourself, and I hope your trip is everything you need it to be." Then I told him, "I hope while I'm away, you find some peace and can relax. I can't wait to see you when I get back. If you start missing me, maybe you could window-shop on the internet for a little welcome-home gift." The next morning, we kissed and exchanged, "I love yous." Then I left.

The Vacation

Scotland was wonderful. Seeing my long-time best friend was a balm. The vacation was working on releasing a part of me that craved joy and hadn't seen sunlight in years. We went for long walks along the North Sea, had tea and pastries in the local fishing town, and visited in her tiny house.

One morning, I asked her about the person whose trailer I was renting. I'd had a strange dream in which a man circled around it before bursting in, getting in bed with me, and trying to snuggle. This happened twice in the dream and both times I angrily pushed him out telling him I wasn't who he thought I was. I was married to someone I loved. I curiously questioned my friend about my landlord: Was there a man in her life whose description matched the dream image? She didn't think so, but she told me she'd ask next time she saw her. We chuckled and continued our day.

That evening, Tim didn't email.

With his OCD and the time difference, we had decided he'd only email once a night: no phone calls—a rule he broke within hours of my leaving, frantically calling me while I was at the airport and later in his first email expressing remorse for "having ruined" our "perfect" leave-taking.

So now, two nights before my return, while it was a bit worrisome not to hear from him, there were practical reasons why I might not. He could be trying to make up for his earlier trespass by giving me extra space. There might be a technology problem—something nebulous having to do with the cloud or somehow tied to the sudden heat wave Chicago was experiencing. Or maybe it was a time difference issue.

Constantly having to walk the fine line between paranoia and sensible concern, I had developed a muscle for pushing back on worry, so I set mine aside. I emailed him again and sent myself to bed convinced I'd see a message from him in the morning. But that didn't happen. On top of it, I couldn't access the numbers in my phone because it was dead and I didn't have a charger. Plus, I was in the middle of nowhere on the edge of the North Sea.

By now, I was leaving the next morning, so I sent yet another email. And like the philosopher's wife I was, consoled myself with Occam's Razor, holding on to the likelihood of tech problems, though I was less and less a believer. When morning came and there was still no email, I couldn't leave fast enough. But matters were about to go from bad to worse.

The planes were, all of them, late and very late. In a cold sweat, I hustled up to an airport kiosk and begged them to let me call my disabled husband on their phone so I could let him know what was going on. They kindly obliged, allowing me both to send an email and to call. But he never picked up. I tried to reassure myself that he was only sleeping (the time difference again) and that his lack of response could be a good sign.

Finally after hours and hours of flying and waiting and waiting some more and flying some more, I got into O'Hare airport. After two more hours eking my way through customs and multiple stymied attempts to find a taxi (in the blistering heat, people had snapped them all up), at last I was lurching through thick traffic, on my way home, seven hours later than scheduled.

Now, through the lens of many years, it seems fanciful how something as simple as immediacy could so completely restore my faith. I marvel at how thoroughly and naïvely reassured I was by the simple fact of my return, as if just my presence back in Chicago somehow conferred a protected status over Tim. I fully expected to find myself throwing my arms around him soon.

At Home

Grinning with anticipation, I struggled out of the taxi, let myself in the bottom door of our apartment building, and wrestled my suitcase up the three flights.

I unlocked the bottom lock on our door and waited for him to come unchain it and greet me. He always did that. That was our routine.

No one came.

I peered through the door crack calling his name. There was no answer.

The thought occurred to me, *Oh, he must be watering the back porch plants because of the heat wave,* and I slyly decided, *I'll just leave my luggage here and go sneak up on him. Won't he be surprised!*

Parking my luggage there at the top of the stairs, I raced down, around the building and up the back stairs.

He wasn't on the porch. That was an unexpected turn.

Fishing out my keys again, I opened the back door and walked in calling his name. Still there was no answer.

Baffled, I began reaching for explanations: *Did he go out looking for me?* I wondered. *But how? He could barely shuffle through the apartment. And where would he even go?*

I kept walking and calling with a growing sense of dread.

Finally, I got to the bedroom.

At first, I didn't see him. He was on the floor between the bed and the wall.

And then all of space-time collapsed.

Dead

Somehow, the days and distance that had been between us turned out to be much, much shorter than the time it took to travel across the room, to see my darling man curled up in rigor mortis, to take in the parts of him that were blue, blue, so blue, and those eyes that had missed nothing, staring off.

I found myself shouting at him, trying to push him flat in order to do CPR before some part of my mind snapped to, stepped aside, and calmly pointed out the obvious: *He won't uncurl because it's too late for CPR.* And the bitterness of betrayal hit me like a club: All these years of taking first aid for work, paying meticulous attention, singing the "Staying Alive" song and counting until it was hammered home—all for nothing because I couldn't even save my own husband. He was so dead, so very, very dead.

I panicked.

I couldn't call anyone—my phone was dead. I looked for his phone. It was dead. In strange slow motion, the thought occurred to me, *Now everything's dead.* And then someone was screaming and it was me. I was running up and down the halls, pounding on doors and shouting, "Help me, help me! My husband's dead!" while in the back of my mind, that stepped-aside voice said, *How are they going to help you, Ellen? He's dead. There is no helping now.* Still, that's what kept coming out of my mouth—I didn't seem to have any control over it.

It was a weekday. Everyone was at work. But finally, mercifully, a downstairs neighbor who worked from home heard me. She had a cell phone. Rushing up the stairs on my heels, she looked over my shoulder and took in the bedroom scene. One of us called some friends, the police, Tim's doctor.

Then everyone started coming.

The ambulance paramedics said he was dead. Yes. Of course.

The police were kind and terrible. They wouldn't let me near him. They wouldn't let me touch him. I hadn't seen him for a week, and they wouldn't let me touch him. They took one look at everything and thought it was a homicide—the shredded mattress, the blood, feces, urine on the walls, floor, everywhere. Finally, a detective satisfied himself that it wasn't a murder and told me I could go to him.

I ran.

He was so vulnerable and dear to me then, lying there completely undressed except for his underwear and left sock. I cleaned him up—I and my two friends.

There are those who think that would have been unimaginably difficult. But to me, it was an intimate and precious moment I wouldn't have given up if someone had laid all the money in the world at my feet. It was the last time I was going to get to do anything for this body I loved. All of those fluids—they became a precious mess to me. It was an unbearably tender time.

My friends helped me turn Tim slightly so I could clean parts that were more difficult to reach while they worked at the stains on the floor and walls and changed the bed linen. But we couldn't turn him over completely—dead weight is heavy—so I was never able to find out what caused the bleeding.

Then the police—oh, how I hated them!—they made me call the funeral home. They refused to let me keep him. One night. That was all I wanted. One last night with the man I'd been married to thirty years and hadn't seen in days. But they wouldn't let me have him. Later, my nurse friend said it had to do with how long he might've been lying there, with bacteria already settling into the decomposition process. Even so, I still hated them for a while afterwards.

Someone from the funeral home arrived and took him away from me, and the next time I saw him he was naked on a metal trolley, covered with a white sheet in a barren room.

Cremated

A series of confusing and hazy events occurred during which I managed to make the necessary decisions about things like the number of certified death certificates I might need and Tim's cremation.

The crematorium was on the outskirts of town. I had no car, so a friend of ours drove. I said my last goodbye to him and they closed the coffin. They put him on a conveyer belt. It was hot and awful, watching them send him into the furnace. I had to keep reminding myself it wasn't him anymore, it was a shell. But still, it was the body of the man I loved. It was hard not to go after him.

In my head, I vowed to him, "I wasn't there when you died, but I am going to be here for you now." So I forced myself to stand there and watch. Foolishly, I thought it would be over in a matter of minutes until the attendant gently informed me that it would take about two hours. It was more than I could bear. Sobbing, I told my friend I didn't think I had it in me to stand there watching him burn that long. So he took me by the elbow and led me away.

Coping

The first few nights were excruciating. The first few days were agonizing. The first few years were interminable.

Initially, many dear friends worried about me having to sleep in the bedroom—the death room. They invited me to stay with them, but I said, "Thank you, no. I want to be in our bed." I had to be in our bed. It was that simple. Still, I could already tell a dark fear of that room, that date, was settling in, and I knew it would overtake me unless I did something to redeem it. Almost immediately, out of sheer need, a kind of "stations of the cross" ritual emerged.

I visited all the parts of the room that had been involved in his death, thanking them for all the good care they took of him for the years before, day after day, and most especially for looking over him while I was away. I told them none of this was their fault, that to me, they were holy, that this room, this place, was holy, would always be holy because it took such good care of him for so long, and I blessed them all. Then I told them I knew I was among friends.

And that is how I was able to go to sleep, if that's what it could be called.

I repeated this mantra over and over until the sacrament took hold in my bones. And on the wall overlooking the niche I found him in, I hung his old framed sepia picture of Notre Dame Cathedral for those moments when I might forget.

Events

Many significant things followed, some precious, some wrenching. Predators emerged, some sadly disguised as friends. Meals appeared mysteriously. Tim's ashes were lost and found. Chalk messages of love from my preschool students and their families poured across the pavement in front of my building. Generous friends, co-workers, and acquaintances donated money to a GoFundMe page. Friends, students, and colleagues collaborated to create the most healing memorial service I could have imagined. Bills came due.

Institutions demanded hard evidence of his death. Finances had to be seriously considered and refigured. Stuff—now artifacts—had to be wrangled, sorted, dispensed, disbursed. The phone calls were endless. Emails hatched other emails.

In the middle of it all, COVID-19 hit, compounding loss with loss when access to my supportive communities disappeared overnight, including my beloved preschool—with all the affectionate hugs of the children, colleagues, and parents—and the agency for refugee high school girls where I volunteered. At a Zoom meeting I told my colleagues, "Now you all are as dead to me as he is." My isolation felt complete.

I took to making a point of tenderly examining the leaves of my many plants and talking fondly to Nietzsche, the mouse that visited each spring, whom I named after Tim's favorite philosopher. From a new angle, I reconsidered old conversations about The Eternal Return of the Same. I had my first chance encounter on public transportation with a man who was his double, and the effort to bully myself into turning my back and walking away wrecked me for weeks.

I began attending a surviving spouse's Zoom support group offered by an organization called Vitas. It saved me. I discovered the strange and unpredictable nature of grief when I found out I didn't need talk therapy or eye movement desensitization and reprocessing after all. Instead, running on instinct, I followed out an intense compulsion: I gathered, framed, and hung every piece of art given to Tim by his art school students and colleagues, and felt surrounded and embraced by love.

In deference to his long-ago request, "If I die first, write me a poem," I wrote a book of them dedicated to him, which is online at https://sites.google.com/view/strike-poemsforthegrieving/home. I asked friends to let me tell them Tim stories about hats, New Orleans, the Kentucky Derby, hospital trips, olive oil, and wrestling. I moved again.

Grace, Goodwill, and Kindness

The support I had during that harrowing time was strong and sturdy. It created a cocoon in which healing could happen. I feel absolutely certain that I would not have been able to move forward beyond that terrible moment without the grace, goodwill, and kindness I was fortunate to have in my life.

I know people often feel awkward around a surviving loved one, fearing they will "say the wrong thing and make it worse." But from my perspective, he was already dead. Nothing anyone said could make it worse than that. And truly, even the most fumbled attempts at comfort were soothing.

Many who knew him and loved him were also mystified and justifiably curious about his illness and death. Who could blame them? His long-time family physician, a man who knew him for decades, was kind enough to officially designate "heart attack" on his death certificate. But I set myself to living with never knowing for sure. After the horrifying abuse of his childhood, I couldn't bring myself to put his body through the further assault of an autopsy. Nevertheless, in a matter of months, I had an answer.

At Preschool

Tim died in July. My school year resumed in September. Despite being an introvert inclined toward approaching sensitive subjects from a discreet angle, I developed a great appreciation for directness from watching and interacting with him. It's one of the many gifts he gave me that I strive to implement in my own life when possible. In that spirit, I chose to confront difficult topics head-on with my preschoolers, and that included Tim's death.

At the beginning of the year, I told my class that my husband had died and that when a being dies, its body stops working. You don't have to worry about the being hurting or needing things because its body doesn't feel or need things anymore. I told them you can go right on loving the person. You just need to find new ways to show it.

The main thing I wanted them to know, I told them, was that if they saw me looking sad, it didn't have to do with them. It was probably because I was sad about missing Tim, since I couldn't see or hug him now. If they felt they wanted to do something kind for me about it, they could just touch my shoulder or give me a hug. They listened attentively. After I finished, a few had questions.

"How did he die?" they wanted to know.

I told them usually someone dies when their body stops working because it's too sick or too injured for doctors to fix, but since I wasn't there when he died, I didn't know for sure what happened.

That satisfied them.

A few days later on the playground, a boy with whom I'd had an especially long and close relationship came running up to me. Out of nowhere, he demanded, "How did your husband die?" So I repeated what I'd said in class. He cocked his head and thought for a minute before replying, "No. His heart popped out and flew off!" Then he ran away just as quickly as he'd run up.

I was in shock. Gathering my wits, I assumed a recent heart attack of a family member or friend had probably prompted his announcement. He was a smart little guy and likely to put two and two together like that. I passed it off as an interesting incident that said more about something he was going through personally than the circumstances of Tim's death.

But then it happened again in exactly the same way. This time his mother was present. After class, I spoke to her about the incident. I asked her whether someone in their family recently had died from a heart attack. She vigorously denied it, saying she had no idea where he had come up with the comment. She was clearly distressed, supposing it upset me and concerned about how it landed. As for me, I was stunned. After telling her the general outline of Tim's passing, we both were stunned. I told her frankly that of all the consoling words I'd received, her son's were the most comforting.

A painful legacy many survivors deal with involves the wheel of guilt, with its endless, "what-ifs" and "if-onlys." A particularly unshakable nightmare I struggled with was, *What if, while I was enjoying my time in Scotland, he was suffering a prolonged, anguished, lonely death there on our bedroom floor? If only I'd gotten there sooner.* . . . The image of it had become unendurably haunting.

Now here was this little fellow who, out of nowhere, appeared to be directly channeling a message of consolation from Tim, delivering it in the intimate language very young children and their caregivers share. I was undone in the best possible way, relieved of a boulder of burden.

A Second Life

It's been over four years now since Tim's death, and I have managed to strike a deal of peace between the life I continue to live without him and his death. It has been difficult to hold on to the demand that it not be a half life, but a full, open-hearted life. I am unwilling to allow bitterness to close me off from love.

I have learned that a person's relationship with a deceased loved one doesn't end when they do. With that, I have made many unexpected, sometimes startling, discoveries about myself and our relationship that have offered insights about people and life in general.

In this "second life," I have had to come to grips with the astonishing and difficult revelation that despite all my efforts to "stand on my own two feet" as an independent person within my marriage, my husband's sudden departure utterly dissolved my axis, leaving me dangerously wobbling, often tilting in the direction of winter. And I have come to realize that that fact was not a failure on my part. When you love someone deeply and widely, they become your home. And losing home makes refugees of us all.

I was also stupefied to realize that simply being married to a kind, good man had somehow provided me an invisible protective shield against predators—a shield I had apparently lived under for decades, entirely unaware, and for which I am now deeply grateful. So our relationship continues in strange new ways.

Still, in spite of my seeming "recovery" and resilience, every year around the time of Tim's death, I find myself reliving it. Then time slowly regathers itself and passes, and I am able to remind myself that neither of us are stuck frozen there. The air lifts slowly, and life resets to the present.

Anniversaries can set off that flashback. So can mirror events: Someone else's mention of their spouse's death leads me to a feeling of deep empathy, while having to retake a CPR class inevitably sends me into a traumatic spiral. But I am here, choosing to go on.

In the early days after I found Tim, I became crazy with the need to understand what had happened, plagued with wanting answers about when he died, and I went searching for clues. The number of chocolate Ensures left in the refrigerator was one. The timing of his last email was another. The number of pills left in his bottles was a third. His state of undress was a fourth. When I thought to check the computer to see the last sites he visited, I found Amazon. He was looking at welcome-home T-shirts with dragonflies. He knew how much I love them.

Many who learn the facts of Tim's illness and death think of it as a tragedy. Certainly the circumstances were. I who knew him best look upon it differently. That my husband went mad was not his fault. That he did so with more self-containment, courage, kindness, and grace than could be rightfully expected or imagined is, to me, heroic. In spite of struggling with demons, he did his damnedest to protect others from all of it, including most especially me. For someone who had been so violated so early in life to manage such a feat strikes me as nothing less than something to be honored and celebrated.

© 2026 by Ellen Palmer

Shirley: Death of My Infant Son

"I had to learn to talk about what happened so that I could heal. When I suppressed it, my body felt that, and I got sick."

Shirley's son died two weeks after he was born. She was devastated, and she shut down, not talking about her son's death for a decade. I talked to her eleven years after he died when she was in her midthirties.

In the Hospital

Shirley went into labor while she was at a regular checkup at a hospital in Chicago. "I had to go to the delivery room on the third floor to have my son. They were waiting for me to become fully dilated to start the birth process, and I was not dilating fast enough. So they gave me something that made me dilate faster.

"I actively started pushing about 5:50 in the evening. I was going through the motions, and then in the middle of it they noticed something was wrong. My son's heart rate was dropping, and my heart rate was spiking, really high. They told me to slow down a little. Then they told me to keep pushing.

"At exactly 7:10 pm, the baby came out. But the cord was around his neck, and he was blue. They didn't let me do anything to him, so I couldn't touch him. All I could do was watch while they were struggling to cut the cords from around his neck. Then they started CPR to try to get him to breathe. At that point, I could see everyone around him, but I couldn't see him. I was bleeding badly, so they rushed me to the operating room to get me stitched up.

"While I was being gotten ready to go to the operating room, some nurses came to me and said, 'Your baby is not doing well.' I kept asking, 'Where is he? Where is he?' They told me that he had to be transferred to Children's Memorial Hospital, also in Chicago, but that they couldn't do that until I signed for it. So I signed the paperwork as I was being taken to the operating room.

"I woke up from the anesthesia about ten o'clock. There was no one in the recovery room, and everything was quiet. This was on Christmas Eve.

"A nurse came, and I asked, 'Where is my son?' The nurse said, 'He's not here. You don't remember signing paperwork to get him transferred?' I said, 'No. I don't remember anything.'

"I have never felt so alone. Everything was so quiet. Yes, there was beeping, I could hear kids crying, and the nurses were going around giving gifts to the new parents. But I was by myself, and it felt as though it was the quietest day of my life.

"I called my mom, crying. She lives some distance west of Chicago, so it was a big hike for her to get to me. Plus, it was at night. I told her, 'I'm just gonna go to sleep. Let's talk tomorrow.'

"The next day, on Christmas, they told me what had happened: 'The cord was around your child's neck, and he lost oxygen to his brain. Children's Memorial Hospital is seeing what they can do.'

"I wanted to get out of the hospital. I did not care that I had just had surgery. I needed to see my child. That didn't happen, though, until the day after Christmas."

Visiting Her Son

Shirley was afraid to go to the hospital her son was in. "I called my mom. She came. It was the first time she had seen me in several months.

"My son was hooked up to a ventilator. That was how my mom met her grandson. I named him DeShawn.

"A nurse told me that because the cord was around him for so long, he might have had bleeding in the brain. They had to cool him down to reduce the swelling in the brain. And then they had to check whether there was any brain activity. I was torn. I had to make all the decisions about him, because I was not married to his father.

"During the whole time, I did not process what my body was feeling. I went through labor and delivery not feeling anything. I was numb.

"I went to the hospital DeShawn was in every day to make sure he was okay. That was very therapeutic for me. I held him, bathed him, and changed his clothes with ones I had gotten at a baby shower my friends had thrown for me. Then I held him in my arms while I pumped milk. I had to pour the milk down the drain, though, because he was hooked up to the tubes of the ventilator. That was hard.

"Normally, you can't hold a child who is on a ventilator because of the short tubes. But they made a way to extend the tubing so I could hold my son.

"They did a test to see whether he could breathe on his own. They lowered the pressure of the ventilator to see what would happen to the oxygen saturation in the blood. It went way down. That told them he could not breathe on his own."

The Decision

Shirley had a meeting with the team at Children's Memorial Hospital about ten or eleven days after DeShawn's birth. "There were eight or nine doctors, along with DeShawn's father and my mom. We were all on a call, so everyone could hear everything. The doctors gave their opinions about what was going on. They had run diagnostic tests. A neurologist had done a complete test. There was nothing else they could do. DeShawn would have to live on a ventilator for the rest of his life.

"As the mom, I had to make the call. I didn't think twice. I said, 'I think we should let him go.'

"I could not be selfish and keep him alive just because I wanted him there. I didn't know how he felt, what type of pain he had. He could not tell me. He could not cry. But I knew there would be no quality of life for him. It felt selfish of me to keep him going.

"When finally I decided that the day for him to go off the ventilator had come, they let me bathe him, change his clothes, the whole routine. Then I told them okay. I held him as they took out the tubing. For the first time, I held him without his being connected to anything.

"His father, my mom, and my best friend were all in the room with me, along with doctors and nurses. They kept checking DeShawn's heartbeat, because they had to announce the time of death. It took less than an hour.

"When finally his heart stopped, I didn't want to let him go. He still felt warm. But I knew I had to."

Change

From that moment, things changed for Shirley. "Everything shut down. I went on autopilot. I didn't feel anything, except for guilt. Even though I knew that logically I had made the right choice, I felt guilty. Who was I to decide who dies? But I suppressed the guilt and went on business as usual. I became numb to the fact that my son had died. I became guarded when talking about it.

"There were other effects as well. I felt no appetite, and I dropped weight. My memory went bad. I was living in a brain fog. I couldn't walk well—I lost strength in my legs, and they became numb too.

"On a visit several months later, my mom said, 'You are sick. You need to come back home. Something is wrong with you.'

"I saw a doctor, who told me to take Tylenol. 'You will be fine,' she said. But nothing changed. I got the impression that she had dismissed me because she thought I just wanted something for pain. I explained to others what was going on with me, but no one understood, which made me feel crazy. Finally, someone recommended I see a rheumatologist.

"The rheumatologist understood what I was saying. I started to cry right there with her. 'I guess I'm not crazy.' I thought.

"I got a nerve biopsy. The results were sent to Mayo Clinic, which determined that I had lupus. I was put on chemotherapy and steroid infusions. I did that for six months. But the side effect of long-term steroids is something called 'avascular necrosis,' which is bone death.

"I started feeling pain in both hips. A doctor said that I might need hip replacement. I thought he was crazy, because I was so young. But the pain became so bad that I had to take morphine three times a day. It did not do anything, though.

"I had hip replacements, first with my left leg, then with my right leg."

Listening and Healing

Shirley felt betrayed by the doctor who had dismissed her pain. "I felt that she had not listened to me. I also felt shut down, in a way, when DeShawn was on the ventilator, because I could not let anyone into my inner life. I blocked everything out. I could not process anything. I had become deadened. I was just existing, and I didn't feel anything. I did not remember DeShawn's funeral.

"Now, however, eleven years later, I have become open to feeling things and processing them and telling others what is going on with me. Earlier, I could not let anyone get close to me.

"I decided that I wanted to be there for those who were going through all the things I went through. I decided that I wanted to listen to what was going on with them. That is why I am in nursing school now.

"The thing that drives me most is the desire to be a voice for people who cannot articulate their feelings. I want to be one who listens to them. I do not want people to feel uncared for by those who are entrusted with taking care of them.

"I have a great support system now with people who listen to me. That also keeps me going, because I can deal with the grief I did not feel when DeShawn died. I can relive the things that happened then. I can go through the entire story without breaking down or shutting down completely and having nothing more to say.

"I had to learn to talk about what happened so that I could heal. When I suppressed it, my body felt that, and I got sick. When I didn't have an outlet to say what I was feeling, it manifested itself in some other way.

"When I was going through the trauma eleven years ago, I would have liked for someone to have said, 'How are you feeling today?' or "Do you want to talk about this?' Sometimes they would not have had to say anything—just be with me. My biggest desire was not to feel dismissed.

"Someone said, 'You're still young. You can have another one,' as though it did not matter that DeShawn had died, as though it was not a life that came out of me that I had lost. Someone else said that his death was God's punishment for doing things out of wedlock. That hurt. It made me wonder whether DeShawn's death really was God punishing me. Still another person said that I should be over his death by now because it had been eleven years since he died. I thought, 'That's your opinion. How I feel is nobody's business but mine.'

"Some days I still live with guilt. I did something against how I was raised. And I was the one who chose to take him off the ventilator. I blame myself for both of these. But when I remember the medical part of what happened, that there would have been no quality of life, I know I made the right call.

"I am healing now because I can articulate my feelings. I can say what happened without breaking down. Earlier, I thought I needed to be strong, and I didn't want people to see me having a sad face all the time. I changed the topic of conversation when DeShawn's death came up. When I did talk about his death, it felt as though what I had gone through had happened to someone else. It had not happened to me. I compartmentalized.

"I know now that I don't have to be strong all the time and that it is okay to cry. I feel everything I need to feel. I am not on autopilot. I relive what happened, sometimes a little at a time. Shutting down is no longer an option."

"Tessa Mae": Swept Up Into the Clouds

"All of a sudden, I felt myself floating upward toward the ceiling. I could see everyone working on my body from above."

When someone is clinically dead, their heart and breathing have stopped. Unlike legal death, which is irreversible, clinical death can sometimes be reversed. That reversal happened to Tessa Mae when she was in an intensive care unit because of a life-threatening neuromuscular disease. She was in her late twenties when the following events took place.

Paralyzed

I had been sick for a few days with a moderate cough, but suddenly one afternoon I went from being able to breathe on my own to needing to use my ventilator. Even with that, I could not catch my breath. A heaviness settled on me, and I knew I urgently needed help. My landlord at the time drove me to the emergency room at a nearby hospital. I had no idea that anything more was going to happen than potentially getting some medicine and going back home.

At the hospital, they took me directly to an individual room in the emergency department, even though the waiting room was crowded. That meant that my condition wasn't good.

In the room, they put me on oxygen because my oxygen level was a little low. They kept dismissing my concern about my condition, though, saying that I must be fine because my oxygen level was okay. But with the neuromuscular disease I have, the oxygen level is not an accurate measurement of what's going on. It is weakness in the diaphragm that is crucial.

To see whether my muscles for breathing were working right, the hospital team needed to be looking at my carbon dioxide levels to make sure those weren't building up. If that happened, I could stop breathing because of weak diaphragm muscles, even though my oxygen level was okay.

But the medical professionals weren't looking at my carbon dioxide levels, and they weren't looking at much else, for that matter. They told me that I was totally fine, even though it had become much harder for me to breathe. So they admitted me to a regular floor in the hospital instead of to the intensive care unit.

That night I "coded." The monitors I was hooked up to showed that I had stopped breathing. A "Code Blue" was activated, and a code team came and intubated me, which restored my breathing. I was transferred from my regular room to the intensive care unit where I had full breathing support.

I was supposed to be in a medically induced coma, paralyzed and unconscious. But I was actually completely awake because even though the paralyzing medications had worked, the medications to put me into a coma had not worked. I could not move anything. I couldn't even blink my eyes to tell them that I was conscious and could feel everything and was in excruciating pain choking on the breathing tube that was down my throat.

They were also flopping my body around, not being careful in the way they moved me. That was bad enough for any patient but especially for one with a connective tissue disease like me. They were dislocating my joints, which put me in even more excruciating pain.

But it was more than just not being able to move or say anything or suffering physically. I felt as though I was being annihilated. It was like I didn't exist anymore. I was not myself.

Even worse, I was appalled to hear the unkind things the people on the code team were saying about me as I was gagging and choking on the breathing tube. They said that I was a burden to the system. With my chronic disease, I was a waste of resources. I shouldn't be getting the kind of care I was getting. They laughed and made crude remarks about things that were important to me.

I was traumatized by their lack of respect and lack of dignity and was dismayed to think how they might treat those who, unlike me, were socially marginalized.

Plus, it felt as though I was drowning. They weren't properly suctioning the mucus that I had from COVID-19 and the pneumonia they had diagnosed me with. The breathing tube was badly clogged. I felt as though I was breathing through less than a flattened straw. I could scarcely breathe at all.

I had the most primal, innate fear you can imagine—no one knowing that I was choking and drowning while everyone was making jokes about my condition.

All this occurred during the first time I coded in that hospital stay. A couple of weeks later I became clinically dead.

Out of My Body

I was intubated for about a week. But they took the breathing tube out far too soon because they did not do a test to check the strength of my diaphragm, which had weakened because of my neuromuscular disease. Nor did they put me on a ventilator, like I was at home. So I weakened very quickly. And because my body was working so hard to breathe, the heart monitor suddenly flatlined. And I stopped breathing.

Another Code Blue was initiated, and hospital staff flooded the room. I could feel my ribs cracking as they did chest compressions. Someone was trying to resuscitate me with a bag-valve mask. They were trying to place a central line into a vein in my neck to give me intravenous medications. They were also trying to put a line into an artery in my wrist that monitors blood pressure with every beat of the heart. That produced sharp pains because it was hitting a nerve.

Machines were beeping. Everything was chaotic, though a controlled chaos to some degree, and I was extremely fearful. Someone said, "How did this happen so quickly?"

All of a sudden, I felt myself floating upward toward the ceiling. I could see everyone working on my body from above, though the sounds were a bit echo-like, far away.

Also suddenly, memories of my whole life came to me. They weren't of events or places, but of all the people I had ever known and loved. They flashed by very quickly, one by one, lingering on people who were closest to me. I remember feeling that I missed them.

I went through a tunnel of memories to a cliff edge on a mountaintop that was completely disconnected from everything else. I stepped off the cliff, but instead of falling, I was swept up into the clouds. They were a pinkish-orange sunset hue.

I instantly felt an overwhelming sense of love and peace. All my pain and fear were gone. I had an assuring, deep-rooted, anchoring sense of calmness and rest.

I met a being of love. He wrapped me in his arms and comforted me. I felt an overflowing sense of assurance that everything was going to be okay. Being wrapped in his arms felt very real and palpable.

The being of love's communication was unspoken, but it became audible when he said that it was not my time yet. I had to go back. When he said that, I felt myself falling back into the place where I was hovering over everyone. And instead of being dreamlike and then waking up from that, it was the opposite. I had felt more awake encountering God. Going back into the room where I was being worked on felt like going back into a dream.

Again, I saw everyone working on me. They had come to the point at which they were giving up on doing anything else. They were saying, "We've exhausted everything we could do. She's not responding." So they were about to pronounce the time of my death.

Back Into My Body

I entered my body, and my bodily pain came back. I struggled to breathe. But I had a deep sense of peace that everything was going to turn out well, though it wasn't as intense as when I was actually with God. My fear subsided.

Then someone exclaimed, "Oh, I have a pulse! I have a pulse!"

There was a flurry of activity when the medical professionals got a renewed sense of hope that they might be able to save me after all. In the end, they succeeded.

After they left, I saw that they had left the crash cart in the room with its emergency medical equipment. The heart monitor was still hooked up to me, plus the defibrillator, which could shock your heart back into a normal rhythm. The defibrillator pads were still on my chest.

I remember hearing the heart rhythm and picturing the heart monitor, how it had been beating and then how it had flatlined. That prompted the thought that once our hearts stop, we are at a crossroads moment, a kind of reckoning. If we had previously chosen to embrace the kind of peace I had when encountering the being of love, we would know that at the end there would be a meeting with that being of love, the being who is close to the brokenhearted and who binds up their wounds. I felt that that was unquestionably real.

The deep sense of peace I had acquired helped me endure the rest of the hospital stay. I had to undergo multiple rounds of plasmapheresis through a central line and dialysis catheter in my neck. My organs failed. I went through agony dealing with the multiple procedures I had to withstand. But having a sense of peace, knowing that I would be okay, made a huge difference.

Faith and Doubt

The biggest thing I took away from that month in the hospital was that it dispelled all doubts about the reality of God. I had previously had a full belief that God was real, but I had strong doubts from time to time, especially in moments of suffering. During the past ten years, I had been through other critical, life-threatening situations, in some of which I had to be resuscitated with chest compressions and arterial lines.

During those earlier life-threatening situations, I felt God's presence more strongly than at any other times in my life. He gave me comforting words of peace, the kind of peace embodied in the scriptural statement, "Do not let your hearts be troubled or afraid."

But I also wrestled with that sense of peace. All of my prayers were coming back to, "God, I cannot go through that again. I literally cannot do it. So if you're going to put me through it again, I cannot believe in you anymore."

Actually, it was stronger than that. If I had to go through another horrendous experience, I would rather have died first. Part of me was amazed beyond belief and so wonderfully glad that I was still alive. Yet it felt as though my body was saying, "Okay, God, I am turning my back on you entirely. I'm not going to have anything to do with you if you let this happen again, because I just can't endure it one more time. I would rather die."

That may sound suicidal. But it was different because it came from a place of desperately wanting to live. It was an extreme plea of my soul to God, saying, "I just can't experience something to that level again. So if you're going to let that happen, just take me home first."

Even though I meant what I said, I was terrified of it all happening again, because I couldn't imagine ever giving up believing in God. And I didn't want to die. I didn't feel that I had lived my purpose yet. I still had people to love and talents that I hadn't fully used.

I wanted to turn away from God in those life-threatening situations, even though I could do nothing but turn to him to have any kind of serenity. So I clung to faith more than ever.

Those situations did happen again, even worse than before. I had to give up things I was passionate about. I had to withdraw from college. I couldn't play the oboe anymore because of my low lung function. I couldn't play the piano because I couldn't hold my shoulders up enough to move my hands. Though playing the cello was easier because it didn't require moving my shoulders up as much, I couldn't hold my wrist up enough to hold the bow. I lost many jobs because I ended up in the intensive care unit too many times. Then I became deaf in my left ear, and now I am losing more of my vision.

I used to be scared of the things I could lose, and I still get scared from time to time. But losing those things has opened my eyes more to what those around me may be going through. Even though my capacities have been dwindling, I realize that giving just a smile or word of encouragement to someone could plant a seed that makes a difference in their life.

I am filled with a determination to use every last ounce of energy in my body to its fullest potential, knowing that every next moment could be my last. That may sound like a cliché, but truly, to wake up another day has become such a gift. I can't take it for granted. I have come to treasure each day and what I am able to do, even if it seems small. I now feel that my greatest accomplishments are the people I have loved.

Two years ago, a friend went through unimaginable pain in a terminal illness. I was able to look her in the eyes and say, "I am so sorry." She started to go into some of her story, then stopped and looked at me and said with a depth of heart that I cannot fully articulate except through tears, "You get it. You get it." Those are some of the most moving words that have ever been spoken to me.

I also have come to believe with certainty that life after death is indisputably real and that death is not something to be feared but is an awakening into real, full, eternal life. It is an entrance into a better love than we could ever dream of or experience here on earth.

When I was encountering God, I sensed him saying to me, "I made you. I love you. And I will sustain you and preserve you. I will not abandon you. I will restore your soul. I will walk with you through the dark valley. You are the sheep of my hand. And at the end of your days on earth, I will carry you home."

I won't say that my doubts about God were entirely extinguished, because I'm human and I still wrestle. But that experience allowed me to be at peace despite dealing with the daily struggles of a life-threatening illness.

I have had to be intubated multiple times since encountering the being of light and now am facing major cardiothoracic surgery. The potential of a medical emergency and the prospect of surgery are sometimes terrifying. But knowing that I have someone who goes through them with me gives me a great deal of peace. I am grateful for each new breath God gives me.

Saved from Suicide

In some of my everyday conversations, I asked the person I was talking to whether anyone had said something kind that had changed the direction of their life. Four of the first five people instinctively thought of an event that had alleviated suicidal impulses. Three of those four had experienced the event decades earlier yet were able to describe it in graphic detail.

Every suicidal person has a unique story. At the same time, every suicidal person has some kind of emotional pain. "Carter," who told me about a suicide attempt a week and a half before I talked with him, said, "As a result of a failed love relationship, I became flooded with hopelessness about my prospects for finding love. I agonized over the fear of being alone with my thoughts." Each of the following persons also experienced hopelessness and agony to such a degree that they no longer wanted to continue living.

A trigger warning: If you have been suicidal in the past or are currently having suicidal thoughts, these stories may prompt suicidal impulses. You should probably not read them. If you do read the stories and are tempted toward suicide, call or text the Suicide and Crisis Lifeline at 988, or talk to someone you trust.

"Annette": The Letter

Annette grew up in Hong Kong, where her parents were missionaries from the United States. She became suicidal when she was a teenager largely because she had been treated badly by her parents. A correspondence she struck up with a college student proved to be a major turning point for her. She was in her late forties when we talked.

Rage and Beatings

"It has taken me many years to frame what I went through as a child, trying both to honor my parents yet be truthful about what they did to me. Their verbal and physical aggression was a daily occurrence. Sometimes there was all-out rage, especially when I had a bad report card—shouting, yelling, grabbing me by the hair, dragging me across the room, beatings.

"It was mostly my mother who did those things. My job was to make her proud of me. And that was wrapped up in how neat my room was, which was usually sloppy, and how well I did in school, which was not good.

"I tried to win my parents' love and approval, but that kept ending in failure. My levels of self-esteem tanked. I tried again and again, but nothing worked. I could not keep them happy. I was dejected all the time.

"Once when I was smaller, my dad got really mad at me for something. Somehow, in a rage, he picked me up by the ankles and hung me upside down. He kept holding me until he got over it. My whole physical self was consumed by an aggressor. I don't know how I got down off that, but I cried on the way to school and could not stop crying at school.

"My teachers at the British public school I went to sometimes asked me what was going on, but I felt pressure to keep quiet. As missionaries, my parents were honored in the community in which we lived. I was supposed to be an emissary of the Christian faith I had grown up in. So I felt an obligation to cover up what was happening at home. When teachers asked, I sat in silence with tears flowing down my cheeks. Or I said that I was sad and that everything was distressing.

"One night when I was twelve my parents went to a parent-teacher conference at school, probably getting another bad report about my studies or my daydreaming and not applying myself in class. I was in bed fast asleep when they came home. I think I was supposed to have done some kind of house cleaning while they were gone.

"My mom was furious. She flung open the door to my room, turned on the light, grabbed my hair, and dragged me out of bed and down the hallway. She shook me hard and threw me against the wall. I don't know whether that was deliberate or a result of her brutal anger. My head hit the concrete wall so hard that I probably got a concussion. All the next week I had to cover the bump on my head so I could go to school. My parents never took me to a doctor for it.

"That was one of the worst things they did, and it was the first extreme physical injury. It made me think that what they were doing to me was not normal. Up until then I had believed that their discipline was justified, because I was the one who had done something wrong. That night I believed I deserved only some of what I got. My mother had gone too far."

Running Away from Home

"For a couple of years prior to that episode, I had been running away from home. I felt horrible and miserable because of the daily rage and violence.

"I never stayed away overnight. Everything shut down in Hong Kong by eleven or twelve at night, including the public transport shelters. My friends could not take me in, because their houses were too small. Also, I stood out wherever I went. I was white in a Chinese city and I had blazing red hair. It was too risky trying to be homeless."

I Wanted to Kill Myself

"After that raging incident with my mother, I became suicidal. I could not see an end to my misery. From my perspective now, thirty-five years later, I realize that misery has seasons and that time changes things. But at twelve or thirteen, my home life felt permanent—an eternity of vicious mistreatment and disconsolate depression. I could not see a future.

"I was familiar with suicide. I had two friends whose mothers had killed themselves. And suicide was common in Hong Kong. Every time after exams, there were reports of 'jumpers,' students who had failed their exams and who had thrown themselves off tall buildings. It was considered tragic, but it was also understood, in a strange way, as natural and normal. I began to accept it as a possibility for me.

"I don't think my parents realized how dangerous a place I was in. I had so much shame for being a bad student that I internalized most of the abuse. That was why self-destruction seemed to be the only out. I dreamed about how good it would be to be done with living.

"I dabbled in suicide attempts. I took a bunch of pills. I went to the tops of a few tall buildings where I had a strong impulse to run and jump. But it took too much courage. I was a failure even at killing myself.

"One time, though, a friend had to take me to the emergency room at the hospital. My parents were horrified. They blamed me for being selfish for wanting to kill myself. That made me feel even more rejected.

"On top of that, there was spiritual abuse: 'God is unhappy with you. You are not pleasing God.' By this time, I had abandoned the Christian faith of my parents. If what they had was Christian faith, I didn't want anything to do with it."

The Letter

"One day when I was thirteen or fourteen, out of the blue, I got a letter from a college student in the United States whom I had never met. She had written as part of a project she and others were doing. They had a missionary handbook that had my family's names in it, and they chose people to write to.

"The person introduced herself and invited me to write back if I had concerns or anything I wanted to share with her. It was a very sweet, kind letter. I wrote back and told her about my parents and everything that was happening.

"It felt safe to tell her those things, because she was totally disconnected from my world and could not get my parents in trouble. I trusted her.

"Here I was, drowning in depression, wanting to end my life, and her letters, which came every two weeks, served as a lifeline. They prompted me to think that I might have a future, because she was a college student, and I had not thought that far ahead. They gave me hope that I wouldn't have to live in pain and misery forever. They got me through the next few years until I could go to college and get out of my home.

"We lost touch at some point. And then we reconnected two or three years ago via Facebook. I told her she had saved my life. She had no idea that she had, because I had never told her about the impact she was having on me."

"Naomi": Coloring in a Professor's Office

Naomi describes an unusual session with one of her college professors that was instrumental in easing her from a deep depression. She was in her early forties when we talked.

"I had become suicidal during my freshman year in college. I didn't have a specific plan to kill myself, but I was in such a dark place that I did not think I could genuinely connect with any other human. That to me made life not worth living. It wasn't going to work for me.

"Maybe that was self-isolation. It was depression for sure. I was in a fog that lasted for weeks.

"At some point during that time, I ran into one of my professors on campus. He must have sensed what I had been feeling, because he invited me to his office to color. I thought, 'That's not going to solve anything.' But I also thought, 'I have absolutely nothing to lose.' So I went.

"I don't remember whether he silently invited me or stated in words, 'We don't have to talk. We can just color.' However the invitation came, I felt that I didn't have to do anything to be with him. I didn't have to say anything. I didn't have to smile or frown. I was free to do nothing other than color.

"We both colored, with crayons and coloring books, for a good forty-five minutes, maybe an hour. We didn't say anything.

"What stood out to me was that I had been offered a free gift of being with someone without having to say anything. That gift was a significant turning point for me. It made me feel that my existence mattered. I didn't have to do anything to earn that sense of worth.

"The experience introduced me to the idea of simply being. I was allowed merely to be even though I didn't produce anything. It was okay to take up my professor's time and be in his space without talking or doing anything. I could simply exist, and that would be enough. I had not realized that before.

"I began to connect with other humans, and my depression lifted."

"Caleb": A Long Hug

In this dramatic story, Caleb describes a chance encounter that turned into a suicide intervention. He was in his early thirties when we talked, several years after the event he describes.

"I was walking down a tunnel of misery, doing miserable things and thinking miserable thoughts about myself. The day arrived when I said, 'Okay, today's the day.'

"A homeless friend of mine, who had sold me weed and who called himself Kevin Douglas Ross, knew something was off that day. But he helped me secure a weapon, saying, 'It's your choice.'

"I drove around, looking for a sign not to kill myself. I put an ultimatum on God. I demanded a hug—a physical hug, not a metaphorical one: 'If you're real, God, you can make it happen. Prove to me that you're real.'

"Half a minute later I drove into a parking lot at Walmart to grab some last snacks. Two women I had never seen before walked out the door as I was approaching it. One of them said, 'Do you know how much God loves you?'

"Thirty seconds later I started bawling. They threw their arms around me and together hugged me for a good two or three minutes as I sobbed.

"I couldn't tell them all the pain that had brought me to that point, but they knew enough to know I had a weapon, which they took with them. They also took much of the self-hate, anger, and acute distress I had. They left with my demons.

"I walked away knowing I was loved."

"Caroline": Moral Beauty

Caroline was in her early sixties when we talked. She had intended to kill herself one summer when she was in her early twenties, but the thought that there might be such a thing as "moral beauty" saved her. That kept her alive for a number of years until she discovered that she wanted to keep living more than she wanted to die.

"When I was in college, one of the participants in a small discussion group I was in read a passage from Leo Tolstoy's *War and Peace* in which soldiers were depicted sitting around a campfire telling tales of moral beauty. The person asked, 'What is moral beauty?'

"The idea that soldiers could talk about moral beauty in the middle of a war was stunning to me. Up until then I had thought that human life was tainted and not worth living. Even the good was tainted, I thought.

"I had been keeping a journal in which I wrote down all the suffering in the world along with my own personal suffering. But the idea of moral beauty prompted me to think that if I was going to be honest and have a genuine assessment of life, I needed to consider beautiful things as well. So in addition to writing down what was hard and painful, I started including instances of moral beauty.

"I was very meticulous about it. I went into a grocery store once and was looking for a particular kind of frozen pizza. They didn't have it. But a store person went out of their way to go to the back of the store to find one for me. That went down in my account of moral beauty. So did a description of someone running after a person on a train platform who had dropped a newspaper. I started keeping track of all these things. That kept me alive for a lot years until I got to a time when I was able to deal with my issues head on.

"Until that time came, I had decided I was going to kill myself on a certain day of the year. I had picked a way to do it. Every year, though, when the date came, I said to myself, 'You're not old enough to make that decision. You need to live some more before you can make it. You don't know for sure that everything is tainted and that life is not worth living.' And then I kept writing in my journal.

"The day I finally resolved the issue of whether to keep living was my birthday. I was thirty-one. I started saying these things and was surprised when I said back to myself, 'Bullshit! You have lived long enough. What you are saying is just an excuse not to think about the matter. So what is your answer? Do you think your life has been worth it, or not?'

"That was a terrifying confrontation to have with myself. I had to answer honestly: 'No, I don't think my life has been worth it.' And then I thought, 'Oh, I guess I have to kill myself.'

"All of a sudden, it seemed as though out of nowhere, I heard a tiny voice in myself say, 'I don't want to die. I don't want to die.' I had never heard that voice before.

"And then I thought, 'Oh, I can't kill myself because if I do, that will be homicide. And I don't want to commit a murder.'

"For years, the part of me that wanted to die had been so loud that I couldn't hear the part of me that wanted to live. After I had that talk with myself, I realized that what I needed to do was to pay as much attention to the part of me that wanted to live as I had been paying to the part that wanted to die. So I started doing everything I could think of to celebrate the beauty of life.

"I took myself to an exhibit of Marc Chagall's paintings in the city where I live, because I love his art. I was practically dancing through the exhibit. People were looking at me as though I was strange because I was laughing out loud at the paintings. I was simply being happy at doing something I loved. I realized that if I felt that intensely about paintings on a wall, I had a lot more life in me.

"Later, I told someone that I had my own three wise men. One was Marc Chagall. One was the author of *War and Peace*. And the other was the person who had brought up the idea of moral beauty in the college discussion group. I would never have gotten to the point at which I could decide to keep living if I had never encountered that idea."

2 Family

"Sara": Betrayed by My Husband

"I never imagined that my life would blow up as we approached our twenty-fifth wedding anniversary."

Just before leaving for a twenty-fifth wedding anniversary celebration trip with her husband, Sara learned that he had been alcoholic and addicted to sex outside their marriage for the previous twenty years. She was devastated, but tried to save the marriage.

Beginnings

Sara grew up in an active, Christian family. "The people in my family were highly involved in church life. My extended family was close knit, and their values sprung from their Christian faith.

"I went to a Christian college. I thought, 'I'll probably make some of my lifelong friends there and possibly meet a spouse in addition to becoming equipped to do something with my life. I assumed that if you met your spouse at a college that required you to have a pretty strong faith to get in, you would be safe.

"I met someone during freshman orientation. We dated all four years of college and got married right after I graduated. We traveled for my husband's job during the first several years we were married, and then we settled down.

"During the next twenty some years, "Paul" and I were involved in church life. We were small group leaders and youth group leaders. We taught Sunday School and were on the missions committee. We organized and ran the first adult mission trips ever done at our church with trips to foreign countries. We even founded a charity that provided support to medical missions in lesser developed countries.

"I never imagined that my life would blow up as we approached our twenty-fifth wedding anniversary."

Suspicions

Paul asked Sara whether she wanted a ring for their twenty-fifth anniversary. "When we got married, we didn't have any money. We were young kids, right out of college, and I never had a nice ring. I said, 'You know what? I'm not a huge jewelry person. Having a ring doesn't mean that much to me. I'd rather have an experience, a memory-building thing.'

"We had been to a number of foreign countries, and we loved to travel. Our children had not been out of the States, and my parents were celebrating their fiftieth anniversary. So I said, 'Let's do a trip, taking our children and my parents, and we'll celebrate both anniversaries.'

"That became the plan. Our children and I learned about the wildlife in the country we were going to and the animals we would see. We got packed and ready for the trip. And I hurried to finish the taxes for our business so that I could be on the trip knowing that everything had been turned in to our accountant before we left, because the tax deadline was in two weeks.

"As I was going over the checkbook register, I discovered some anomalies. There were a lot of cash withdrawals, and we hardly ever spent cash on anything. So the withdrawals didn't make sense. Plus, they were for $500 to $1500 at a time. I totaled them up for the checkbook I was working with, which covered only four months, and the total came to $16,000 to $18,000. That didn't make any sense.

"I pulled out the ATM receipts. My husband had been traveling to a large city two times a month for five days at a time. All of the ATM slips, I noticed, were from his trips to that city. At first, I thought he was taking taxis, maybe paying cash at restaurants, and the like. But the amounts withdrawn were huge. So I took a closer took at the ATM receipts and quickly realized they were from really late at night in the really bad parts of the city.

"I knew something was very wrong. My whole body tensed. I was shaking."

Revelations

"I approached Paul with the stack of receipts and said, 'Would you like to explain where you spent $16,000 in four months when you were away?'

"He said that he had been drinking heavily and that the cost for that was really high in the city he had gone to. He had been going to fancy places and buying expensive bottles of wine. Plus, he had been treating people and eating extravagant dinners, taking large UberX cars to get to the restaurants, trying to feel like a big deal. He had been keeping it from me, he said, because he knew I wouldn't like all that spending.

"I started thinking it through—'You could drop $200, $300, $400, maybe even $500 on a fancy meal and expensive wine, especially if you're treating a bunch of other people to drinks, but not $1500 a night. And not a couple of those in one three-day business trip. So I went back to him and said, 'That's not everything. I can tell.'

"He then said that he was a closet alcoholic, a binge drinking alcoholic.

"I didn't even know there was such a thing. I imagined alcoholics as day drinkers who are hung over every morning and miss work. But he had never been like that. So what he said was a shocker.

"He said that he had been a raging alcoholic for nearly twenty years and that he did his drinking on trips when he was away from me or at home when I was already in bed or when I was out. He had removed bottles from our house, he said, so that I did not see wine or hard liquor bottles in the recycling bin. Also, when he was commuting by train, he was drinking in the bar car on the train the whole way home. I had no inkling of any of this, because his tolerance was so high that I had never seen him drunk.

"With much prodding, I got the admission that he'd been buying drinks for women. But he said that was all—he just bought drinks for them. He never left for any place with them and had no physical contact with them.

"That still didn't ring true. I kept at it until he admitted he had been drinking in strip clubs, which are like a vacuum cleaner for your wallet. You can easily drop a thousand to fifteen hundred dollars between drinks and tipping. He had been doing that once or twice on every business trip for a really long time.

"That piece of news was devastating. I couldn't imagine leaving on the trip to celebrate our anniversary the next morning, especially with kids and parents in tow."

Harmful Counseling

Sara called the church she and Paul attended, and they met with the counseling pastor that night. "Instead of having a healing experience, though, it was very damaging. The counselor immediately tried to distribute blame equally—'Let's talk about what you may have done in the marriage to contribute to this problem.' The counselor also immediately assumed I was codependent when Paul said he was an alcoholic. I have done a lot of therapy since that time, and I know now it was not true that I was codependent.

"The counselor would not allow us to leave the office that night until Paul looked me in the eyes and said that what he had done was wrong, that I didn't deserve it, that he was sorry, and would I forgive him. Paul said this in the way I could imagine our older child talking if I took him by the scruff of his collar and held him up to our younger child and said, 'You tell him you're sorry for hitting him.' My husband simply said, 'Sorry.' There was nothing contrite in him. No compassion or empathy. No desire for forgiveness. He wanted to get out of that office and nothing more.

"I said, 'I'm not ready to forgive right now. This is all new information. It feels like the tip of the iceberg. It doesn't feel like I have all the information, and I really can't say I forgive you when I don't even know what I'm forgiving.'

"The counselor said to me, 'Sara, in light of all your sins, every sin of your whole life, picture them at the foot of the cross and then tell Jesus you can't forgive this man for what he did, even though Jesus has forgiven you for all your sins.'

"That counselor shamed me when I was already broken.

"I was nowhere near being able to forgive at that point. Forgiveness needs to occur much later when you have a full understanding, or it doesn't mean anything. So what the counselor asked me to say only served to make me feel worse, and it did nothing to facilitate further communication or any healing between me and my husband. I left feeling beat up and guilty."

Compound Trauma

Sara and her family left on the trip the next morning. "At this point I was not ready to explain to my parents or our children what was happening. They were all packed, had gotten passports, and were ready to go. So I had to go.

"I did not sleep the night before we left and did not eat the next day, the day we were traveling. Nor did I sleep the following night, at the hotel in our destination country. I paced the bathroom all night long, writing out a thousand questions. My husband, though, had drunk a bottle of wine and instantly fallen asleep, snoring.

"After two nights at the hotel, we drove to a resort where we were given a room on the third floor of an A-frame built into a hillside overlooking the ocean. Our children ran ahead of us into the room, and before we even got inside with the luggage, our younger child fell from the balcony. He landed three stories below on a little grassy area that was sloped. He was unconscious. Fortunately, he had not hit his head, but we were concerned about a spinal injury, so we called an ambulance.

"The hospital was open air, because it was in a remote rural area in a lesser developed country. It didn't have any food, water, or medication, not even a painkiller. After going back to the resort to get these, a half-hour taxi ride each way, I stayed there all night in a folding chair by the crib my child was in. It was super hot and muggy all night.

"That was the most miserable night of my entire life. I had not slept previous nights, had gone a couple of days without eating, now knew about my husband's secret life, and was concerned that my child was brain damaged or paralyzed.

"In the morning, my child and I were taken by helicopter to a hospital in the capital city, where there were CAT scan and MRI machines. Everyone else drove all day to get there.

"I sat in a tiny curtained cubicle, alone, thinking the hospital pediatric neurologist was going to tell me my child would never walk again or had a skull fracture or serious brain injury. In the end, they found nothing other than a mild swelling on my child's neck. It felt like a miracle.

"The next day we were all on a plane home."

Trying to Save the Marriage

Sara took steps to save her marriage. "After getting back from that traumatic trip, all my efforts went into trying to save the marriage. To do that, we had to get my husband sober from alcohol. You can't make good decisions when your brain is affected by alcohol. And he also had to become sober from all the sexual stuff.

"Paul said that he was on board and that this was his desire. He was ready to be healthy. He for sure wanted to stay married and in the family. He had been dreading being caught, but was relieved when he finally was.

"I came up with five basic things I needed from him in order for me to stay in the marriage. I needed full disclosure—he had to answer all my questions. He had to be accountable to someone. We set up filtering programs on his cell phone and the computers in our house. He was not going to travel alone anymore. And I was going to have a lot more involvement with the money. For someone who was in his position, considering what he'd done, these were not all that invasive, especially since he had said he wanted to stay married.

"But he balked at a lot of them. He didn't want to answer all my questions. He kept saying that he had said enough.

"We selected a person to whom he could be accountable, and he set up coffee dates with him. But they just chatted, and he never opened up about any of the important things. So he wasn't actually being held accountable.

"He agreed to start counseling, but he went for three or four times and then quit. He did this with several counselors. He didn't like them, he said.

"I gave him a lot of leeway on this last one, because I thought he was overwhelmed, ashamed, embarrassed, and full of guilt. It was hard giving up more than one addiction. He was, though, going to Alcoholic Anonymous meetings and to another recovery program's meetings every night."

Betrayal Trauma

Sara suffered. "I wasn't able to think straight. I had an upset stomach and could not eat well. I felt sick all the time and dropped thirty pounds. I spent extra time with our business to allow Paul time to get healthy and sober. My heart was broken.

"When you have a sex addict in a marriage, I have heard it said, it's like the addict has driven a large truck through your home, through your whole life, leveling everything. And then he puts the truck in reverse, running over you. When the ambulance shows up, he gets in, leaving you lying there. That is what happened to me. The whole focus is on the man and getting him better. I now know, after many years, that I suffered from betrayal trauma, which, I have learned, has very real effects on the brain.

"I had a brain scan, which showed my brain lighting up like a soldier who has just gotten back from Iraq with PTSD. I also tested positive for raging ADHD, which I've never had, and which you don't just suddenly contract in your fifties.

"The trauma is such a visceral, deep, painful, difficult thing that affects every area of your life—your present, your future, your past even. It is all called into question. You go into a heightened fight or flight mode. Life becomes about survival. What happened was done by the person who was closest to you, the one you trusted, the one you should be relying on to help you through the trauma.

"The most problematic part of the trauma is its effect on the hippocampus, the card catalog of your brain. It's where you store all your memories, the narrative of your life, in order. When someone tells you that they've been lying to you for decades and that your assumed reality was not the actual reality for that length of time, it's as though the whole drawer of memories has been dumped out onto the floor. Not only are they all out of order, there are new cards in the card catalog with terrible pieces of information. You don't know where anything fits together.

"Everything about your history together is called into question. And the only person who can sort it out for you is the addict, whom you now have to trust as being honest with you after decades of not being honest. But he is not interested in helping you order all that information, because it doesn't look great for him. So you stay in a heightened state where you are trying to figure it all out and piece your life back together.

"Now that all the hopes and dreams and everything you've worked for are demolished, you're trying to determine what kind of future you can have. How do you get through today? And what actually was your past? It's as though you wake up being an amnesiac who doesn't understand your history. None of it.

"For eighteen months, I lived in all this while my husband got sober from alcohol and all the sexual things, including pornography. So he said. There was no way for me to know for sure. Later, I realized he never really stopped lying to me or shut all the doors to his addictive behaviors. So I don't know how much was and wasn't going on, even though he was telling me he was sober from those things."

More Revelations

During those eighteen months, Sara got more revelations about what her husband had done. "In the beginning, all Paul would admit to was strip clubs and pornography. But with the amount of money he had spent I knew it could not just have been that he was watching dances and giving out dollar bills. He had to be doing more than that at the strip clubs, or there had to be something further and deeper.

"On five separate occasions, we sat down and I learned more and more. Each time he said that it was everything, a full disclosure, and you can ask all your questions. Each time it got worse and worse. He had participated in every form of commercial sex that is possible, in the worst and most pernicious ways, for nearly twenty years.

"Some people think that women with cheating husbands know on some level that their husbands are cheating—there is no way they can hide it from their wives. But that is not true. I've learned from my own experience, from counselors who are trained in betrayal trauma, and from many other women I've met in various programs who are partners of sex addicts, that men who are sex addicts are able to live a dual life. They compartmentalize. They very carefully keep everything separate.

"That is what Paul admitted. When he was away from home on business and mission trips, he was living a bachelor's life. But when he was back home, he was the married father of two and a practicing Christian. The two realms were completely separate for him. One world never crossed over into the other world."

An Ultimatum

Also, during those eighteen months, Sara was checking on everything. "I had locked everything down pretty tight, so he didn't have a lot of freedom. If I was going to stay married, I would have to be hypervigilant. I tracked Paul's locations on my phone. I looked at the charges on our credit card. I checked his phone and his computer. It would have been pretty tough for him to be acting out in his addictions at that stage.

"However, he was not doing the five things I had asked for, at least not completely. He made steps on some of them, but he would quit. It was only I who went to the counseling that was supposed to be for the two of us. And I didn't believe I had ever had a full disclosure. He seemed so sincere and genuine when we had conversations that I thought, 'Okay. This is it. This is really all of it now.' And then I discovered some new piece of evidence that I wasn't even looking for that proved something large in the last conversation was still a lie. That kept happening.

"I finally gave him an ultimatum.

"I had found a prepaid credit card, which he should not have had. When I asked about it, he said it had been a gift from his mother who had sent it to him from another state. But I could see the name of the company that issued the card right on the card, and it was not a company that had a store in the other state.

"He said, 'Oh, just take the card. Whatever the balance is, you spend it. I don't need it. It was a gift. If you're going make a big deal out of it and act like it's something that it's not, I don't even want to look at it. You take it.'

"What he didn't realize is that those cards have unique numbers, and you can see when and where they were purchased and on what date, plus all the charges. I had looked them up and had seen that the card was purchased recently at a store where we live and that the charges were for hookup sites.

"At that point, I threw the card down on the bed and said, 'You need to sit down with me right now and answer all my questions, even the ones you've answered before, because everything's in question again—all my questions, until I'm finished and the whole truth is out here on the table. Or you have to pack your bags and leave, because I can't spend one more night in the house with a liar, with someone who is still lying to me after all this time.

"He chose to pack his bags and leave."

Divorce

Sara stayed married for the next two and a half years. "We lived separately, which was devastating to me, because I became a single mom of two young children. I could not keep the house, which was heartbreaking, because it was my dream house. I had designed it, planning out every single thing about it. I had to pack the whole place, sell it, find a new place, and move, with no assistance from my husband.

"At two points during the two and a half years of separation, I told him, 'I'm going to file for divorce. You're still not doing the things I asked you to do. There's no reason for us to keep being married.' Each of those times, he'd make a big, grand gesture. He still wanted to be married and wanted our family back together, he said. 'You are the only woman going forward for the rest of our lives. I'll go to the sex addiction workshop. I'm going to do the men's group, the couple's group with you, and then I'll do whatever follow up they say. I'm really going to work this plan now.' But he didn't do much about any of these, and everything fell away.

"The final straw came when we gave our older child a cell phone. We three were on a family plan, and the first month's phone bill went crazy. I got online and discovered that my husband was using a large amount of data. I could also see that he had called or texted three numbers forty to sixty times a day, including on his birthday when all four of us were at the beach for the day. I called the numbers. They all belonged to women.

"That was the day I marched over to his house—we were living in the same neighborhood—and said, 'Would you like to tell me who this person is, who this person is, and who this person is?' He was stunned. He said they were people from Alcoholics Anonymous and he was making arrangements about who was making the coffee or unlocking the church.

"I said, 'Sixty times a day, every day?! I don't think so.' When he still wouldn't tell me the truth, I said, 'It's time now.' I filed for divorce."

A New Life

Sara started life over. "For a number of years, both before and after the divorce, I was pretty much floundering. I felt stuck and was crying every day. I had to give up my dreams. I'd always believed there would be no divorce with my family. I had signed on for life and wanted to be with one man only and forever. I wanted thirty, forty, and fifty-year anniversaries. I wanted our children to have a dad in the house. I wanted to stay in the gorgeous house overlooking water and woods that I had designed. All of that was taken away.

"As for my emotional health, there was a whole lot of healing that should have started all the way back at the time of discovery but got sidelined in order to get my husband sober and healthy and then to resituate my kids and myself. I finally started my healing journey a couple years ago when I learned about betrayal trauma and how it affects spouses of sex addicts.

"I read a lot about betrayal trauma, listened to podcasts, watched videos, and went to workshops. I found counselors who had been trained in betrayal trauma. Regular counselors or clergy without that specialized training, I learned, can do way more harm than good, as happened that first night with the counseling pastor at our church.

"I also found my way to a Christian twelve-step recovery program for people who hurt. I met other women who were struggling. Most of them had husbands with porn addiction, and one or two had husbands who'd crossed the physical line. I don't think any had husbands who had a full blown sex addiction. But some women had been through something like what I had been through. And there was a really good leader. The whole experience with the program was a lifesaver for me.

"The most peaceful, most joyful, most fulfilling time that I have had in the last seven and a half years, two and a half of separation and five of divorce, were the years when I was a table leader at that twelve-step recovery program, helping other women who were just entering the process of recovery from situations like mine. I did nine sessions, which was very fulfilling.

"I am still heartbroken. But I have forgiven Paul and pray for him daily. I am grateful to have a home, though it is not the one I wanted. I'm grateful for a job that allows me the flexibility to get my kids ready for school in the morning, pick them up in the afternoon, and go to their basketball games and cello concerts.

"At some point I want to write about my experiences so as to help other women. It is not an easy subject to be honest about. It's humiliating. It's embarrassing even to be a partner of a sex addict. The details are pernicious and disgusting. Everything about the story is sad and ugly. Still, by telling my story, I can give purpose to my pain."

"Bella": Extricating Myself from Domestic Violence

"For two years, I kept going back and forth, to and from, that relationship. It got worse and worse and worse."

Bella experienced firsthand how hard it is for recipients of partner abuse to leave their abusers. She also experienced firsthand the emotional toll that repeated abuse exacts from its recipients. We talked several years after she graduated from college. She is now working at a job she loves.

The Beginning

The mistreatment Bella experienced began while she was in college. "At the college I went to, there was a 'ring by spring' culture, which encouraged students to become engaged by the spring semester of their senior year. This meant relationships had a particular weight on them. This dating culture felt exclusionary toward people of color, which I am, so I looked for a relationship through an online dating service.

"I found someone when I was a sophomore. We hit it off. But after a couple of years, things took a turn for the worse. I found out that my partner had drug challenges. I don't want to say he was wrestling with his own demons, but that's what it was like.

"He became highly unstable. He smoked weed and did hard drugs. He rented a motel room to do drug exchanges. Sometimes he hung out on the streets near where he lived, and sometimes he called me in the middle of the night because he needed someone to pick him up so he could get back home, where he was living with his parents.

"I was brought into a whole new world, which I never thought would happen—not that I was actually a part of it but that I was connected to it, in a way, as an extension of my partner. At the same time, I was trying to do school so that I could graduate at the end of the semester.

"One night during that spring semester, I was at my wits end. I was done with being just the one who picked him up. So I ignored his messages and phone calls and put him on block. Somehow, though, he navigated a way to get in contact with me. He kept calling, calling, calling, telling me how much he needed me to come get him from wherever he was. I finally relented.

"It was 2:00 am and pouring rain. As I was getting off the highway to get to the town my partner had gone to, my car spun off the exit ramp, and I landed in the ditch beside it. I saw that my phone was buzzing—my partner was begging me to come get him, rushing me, after he had done drugs or whatever it was he was doing: 'Hurry up. Hurry up. I need you to pick me up now.' I was terrified.

"In that moment, I took a step back. I realized that I needed to get away from the relationship because it was becoming so detrimental to me. I didn't want to have to call my mom, who lived in another state, and tell her what was going on. She and my dad didn't know anything about it.

"By the grace of God—I didn't know whether it was a good or a bad thing at that point—two men saw my car in the ditch and came down and pushed it out. I was still able to drive it. It was just covered in mud from the rainy day.

"I ended up meeting my partner, picking him up, and taking him home. But we both had to sleep in my car in his driveway the rest of the night, because his parents wouldn't let him inside the house."

Emotional Toll

As a result of what had been happening, Bella experienced a good deal of emotional distress. "There were multiple occasions that last semester of college when I had to pick up my partner. It made me less of a student and even less of a person. I started to become more and more a shell of myself. I was only a go-to person, running here and there to meet his every need. Nothing more.

"He became verbally abusive: 'You're never going to amount to anything. You need me, and you won't be able to do anything without me.' His parents also put a lot of pressure on me. At first, they had been very open to me. But as time passed, my relationship with them became contentious. I felt that I was always trying to prove in some way that I was good enough for them and also good enough for my partner. That, I think, was a big reason why I was going out and doing all the things I did to support him.

"I wished I could just have focused on my studies. I loved my major, and I loved what I was reading and researching in my major courses. I would have liked to spend time on the basic things of college life, such as being with my friends, going to the dining hall and having a nice meal, going to the gym—simply doing routine and mundane things rather than being exposed to my partner's being high and my not knowing what to do about it.

"I didn't sleep for weeks on end because I was trying to keep up with my studies and tend to my partner's needs, not thinking about my own needs. I didn't have any grasp of self-care. I didn't even know whether I would be able to graduate at the end of the semester, because I was falling behind in all my classes. I didn't have a sense of the future. Everything he had said felt true. I wasn't going to amount to anything.

"I got through the semester. My professors were understanding. I graduated and found a good job, which was more than I thought I would get at that time."

A New Start

After Bella graduated from college, she cut things off with her partner. "I got an apartment and started working. For the first time, I felt like myself. I was starting a new life.

"I began to have a sense of who I was, a sense of my own personality. I did what I wanted to do—simple things like cooking and hanging out with friends. I regained community connections, which had been set aside during my senior year. I was able to focus on myself again.

"One day as I was on my way to work I sensed that I had been having less mental fog. I was actually feeling productive. I could solve problems on my own outside the abusive relationship. That made me feel alive again. I was getting back to some sense of normality."

A Return

Unfortunately, this new beginning did not last long. "There's a saying that someone who has experienced some form of domestic violence tends to go back to the person who caused the violence an average of seven times.[1] That saying is very true, I learned.

"It's like the Stockholm syndrome, which occurs when people who are held captive 'form a psychological connection with their captors and begin sympathizing with them.' It also occurs when 'there's a bond between the abuser and the person being abused.' The 'positive feelings toward their abuser . . . [are] a coping mechanism that [the abused] uses to survive the days, weeks, or even years of trauma or abuse.'[2]

"Although my partner had been hurting me, he was the one person I felt I would receive love from. Being with him was the only place I felt loved.

"He texted me and called me. It was very difficult to ignore him when earlier we had had such a deep relationship. We had bonded to each other when we first met. There had been a spark, a fire of connection, and he had been very kind and sweet to me. That was hard to let go of.

"So when he reached out to me after I graduated, found an apartment, and gotten settled, it was like, 'Let's go on a date, let's just meet up, spend time together.' I found that I wanted to prove to him, and to myself, that I was in a better place. I wanted to say to him, 'The things you said I wouldn't be able to accomplish, I have.' I wanted him to see that.

"He came back into my life."

Worse

Things got worse. "My partner started living in my apartment. He quickly escalated from being verbally abusive to being physically abusive. There were days when I couldn't go to work because he would not let me leave my apartment. At times I became afraid that I wouldn't walk away alive.

"One day he took my phone when he left the apartment. At that point, my sense of confidence shattered. I had no control. I could not do anything.

---

1. Respond: Seeking to End Domestic Violence. See also National Coalition Against Domestic Violence. "Why Do Victims Stay?" The National Domestic Violence Hotline is 1-800-779-7233.
2. Cleveland Clinic. "Stockholm syndrome."

I lost my voice. The only way I could communicate was to use my computer. I contacted my friends to let them know I needed someone to help me. A family friend who themselves had experienced domestic violence said that I could file for an order of protection.

"I filed for an order of protection through the domestic violence court where I lived. They granted it for six months. I felt safe again.

"But after those six months, I had him back in my life. There was more physical abuse. For nearly two years since graduating from college, I kept going back and forth, to and from, that relationship. It got worse and worse and worse.

"It wasn't until he spat on me that I thought, 'If he spits on me, he's probably going to kill me the next time something comes up.' That triggered the thought, 'I need to stop engaging with him completely. Not at all, forever.' I finally had had enough. I felt that I had to have a complete change in my life.

"I went to the nearest police station. I told them what was going on, and they started my case. I got a second order of protection, this time for a year. I moved from my apartment. I switched jobs. I got information about myself—my address, my place of work—removed from the internet, so that he could not contact me after the protection order ended. I went under the radar completely. I made a clean break. And I never engaged with him again. That was about four years ago."

Looking Back

It had been very difficult for Bella to extricate herself from the relationship for several reasons. "There were a number of feelings I was trying to work through. I think the biggest thing I struggled with was feeling that if I left him, no one would love me. The shame and guilt I felt at not being able to leave him made me realize how much I had been codependent on others throughout my life. I had not felt empowered to do things on my own.

"I discovered that I was prone to having a freeze response whenever something happened with my partner. I would just freeze, meaning that I would not think about what had happened and would do nothing. Or I would run if I could, get away from him.

"I realized I was not assertive or communicative about what I needed or what I was feeling. I discovered that this showed up in all my relationships, even at work. I did not feel I could share an idea or share how I was processing something.

"There were times when I felt extremely suicidal, either because I could not get out when I was with my partner or because I did not have a sense of belonging in the world when I was not with him.

"I also felt I had let my Christian faith down. It made me feel less of a Christian to have been connected with someone who was doing all that illegal activity and who stayed in my apartment even though we weren't married."

Learning New Patterns

Bella has been unlearning the patterns she had exemplified. "I am taking steps to communicate my needs without being afraid that the response will be anger or abuse. I am surprised now when someone says, 'Okay, that's fine. That's understandable,' instead of my being physically threatened or verbally abused when I set a boundary of some sort. I am trying to voice my thoughts, not fearing being told that I'm stupid for thinking the way I do. I am regaining the voice I lost.

"Also, I am feeling more empowered because I went to the police and filed for a protective order to say that enough was enough. Doing this helped mitigate the freeze response I had with my partner. It also made me realize how important my needs are. I recognize now that I need to do things that satisfy myself. I don't want to have a life of abuse, and I feel more enabled to sustain the life I want.

"Because of the abusive relationship I had, when something comes up now with a friend or my current partner, my gut reaction sometimes is not to trust them. At first, my emotional safety feels jeopardized—they are not going to be there for me when I need them. But I have become mindful of this initial reaction and resist it instead of simply letting it get hold of me.

"I am encouraged when I am an advocate and a voice for others. When my friends tell me about something that is going bad in their relationships or when I engage with people who are in the middle of something traumatizing, I try to affirm them and validate them. 'You know that yucky thing that just happened to you? That's truly a red flag. Don't feel self-doubt about it.'

"I think there are stages as you move from being a victim to being a survivor. Right now I'm not too far removed from being a victim. But I am able to live free from abuse and also to be an advocate and a source of validation for others. I am exercising more self-care."

"Stephanie": A Schizophrenic Mother and an Abusive Father

"I realized that the harmful things she had done to me were done out of love, unlike the things my dad had done to me."

Stephanie left home the day after she graduated from high school because of the severe trauma she had experienced at home. She never spoke to her father again, though she saw her mother from time to time as an adult. She was in her early fifties when we talked.

Feeling Like Two Persons

Stephanie thinks of herself as having two separate parts. "When I filled out my college application, I wrote an essay with the title, 'What do you get when you cross a schizophrenic mother with an alcoholic, abusive father?' In it I described how I felt like a split person. I still feel that way.

"On the one hand, I have horrific scars from childhood traumas. I have painful and debilitating memories of them. Sometimes I feel very insecure and am a people pleaser at the expense of my own needs. On the other hand, I attended a highly regarded university. I was nationally ranked in tennis and saxophone. I have my own business now and can work at home, travel, and set my own hours. I have a beautiful family with four wonderful kids.

"The overarching theme of my life is that I don't have just one piece in it, but two. However, I do not let the bad piece define me. I am not simply the Stephanie who got pregnant by her dad at fifteen and got an abortion. I am so much more than that."

Before My Dad Left

Stephanie's parents divorced when she was young. "My mom and dad had my two brothers and then me. They divorced when I was about four because my dad was an alcoholic and wasn't showing up. I remember him drinking a lot. I also remember him hitting my mom and using wire hangers and duct tape to tie up my brothers, who were sometimes a little wild. We lived with my mom after the divorce, and my dad was not in the picture."

While My Dad Was Away

Stephanie's father stayed out of the picture for a couple of years until Stephanie was in first grade. "He had gotten remarried, and his new wife said that he should have a relationship with us kids. So we did the visit-dad-on-Sundays thing.

"During the next two years, I noticed that my mom was doing things that were not normal. I knew they weren't normal because I saw how my friends' moms acted when I visited them. Before supper my mom made me and my brothers wash our hands, dip them in bleach, wash our hands again, and then do another bleach dip. When I went to one of my friend's house, I saw that they didn't use bleach before eating. I asked my friend about it, and she said that washing your hands with soap and water was fine.

"My mom was a hypochondriac. Anytime there was any little thing wrong with me, it was doctor visits and tests. So I grew up hiding sicknesses because my mom totally overreacted and I didn't like missing school because of that.

"As more of these little instances happened, I came to believe that what she was doing was not right. When I was in the third grade, she got hospitalized.

"One day I got sick at school, and the school couldn't contact my mom. I said, 'You can't get hold of her because she's in the hospital.' That, of course, caught their attention: 'Why are those kids home alone?' They were going to call DCWS, the Department of Child Welfare Services, but I said, 'Wait. Call my dad.'

"That was a turning point, because that's when my dad got temporary custody of us kids. Then he went for full custody. My mom didn't go to the custody hearing. So in the middle of third grade, I and my two brothers started living with my dad.

"Later, I felt that I deserved the bad things that subsequently happened to me, because I was the one who said, 'You can call my dad,' when I was sick at school.

Living with My Dad

In the new household, there were six children—two young daughters of the woman Stephanie's father had married, Stephanie and her two brothers, and a girl her dad and the woman had together. "I kind of liked the situation, because I had a mom who wasn't schizophrenic. I was important to her, and we ended up having a close bond. I absolutely loved having younger sisters. One of them had Down Syndrome, and she loved on me. And I loved the child my dad and stepmom had.

"Unfortunately, my dad didn't stop drinking. And when he drank, he got abusive.

"One time we were having barbecue ribs and mashed potatoes, and my dad smacked me in the face for some reason. I cried, not because the smack hurt, but because my potatoes got bloody from the bloody nose I got from being smacked. So I couldn't eat them, and there weren't any more, because we didn't have a lot of food.

"My dad was very controlling with the food we did have. One thing we did was to can pickles. I was starving one day and went down to the basement and was eating pickles when my dad came home, which I was not expecting. I dropped the jar of pickles. It broke. My dad came downstairs, grabbed me, duct taped me to a metal post in the basement, then left. I had glass in my bare feet, plus pickle juice on them.

"My dad was gone overnight. Because I was sweaty and small, I was able to wriggle out of the duct tape. I used the duct tape to get the glass out of my feet. Then I cleaned the mess up so that you couldn't smell the pickles. When my dad came back, he acted as though nothing had happened. "Another time, he hit my stepmom. My older brothers weren't around, just the sister with Down Syndrome. The sister got upset. I was ten or eleven and petite for my age, but I stood in front of my stepmom and said, 'You can't hit her. You gotta stop.' I don't know what I expected, but, of course, I got hit too.

"Then two days later a very traumatic thing happened. I woke up and my stepmom was gone. She had taken my three sisters with her. I didn't care about my brothers because they were jerks and were misbehaving. But my sisters were an important part of my life and a source of stability. So I was very upset. And I was mad that my stepmom had not taken me."

Survival

When Stephanie was fifteen and a sophomore in high school, her father raped her. "I got pregnant and had an abortion. I had a lot of guilt about that, but I dealt with being pregnant the same way I dealt with everything else that was going on: 'What do I need to do to survive?'"

"My dad had beat me countless times, and I had gotten through that. He gave us kids marijuana and had done other things before he raped me. My main reaction to being raped and becoming pregnant was, 'Is this going to stop me?' My answer was, 'No.' I had overcome everything else so far and was not going to let this last thing keep me from going to college. That was my ticket out of the house.

"I was number one in my high school class. I was state ranked on the saxophone. I knew I had an opportunity to go to college. Plus, I knew, even then, that genetically there could be issues with the child. I felt as though I was at a fork in the road: 'This is going to make me or break me.' The pregnancy was one more thing in a long list of things I had to overcome. That is how I looked at it.

"It's not that being pregnant didn't matter, but I had to focus on getting food and other basic needs. I needed to know where I was eating and whose friend's house I could sleep at for the weekend.

"School became a safe haven. I always got positive attention at school, because I did well in it. I was active in every club and sport possible. I had a teacher who gave me free music lessons. He said, 'If you practice, I won't charge.' He's the one who got me into a highly selective university."

Repressed Memories

After Stephanie graduated from the university, she became a teacher, got married, and had children. "When my daughter got to fifteen, I started having weird memories, which I learned were flashbacks. At first I thought, 'Why am I having these dreams about myself when I was a child?' I talked to one of my brothers, and he said, 'Those weren't dreams. They really happened.'

"I went to therapy for two years. There I learned that if you're in a safe environment, it's natural for painful memories to surface. I was married to a very nice person who was a good provider. We had four great kids. That's when everything in my childhood started to come out.

"I dealt with that by doing competitive running, including marathons, which got my mind off the painful memories for a time. I did yoga twice a week. I worked hard. And I got great satisfaction from knowing that I gave my kids an idyllic childhood. They had everything they needed to succeed, because my husband and I were upper middle class. If our children wanted to do a sport, they could do it. We did vacations. I was able to do everything with them that I never got to do as a child. Knowing that I had broken the cycle of terrible abuse was very rewarding. Focusing on that was a big thing for me when the memories started spilling out.

"The flashbacks were foggy at first. But then they came into focus when they came back again. Every time I had a flashback, I wrote it down, and my therapist and I went over it.

"The hardest thing about the flashbacks was regret at not having done more to protect myself from what my dad did to me. When he first got custody of us, when I was nine, I remember him having an erection when I was sitting on his lap. I didn't understand what that was at the time—what nine year old does? And then there were times he unzipped my pajamas. I was mad about that because they covered my feet and were cozy and warm. I tried to protect myself once, but big things happened as a result.

"One time my dad was passed out on the couch. Besides drinking, he did heroin. I saw his black briefcase where he kept stuff. I opened it and discovered that there was a gun in it. I took the gun, pointed it at him, and pulled the trigger. But it didn't go off. I pointed it at myself, and it didn't go off again. I was fifteen and a half, I think. Much later, I wondered what would have happened if the gun had gone off."

My Mother

Stephanie's mother was in a home for impaired adults. "I visited her there as an adult. She got to meet my kids, which I was thankful for. It was always a one-way relationship, though. I know it sounds terrible, but I didn't get anything from her being a mother when I was young. She didn't talk to me about boys or how to do my hair or anything like that. I feel cheated.

"About ten years ago, my mom traded cigarettes for the medications people in the home had. Then she took all the meds at once. She knew her condition had been worsening, because she was cycling through meds very quickly. When she wasn't on them, things were very bad. I am sure her reality was so much worse than I can imagine.

"After she died as a result of the overdosing, I found my name and birthday, and all my kids' birthdays, in her address book five times, under "Stephanie," my maiden name, and my married name. No one else was in her address book that many times. When she was alive, she couldn't express herself emotionally, couldn't say she loved me, wasn't there for me the way a mother could be. But when I saw my name in her address book five times, I knew I was important to her. She had done the best she could in spite of her incapacitating condition.

"I realized then that the harmful things she had done to me were done out of love, unlike the things my dad had done to me. Those were done out of selfishness and a desire to control me.

"People have asked me whether I was sad when my mom died. I wasn't sad that she had died, because I knew she was no longer struggling with pain. But I was sad that I never got the mom I deserved. And she never got to be the mom she wanted to be. It was very obvious to me that in her own way she loved me and my brothers. It probably broke her heart that she couldn't take care of us.

"I still have the address book."

Never Again

"I tried to visit my mom once a year," Stephanie said, "but I never saw my dad again after I left home. And I never talked to him again. The last time was thirty-five years ago.

"I moved out the day after I graduated from high school. I declared myself financially independent, because he wouldn't sign the financial aid forms for college. He thought I was too uppity. When he heard that I had graduated from college, I heard, through one of my brothers, that he said I was a conceited, spoiled brat. He did not believe anyone should go to college. When I did my own taxes, he got into trouble, because he was still trying to claim me as a dependent.

"Later, he requested that I be a Facebook friend. I messaged him back, 'If you have anything to say to me, you can write me a letter and we can go from there.' I was not going to be his friend. He never wrote me.

"Four months ago, one of my brothers told me that my father was very sick and did I have anything to say to him? I said, 'Does he have anything to say to me? If he does, I'll listen to whatever he says.'

"I thought, 'I'm not so insensitive that I will let him die without any contact. He has not spoken to me for over three decades, and he has never met my children. If he wants to do a video call, I am open to that.' My brother got back to me and said that my father had nothing to say to me. He died two months later.

"I never found out whether he remembered what he had done to me or whether he felt guilty for it. I always left the door of my heart open for forgiveness. If he had said, 'I know what I did and I am so sorry,' I would have been okay with that. I am a little angry that he never wanted to talk to me, even when he was dying. Maybe he was just chicken. But I realize that I could not make him do what I wanted him to do.

"His death did not affect me. It made no difference in my day-to-day life.

"I talk about all these things matter of factly, as if they don't matter. In fact, they have had a very damaging impact on me. So I have to separate them off when I describe them.

"I don't want to say that the little girl who had such appalling things happen to her is dead. In some ways, I feel the same now as I did then. But in other ways I'm a different person now. It's a mixed thing.

"Though I've had a rough life, my four kids have made it beautiful. My daughter is incredibly brilliant and went to college early. My oldest son works at a good place plus spends a lot of time exploring the outdoors. My next son is becoming certified to do welding underwater. My youngest son is in high school figuring out his way. He's emotionally intelligent. Without my saying anything, he'll sometimes come over and sit next to me and say, 'Mom, what's the matter?' I am so amazed at it all."

Lora: Homeless as a Child

"I am grateful to be alive. I have learned to honor my own suffering with compassion and kindness."

Lora's mother could not hold a job for long, which meant that the two of them frequently had to move and at times were homeless. Lora never knew her biological father. She is now a therapist. We talked when she was in her midfifties.

Me and My Mom

Lora's mother was twenty-eight when Lora was born. "From the very beginning, we had economic and housing insecurity, though I wasn't aware of it until much later. I know now that my mother was probably prostituting to support us two and that that was probably how she conceived me. So from the beginning my mother was in dire straits with no outside support.

"She married and divorced a couple of times when I was very little. For about four years, from the time I was three or four years old, she was in a long-term relationship, which was the longest period of stability we had. I thought of her partner as my dad, and I loved him very much. But he was also an alcoholic, and their relationship became more volatile and unstable. They broke up when I was about seven. From that point on, we stayed in different apartments for short periods of time, depending on how long my mom could pay the rent. We got evicted, and she found another place.

"That was also a period of mental health decline for my mom. She was hospitalized a couple of times and diagnosed with schizophrenia. She didn't want me to go into the official care of the state when she was hospitalized, because she thought she would have a hard time getting me back. So I stayed with neighbors, twice. Their daughter, 'Roxanne,' who was a few years older than me and who was developmentally disabled, was my friend.

"The first time my mom was hospitalized, I came home from school and was told, 'Oh, you're going to Roxanne's house.' I didn't know why.

"Roxanne's family lived in horrendous squalor with filthy clothes and dirty dishes everywhere. Roxanne slept on a bare mattress in the basement that had a big, chronically wet spot from urine a little off toward one side. I slept with her on that mattress, on the other side from the spot.

"While we were on the mattress one night, her dad came down to the basement and beat her younger brother in the other room with his belt. I heard him screaming, which was terrifying.

"I stayed there for about three weeks. A few months later, I stayed there again. My mom had what was then called a nervous breakdown. Her stress levels were high, and she had no resources, because she had broken up with her partner, the one whom I had loved as a dad. He had attacked my babysitter in an alcoholic rage once when my mother was out.

"While I was at Roxanne's again, I visited my mom in the hospital. She gave me a soft, furry, little bear with a red ribbon. I held him every night when I went to bed, crying and missing my mom. I still have him. He has been well-loved over the decades since then."

"I don't remember what happened next, but we ended up moving again. This time, we were short on food, quite short. My mom went to Social Services to try to get assistance. Every day she waited all day, and at the end of the day they said, 'Come back tomorrow.'

"After a week of doing this, she put a knife into her purse when she went. I was in the apartment playing games all day, dressing up as Charlie's Angels, goofing around. The police came to the door. They asked whether I was so and so. I said, 'Yes.' They went away, then came back later and said, 'You need to come with us.'

"I didn't know what had happened, but there were articles in the newspapers that told the story. My mom had gone to Social Services and taken a social worker hostage to try to make them give us help. She was probably arrested and determined to be mentally ill, because she spent several months in a mental institution. During that time, I was in official children's homes.

"I'm not sure how my little bear went with me, because a lot of our stuff disappeared when somebody came and packed it. I don't know who took it, but my little bear made it through.

"That was about the time I learned that my mom was prostituting and that she had been doing it for many years.

"Each time we moved, things got a little worse—a worse neighborhood, a worse school system, more crime in the neighborhood, fewer nearby resources. Our becoming homeless was a confluence of these downgrading conditions."

The Launch Into Homelessness

Lora's mother wanted a fresh start. It was the end of a decade, in December, and Lora was eleven. "My mom was hopeful. She got out a map of the United States and asked me, 'Where would you like to go?' I knew nothing about where we could live. But I had heard John Denver sing the West Virginia song, so I said, 'How about Virginia?'

"My mom sold everything she could possibly sell, earned whatever money she could, and bought one-way plane tickets to Virginia. We had our cat in a box and what we needed of our belongings in boxes and plastic bags. We landed looking forward to a new beginning.

"We didn't know anyone in the city in which we landed, and my mom had less than a hundred dollars on her. We stayed at a hotel for a day or two, and then for the next six months we had no permanent housing.

"We went to a social service office and spent the day there. They put us in someone's home or a halfway house for a night, sometimes for a week. Once they put us in a motel where we were able to stay for two months.

"One of the big things about being homeless is that the most mundane things you would otherwise take for granted required extraordinary effort. Before that period of six months, my mom had sat at the kitchen table in the morning and written her little list for the day. She smoked a lot of cigarettes and drank a lot of coffee as she sat at the table. That was part of her gathering herself for the day. But when you are homeless, where is a place you can gather yourself? And where can you go to the bathroom?

"We had our cat with us wherever we went. I had gotten her when I was three and a half, and she didn't die until I was sixteen. Amazingly, we were able to keep her through all of our moves. We also had bags of dirty laundry that we hauled with us from place to place, because we didn't have the money to wash it.

"As we walked the streets, I looked for spare change and sizable cigarette butts. I grabbed those butts for my mom, because that was what she needed. Even to this day, I still look at sidewalks for coins and butts or think as I walk along, 'Oh, that's a really warm grate I could sit on and be warm.'

"I spent a lot of time walking the streets, sometimes with my mom and sometimes without. Now and then we found a place where we could stash our things so that we wouldn't have to carry them all the time. Sometimes we crashed wedding receptions and got a good meal.

"Once we stayed in a halfway house where one of the men who was also staying there brought home some leftover food, including fish. I was so hungry that I ate two or three servings. The man didn't tell us until the next day that he had found the food in a trash can. I got food poisoning and was very sick for weeks.

"At some other halfway house, I had asked my mom whether cockroaches crawled on beds. My mom said, 'No, they never get on beds.' So when I got sick because of the trash food, I was able to sleep. I learned much later that cockroaches did, indeed, get on beds.

"One time, we had all our belongings and our cat piled on a sidewalk. Some guy saw us and said, 'You look pathetic. Why don't you come to my house?' So we stayed with him for a couple of weeks.

"A big thing you don't have when you are homeless is a place to put your stuff. It feels good when you do have a place like that, even if it's in somebody's house for a little while."

School

Lora was in and out of schools both before and during her homeless period. "I had gotten kicked out of school a month or two before we moved to Virginia. I had thrown a snowball at a brick wall that was part of the school. They told me, 'You can't throw snowballs at the school, and you have to write, "I will not throw snowballs at the school," five hundred times. You can't come back to school until you do that.'

"My mother and I agreed that that was ridiculous. So we said, 'Okay. I'm not going back.' When we went to Virginia, I went to school for a total of eight days between January and June. We were in a couple of places just long enough for me to get enrolled. Then things blew up.

"In one place, my mom had a nanny job for maybe a week. But she wasn't stable enough to keep it. In another place, I went to a science class where we were given an assignment for which we needed batteries. But my mom couldn't afford batteries. So I didn't do the assignment, and we moved on."

Looking Older

Lora was scared a lot during the six-month period of homelessness. "I was getting taller and starting to look older, because I was getting closer to twelve. I became afraid of my mom. She was becoming more violent to me, more verbally abusive, and less contrite about it. Up to that point, there had been episodes when she'd get angry and abusive, but then she'd feel sorry about it and remorseful. But during that period of homelessness, I think she started seeing me as an adult who was not pulling her own weight.

"I didn't understand, though, what she wanted me to do. She seemed to think I understood, but I didn't.

"After we were in Virginia for six months, my mom met a sailor who lived in a city in Wisconsin. He said we could go there and stay in the house he lived in. So we got in the back of his pickup truck, along with our bags of stuff and our cat plus the puppy we had picked up, and rode to Wisconsin.

"Shortly after we got there, my mom sent me out the door, saying, 'Go get food. Go get money. I don't care how you do it.' I was twelve by then.

"I had a horrifying feeling of abandonment. I thought, 'I could go to the bars and prostitute, because I know that's what Mom does.' But then I tried playing that out in my mind. I was still innocent, and though I'd seen a lot of stuff, I hadn't done anything. I didn't know how the whole prostitute thing worked. So instead of going to the bars, I went door to door in our neighborhood and asked for food money.

"It was a dark time."

The Last Night with My Mom

Shortly before Lora turned thirteen, she became deeply involved with an evangelical Christian church. "I had a powerful conversion experience. I gave myself to God and suddenly felt connected to something bigger than myself.

"My mother was enraged by my conversion, and she became physically very abusive to me. She justified hitting me by saying things like, 'You mouthed off.' The church people became aware of what was going on. After the minister of the church saw a big bruise on my face, he told my mom, 'If that happens again, I will intervene.'

"I had just turned thirteen when I spent my last night with my mom. The church wanted to fundraise, and I was given a box of light bulbs. We were to go door to door and sell them. I walked home with the box, which I put outside the door, and said to my mom, 'I have to do some fundraising.'

"She was infuriated. We were struggling to have enough food to eat and to pay the rent. And I wasn't contributing. I was going to raise money for the church. At the time, it didn't register with me what I was doing.

"My mom spent most of the night beating me. She poked me in the eye, and I got blood under the surface of it. She scratched me and hit me.

"The next morning a couple of church women came by to take my mom grocery shopping. That had been prearranged, but she'd forgotten about it and was still upset with me. She hit me in front of them.

"They said, 'Why don't we take Lora shopping for you? She knows the kinds of food you like and what you can eat.' Although my mom was still upset, she let me go.

"The two church women took me to Social Services. They took me to a doctor. I testified in court. And I went into foster care."

Compassion for My Mother

When Lora was younger, her mother had told Lora about some of her own experiences of being abused. "She was sexually molested as a young child. Her own mother was a prostitute, and her sister prostituted as well. She was exposed to horrendous things. So as an adult, she became a trauma survivor. But she was an unhealed trauma survivor, trying to raise a child. She had no good parenting models.

"My mother told me those things long before I was able to absorb them. But later, I found it easy to have compassion for her."

Compassion for Myself

Although it was easy to have compassion for her mother, Lora continued, she downplayed her own suffering. "It took me years to acquire compassion for myself. I told myself that what I had gone through wasn't as bad as what my mother had gone through. I felt I was a burden to her. My very existence, I thought, was part of what had caused her to suffer when I was growing up.

"Healing for me has meant having deep compassion for my own experience. I had to recognize that my mother's suffering wasn't my fault. I had to extricate myself from an acute feeling of shame that my presence had caused her suffering.

"After my mom was pregnant with me, she thought about having an abortion. She actually got a black market pill to abort her pregnancy. But she was afraid, and she didn't take it.

"I think her life might have been a kinder, gentler one if she had not had me.

"But I am grateful to be alive. I have learned to honor my own suffering with compassion and kindness."

Compassion for Others' Suffering

Lora's experiences, she said, have also given her the ability to recognize other people's suffering. "I don't look like someone who has gone through what I've gone through. But I've gotten a peek behind the curtain hiding those who are not privileged in our society.

"Although I am not black or brown, I believe it when black and brown people say they are not treated well by the system. I've seen the backside of the system, with its failures and prejudices. When I got educated, cleaned up my language, dressed properly, and learned social norms, I could pass for normal. I could succeed. But if I had been a black or brown woman, I might not have had an opportunity to succeed.

"Now in my work as a therapist, I draw upon my childhood experiences to understand my clients, including women and men I served as a therapist in the prison system. I have felt the profound impact of my trauma. And I have been through the process of healing from it. I pass the knowledge I have acquired from it on to my clients from a place of empathy and compassion."

Katie: Finding My Birth Family

"My birth mother came out of the house and immediately hugged me and started sobbing. She kept sobbing while we held on to each other."

Katie was in her late thirties when we talked, about two years after she met her birth family. She went through times when she rejected her Korean identity and other times when she embraced it. It took her a number of years before she finally took steps to find her birth family. In what follows, she refers to her adopted family members simply as her mom, dad, sister, and parents and to her biological family as her birth mom, dad, and sister.

Adopted

Katie was born in South Korea and adopted into a Caucasian family in the United States when she was six months old. "I knew from the time I was two years old that I was adopted. I was looking in the mirror with my mom and asked, 'Why do my eyes not look like yours?' That's when she explained to me that I was adopted.

"My parents adopted me because my mother couldn't have any more children than the three she already had. At a church service, they had heard a talk about the plight of children in India who were in need of homes because their families were deeply impoverished. A couple of days later, my mom said to my dad, 'You, know, I've been thinking about adoption.' And my dad said, 'I have too.'

"They started talking to friends who had adopted and then decided to move forward on it. But there was soon a pause on adoptions from India because children from there were dying on flights to the U.S. or had severe medical needs when they arrived because they were so malnourished.

"So then my parents decided to adopt from South Korea. The process took about a year, from the time they started to the time I was in their arms. I was brought over on a plane with a social worker, and my parents went to the airport to get me. That happened on August 31 nearly forty years ago. We call it 'gotcha day.'"

Belonging

Katie always felt that she was a part of her family. "My parents did a good job of creating a sense of belonging, saying, 'You're one of us.' When I got older, though, that sometimes resulted in my erasing my Korean identity. My parents didn't intend to separate me from that identity, but that is what happened. I didn't want anything to do with it, and didn't even want to say that I was Korean.

"My mom volunteered at the school a lot. So when my classmates saw her, they said to me, 'Why don't you look like your mom? That's not your real mom.' I got mad when they said that and got into little arguments with them. When I came home from school, I said, 'Someone said that you are not my real mom. But you are my real mom.'

"I have an older sister who has blonde hair and blue eyes, which is what I thought the quintessential American girl looks like. I look nothing like her, and everyone at school was pointing that out to me: 'Are you Chinese? You have a flat face. Why are your eyes so slanty?' When someone said, 'Where's your real mom?,' I said, 'If you mean my biological mother, she's in Korea.'

"All that was difficult for me. I was glad, though, that my family did not brush it off as though it wasn't important. They said, 'Oh, they're just being stupid and rude. Ignore them.' But I wasn't taught to process it.—'What did it mean to my identity? Is it okay to be different from my family because I look different? Am I actually welcome even though I am different?' And it wasn't just the way I looked that was different. It was my personality and skills as well, neither of which anyone in my family had.

"All that took place in elementary school—knowing that I belonged in my family but also wondering about it."

FAMILY

Embracing My Korean Identity

Katie still felt conflicted at the beginning of her high school years. "At the church I went to, I had a lot of friends who were adopted. We shared our experiences with each other, which was helpful. At the same time, I didn't want to be known as Korean. 'Even though I was born in Korea,' I thought, 'I'm American.' I did not want to learn more about Korean culture or be associated with Korea. I just wanted to belong to my family.

"People tried to figure out where I came from and why I was different from my family. Why did I have a last name that didn't sound Asian? Sometime I told them, joking, that I was German, because my mom was of German descent. When they asked about my dad, I'd say, 'He's Danish.' I don't know why everyone thought it was their business to try to figure out why my last name was not Asian and why I was in the U.S. They acted as though I owed them an explanation.

"When I was a sophomore in high school, I met someone my age who was half Korean and half Caucasian. We hit it off. I spent a lot of time with her family, participating in some of their Korean traditions and sometimes going to the all-Korean church they went to. Korean culture was very much part of their household.

"They said, 'How do you not know all these things?' My friend's mom said, 'You need to learn how to speak Korean.' They taught me Korean words from time to time and took me to restaurants where there was Korean food.

"I learned how to use chopsticks for the first time when I went to the Korean restaurant owned by the mother of another Korean friend. When the mother brought the food to our table, I asked for a fork. The others at the table looked at me as though to say, 'What is wrong with you?' I was completely confused. My friend's mother asked, 'You don't know how to use chopsticks?' 'No,' I replied. 'I'm White.' She laughed and said, 'You're learning today.'[1]

"I was starting to enjoy the practices and family traditions of the Korean world, and I began to appreciate them. My mother seemed a little offended that I was embracing this new world. She never explicitly disapproved, but I felt that she and the rest of my family were having an unspoken conflict between their desire for me to be part of them and their desire for me to know my Korean culture.

---

1. Katie reports that the Chinese and Japanese use chopsticks for rice but that South Koreans use chopsticks for everything but rice.

KATIE: FINDING MY BIRTH FAMILY

"Both of my parents had always encouraged me to explore my Korean roots. They said they would help me go to Korea if I ever wanted to find my birth family. I believe they meant what they said. But when it came down to my actually embracing that culture, they didn't seem to be fully accepting of that. So I was a little worried about whether they were okay with my liking Korean culture. I didn't want to disappoint my parents or for them to think I didn't love them.

"Despite the tension with my family, those high school years were formative for me. I learned about Korean culture and became proud that I was Korean."

Do I Want to Find My Birth Family?

For more than a decade, Katie wondered whether she really wanted to find her birth family. "After college, I went to the wedding of a friend who had been adopted. Both her birth mother and her adoptive parents were there, which made me realize that she had something I longed for.

"I put that emotion into a little file folder, which is how I typically handle emotions I don't know what to do with. Still, I felt drawn to her experience during my early adult years, even though I didn't consciously think I wanted to look for my birth family.

"Then, some years after I was married, in my late twenties, when my husband and I were talking about having children, I thought, 'Maybe I need to reconcile my conflicting feelings about finding my birth family.'

"I talked to a friend who had been adopted. She had hired a private investigator to find her birth family. But her birth mother said, 'I never had a child. She's not mine,' and completely rejected my friend. That was a terrible experience for her.

"I found other adopted people who were willing to tell their stories. I don't think I would have had the courage to try to find my birth family if I had not talked to them.

"It did take courage. I was afraid my adoptive parents would wonder whether I was replacing them. I was afraid I would not find my birth family or find that they were no longer alive. I was afraid they would not want to meet me or say what my friend's birth mother said to her: 'She's not mine.'"

Procrastination

Katie was on and off for another seven or eight years. "We were about to have our first child, at twenty-nine, and I said to myself, 'I need to do this now. If I'm going to start my own family, I should understand where I came from.'

"My parents had given me all of my adoption papers, so I knew the adoption agency in South Korea I should contact. I also knew the name of my birth mother. But there was no address or other contact information for her. Plus, there were lots of people with her name. My birth father's name was not in the file.

"I filled out the form you have to send to the adoption agency. But I never emailed it.

"After our first child was born, I thought, 'I'm a new mom. I can't focus on finding my birth family.' So I put it off to the side. Then about the time we were going to have our second child, three years later, I had an updated draft of the adoption agency form ready to send. But, again, I didn't send it."

"The Time Has Come"

"The pivotal point came when I was thirty-six," Katie said. "My husband and I were at an outdoor gathering in August, and suddenly I felt a strong sense of dread and anxiety, as though something heavy was going to happen. My stomach became upset, and I felt as though I was going to throw up. I didn't know where that came from.

"Later I talked to my therapist about it. She wondered whether something had happened around that time. I said, 'Yes. My gotcha day was coming up, when I came to America.' 'Well,' she said, 'the body keeps score.'[2]

"We talked about what it was like for me as a six-month-old baby suddenly experiencing different surroundings. I was probably scared to leave my foster mother, who had been a real mother to me. I was taken on an airplane with someone who was a complete stranger. At the layover in the U.S., another stranger took me to the city where my new family lived. And then I was placed in the arms of that family, whom I had never seen before. And as they were taking me to their home, I cried out 'Umma, Umma,' which is 'Mommy' in Korean. I was crying for my foster mother.

---

2. Van der Kolk, *The Body Keeps Score*.

"After recounting all this, it occurred to me that I had struggled with separation anxiety ever since I was a child. I was attached to my mom like nobody's business. I had a fear of abandonment that had come from a separation I couldn't remember.

"That was the point at which I vowed, 'Okay. I have got to try to find my birth family and figure out a way to connect with my history. So that I wouldn't delay again, I immediately filled out an updated form and sent it off. I told Devlin, my husband, that I had done it, the thing I had been trying to do for years. He said, 'Wow! That's big!'"

News from the Adoption Agency

The adoption agency replied within three days. "'We are initiating a search and will reach out to your birth family if we can find them.' They also had information that I had not known. My birth parents were married when I was born, and I had three older sisters who were then ten, seven, and four. Also, I had a younger brother who was only eleven months younger than me. That shocked me. If I had a younger brother, why had they put me up for adoption?

"A few days later, the agency found my birth mother's address and contact information. They wrote to her to say that I would like to be in contact with her and asked whether she would like to be in contact with me. The agency then wrote me to say that my birth mother had called them to say that she needed a week to think about it, because my birth siblings did not know about me. And she wanted to talk to my birth father.

"I tried to make sense of that. My ten-year-old sister in Korea would surely have known that my birth mother was pregnant with me.

"The very next day, my birth mother called the agency and said, 'I've told my other children, who were very surprised. We want to be in contact.'

"My first thought was, 'Whoa! She is a high action person. She went around to four siblings in fewer than twenty-four hours and made the decision to be in contact with me. That sounded like something I would have done. It was one of the first moments I recognized myself in someone other than my children."

Writing Letters

Everything was shut down then because of the pandemic, so Katie could not go to South Korea. "The agency said, 'Why don't you start by writing a letter? We will translate it and send it to her.' So I did that. And my birth mother wrote back. We kept writing.

"At one point, my birth mother wrote that she would never forgive herself for having given me up for adoption. 'You've told me that you have children. So you understand what it is like to care for your children and what an unthinkable thing it is for a mother to give her child away.'

"I had never felt anger toward my birth family. That is because my parents, my mom especially, had told me numerous times that my birth family had given me up for adoption because they loved me and wanted me to have the best life I could. My mom always said, 'Think of your birth mother on your birthday and how she must feel.' So I always had kindness toward them, never any resentment.

"Through our letters, I learned that my birth siblings liked to draw and sing. My birth father also liked to sing and was left-handed, which I am. My next oldest sister had severe disabilities.

"After a while, my birth mother said, 'It is taking too long to go back and forth through the agency. Would you be willing to be in direct contact?' So we started using an online translation service so that we could email each other directly, which was much faster. Later, we switched to an instant messaging app that Koreans use. I wrote to my siblings as well and connected with them on Instagram. I wrote to them all at least once a week."

Visiting My Birth Family

Katie traveled for her job and was scheduled to go to Malaysia after the pandemic had died down, in early 2023. "I thought that might be a good time to go to South Korea. But immediately I was afraid to say anything to my parents. Earlier, I had been afraid to tell them I had gotten in contact with my birth family. But when I finally did tell them, they were very supportive. And then when my mom learned I was going to Malaysia, she said, 'Why don't you go to Korea to meet your birth family?' I thought, 'Oh! I've been worried about bringing that up to her, and here she brought it up to me.' She said, 'I completely support you if you want to do that. I'll watch the kids while you and Devlin are gone.' And my dad said, 'I'm so glad you have the opportunity to see them. We're here for you and are so proud of you.'

"I told everyone I knew about going, even the CEO of the company I worked for. They all were happy for me, and I felt a lot of embrace.

"I flew to Malaysia for a few days and then to South Korea, where Devlin met me."

Meeting for the First Time

The very first meeting with Katie's birth family took place at their home in Daegu, a city in southern South Korea, about a three-hour train ride from Seoul. "We had hired an interpreter to go with us the whole time we were there because my birth family only speaks Korean, and I don't speak Korean well enough to talk to them.

"The first thing that happened when I got out of the cab at my birth family's home was that a woman grabbed my hand and started crying. I didn't know who she was, because she didn't look like anyone in the pictures of my family. And I was surprised, because I had not expected to see anyone right when I stepped out of the cab.

"I said to the interpreter, 'Who is this?' She said, 'This is Hee-Jung, your oldest sister.'

"I exclaimed, 'Oh, my gosh!' It felt so surreal, like an out-of-the-body experience. I felt as though I was watching myself as she walked me across the street to my birth family's home. She kept crying.

"Hee-Jung had called our mother, and I was thinking as she did, 'This is the moment I am going to see my birth mother for the first time. For real. In person.'

"She came out of the house and immediately hugged me and started sobbing. She kept sobbing while we held on to each other. I introduced her to Devlin. We went inside, where I met Yoon-Jung, my second oldest sister. Then I met my birth father, who uses a walker because he had a stroke a few years ago.

"The first thing he said was, 'This is all my fault. It was because of me. I have never forgiven myself.' I didn't know what he meant by that. But while he was talking, my birth mother nodded her head in agreement as though to say, 'Yes, this was his fault.'

"My sister who is just above me in age, Hyung-Jung, the one who has severe disabilities, was hesitant to come to me. She sat in a corner, feeling nervous and anxious. When she was ready, she came to the table in the kitchen where we were sitting and grabbed my hand and looked at me as tears streamed down her face.

"She is non-verbal, but she can respond yes or no by nodding or shaking her head. 'Are you excited to see her?' my birth mother asked. She nodded her head and cried more tears. She sat down again and looked at me. Every time I noticed her doing that, I'd smile back at her, and she quickly looked away, as though she wasn't looking at me, a sign of her shyness.

"When Dong-Won, my younger brother, came home later, he kept saying, 'I can't believe it's actually you.'"

A Photo Album, My Height, Similarities, a Tattoo, and a Weekend Together

Katie's mother and father had given her a photo album to give to her birth family. "It contained pictures of me growing up. Also, my parents wrote a letter to my birth family, which I had translated into Korean and which they and my siblings all signed. My birth family was thrilled to get the photos and the letter. They said, 'Please tell your parents how grateful we are to them for giving you such a good life.'

"I am only five feet tall and am usually the shortest person wherever I am. But I am taller than some of my birth siblings and definitely taller than my birth mother, who is about the same height as my nine-year-old son. And Devlin was towering over them all at six-one. I thought, 'Wow, I've never been in a place where I'm taller than others.'

"When I was growing up, I never had people say to me, 'Oh, you look just like your mom or your dad or your siblings' or 'You two are like two peas in a pod.' So it was satisfying to find that my younger brother and I looked alike and had the same smile. Plus, it was cool to see certain qualities in my birth family that our two children have.

"Before we went to Korea, I had asked my birth mother to give a Korean name to each of our two children. So she did—Min-Jun and Min-Seo. I had also asked her to handwrite their names and my name in Korean and send me a picture of them. I didn't tell her why I wanted that. I got a tattoo of them on my left forearm: Kang, Yoon-Hee, Min-Jun, and Min-Seo. When I showed it to her, she exclaimed, 'Oh! That's my handwriting! That's why you asked for it.'

"For me the tattoo was about keeping my birth mother near to my heart. It represents who I am, and I am proud of it."

"My birth family had rented a house in a nearby tourist city, where we all spent a weekend. We interacted in numerous unspoken ways that went beyond spoken interaction. They cried when I sang and played the guitar for them. We laughed together until our stomach muscles hurt. I formed an amazing bond with them."

Why I Was Given Up for Adoption

Katie felt weird asking why she had been given away. "While we were eating supper after we had gotten back to their home in Daegu, my birth father said he wanted to explain why, 'not to give an excuse,' he said, 'but because we owe you an explanation.'

"'Long before you were born,' he continued, 'my mother lived with us. My father had died when I was fifteen, and in the following years my mother had spent the family savings and lost the house.

"'When our first child was born, my mother was very critical of your umma for not having a son. And when our second child was also a girl, my mother said to your umma, "What kind of woman are you not to have a son? You need a son." After our third girl was born, my mother said, "You don't need that many girls in this house." On several occasions, she had tried to sell our second girl or give her away when she was a baby. Your umma and I rushed home from our jobs, worried that my mother had done something to one of the girls while we were gone.

"'There were times when we couldn't find our third girl. My mother had said that because of her disabilities, no one would buy her. "She's no good," she declared. Plus, she didn't allow our second girl to go to kindergarten, saying that she too would be no good in this world. My mother never gave any of the girls anything.

"'Then when your umma was pregnant with you, we didn't know that you were going to be a girl, because we didn't have that technology yet. If you were going to be girl, your umma and I thought, my mother would try to kill you or sell you or give you away. She would not let us bring a daughter home.

"'We were afraid for your life. So we made the decision that if you were a girl, we would give you up for adoption. That would be the safest thing we could do for you.'

Katie asked, "How did you explain that Umma came home from the hospital without a baby?"

"'We told your sisters and my mother that you had died. And we never told your brother that your umma had been pregnant with you.'

"That gave me a lot of compassion for my parents," Katie said. "I couldn't imagine being faced with having to make a decision like that. I had wondered why my mother had been married, with three other children and then a fourth after I was born. Most mothers who gave their children up for adoption, I had thought, were young, single, or very poor. So hearing the story of my adoption was immensely clarifying."

The Missing Nine Days

But there was another mystery. "Before I went to meet my birth parents," Katie continued, "the adoption agency told me that there was no record of where I was for nine days after I had been born. 'Was I in transport? In temporary housing?,' I asked. They said they didn't know.

"That had been hard for me to hear, because it made me feel as though I was nothing for those nine days, and no one's. Actually, it felt like a declaration that I had never belonged to anyone.

"I prayed, 'God, why would this happen? I know it's only nine days, but it feels traumatic and confusing.' As I was praying, I was listening to the words of the song, 'You Know My Name,' by Tasha Cobbs Leonard. And it felt as though God was answering me: 'I knew where you were, because you belong to me. I took care of you. I protected you. And I knew your name.'

"Then when I heard the story of my adoption from my birth father, I realized I was likely with my birth parents during those nine days while they were away going through the process of putting me up for adoption.

"I also learned that when I was with my birth parents they had given me their last name: 'Kang.' I had always thought that the adoption agency had given it to me. Also, my birth parents had named me Yoon-Hee after my two oldest sisters, Yoon-Jung and Hee-Jung. That gave added meaning to God's answer to my prayer: 'I knew your name.'"

"I Forgive You"

Katie wanted her birth parents to know that she did not have any ill feelings toward them. "I felt they needed to hear me say that I forgave them and was grateful for their having saved my life. I didn't want them to torture themselves over the decision they had made.

"I told them individually. My birth father didn't show much emotion, but I could see that he was trying to hold it back. Later he sent me a message through one of my birth sisters that my extending forgiveness to him meant a great deal to him. For the rest of the night, he had cried his eyes out. 'It was one of the best gifts I could ever have received to meet you and see that you were well.'

"My birth family all loved Devlin. It made them extremely happy to see that I was happy and that I had a good husband and a good life."

Falling in Love

When we think of people falling in love, we often visualize happy faces with big smiles. There is enchantment. Charm and excitement abound. As Cristina put it, "I suddenly noticed a boy I had never seen staring at me as though he was mesmerized."

If excited enchantment were all that falling in love involved, life would be eternally and wondrously idyllic. To be sure, falling in love is, indeed, wondrously idyllic, but often only in snatches. Happy faces have frequently had to get past obstacles. Those faces have had to be set aside when engaging in serious effort to overcome barriers to love.

The following stories depict two such efforts.

Ruby and David

Ruby and David met in 1995, got engaged in August of 2000, and were married in 2001. Ruby lived in the U.S. and David in Tanzania.

Background

When Ruby was a sophomore in college, at Asbury University in central Kentucky, she dated a classmate. "I should never have dated him. We were not at all compatible. When we broke up, I wondered why I had been so stupid to go on a first date with him.

"During my junior year, I was dealing with the social pressure of having a 'ring by spring.' How was I going to have a ring by the time I graduated if I didn't have a boyfriend? That pressure prompted me to wonder what made me worthy. It was hard to tell myself I was okay when the culture around me was telling me otherwise.

"Finally, by about mid-spring of that junior year, I came to the point at which I was content to be where I was. I was enjoying being single and enjoying my friendships. I was okay even though I had no significant other.

"About this time, I decided I wanted to work at a summer camp between my junior and senior years. That would give me the opportunity to work with children, which would fit with my elementary education major. I chose one that was about an hour and a half away from my home in western Pennsylvania.

"Also, about this time, a Tanzanian named David, was deciding what he wanted to do for the coming summer. Tanzania is just south of Kenya in eastern Africa. It uses the British educational system, and David had just finished advanced secondary education in it, which meant that he was about my age. He wanted to take a gap year before he went to a university, and he wanted to network here in the States so as to find a university in the U.S. he could go to.

"David had a childhood friend whose sister was working at an organization in his hometown called Camp Counselors USA. The organization has exchange programs for lots of different kinds of camps around the world. His friend said, 'Why don't you talk with my sister about applying?' So David did. He applied, interviewed, and was approved to be a counselor at the very camp I was going to be at."

At Camp

Camp started the first week of June. "I was feeling free and light, happy to be away from campus. David was in awe that he was in the U.S.

"It wasn't long before David was coming to see me while I was on 'lane duty.' It was called that because the four cabins in each of the four 'villages' at the camp were connected by a road that we called a lane. The lane in each village was shaped in a semicircle. Each night, from 9:00 pm, at lights out, to 11:00 pm, one of the counselors from each village would stay near the four cabins in their village to ensure the safety of the campers.

"David and I had been assigned lane duty the same nights at the beginning of the summer, which meant that we would each have to be in our own village of cabins those nights. But all of a sudden David started asking me after supper whether I would like for him to bring me a nighttime snack during lane duty.

"I thought that was peculiar because he was supposed to be staying at the cabins in his village. But I said, 'Sure, if you have a way of doing that.' So he brought me a snack, and then he stayed to talk. I thought, 'What is going on? He shouldn't be staying, because who's watching his kids?' This kept happening the next times I had lane duty. I later discovered that he was on lane duty when I was not.

"I mentioned this to one of my counselor friends, who said, 'Ruby, he switched his lane duty so that he could be with you during your lane duty. He likes you.' My response to this was to exclaim, 'Oh, don't even talk about that! I'm not interested. I don't want a boyfriend. I am enjoying being friends with everyone here and not having the awkwardness of "Does he like me? Does he not?" I don't want to deal with that.' But David kept coming around.

"I thought, 'My friends were wrong. He just found a friend in me because I was asking questions about his homeland, his language, and his culture and was showing an interest in his life. I had lots of questions, because at one time his family had lived in Uganda, where there was a civil war, and then in Tanzania, where he grew up. He does not actually like me, I thought, and that's good. I'm not looking for that.

"In addition to his visits, he always came with me and others to my parents' house when we counselors had to leave camp in between camping sessions. Again, I was naïve. I just thought he had gotten to know my parents' house and was comfortable visiting it.

"On one of these breaks, a medical issue for me came up, and the doctor said I should not be driving the two hours back to camp the day we were supposed to be there. I could go back the next day if I was okay. The other counselors would go back by themselves in another car and I would go the following day. I said goodbye to them all and went upstairs to my room to lie down, as I was feeling woozy. But David came upstairs and gave me a kiss on the cheek, then said, 'I hope you feel better.' I said, 'Thanks.' Naïve, yet again—I just thought he was a sweet guy and that the kiss was cultural.

"Back at camp—about halfway through the summer—David asked a couple of times, 'How do you feel about dating?' I said, 'I'm not interested. I've got my senior year to do, and then I'm going to begin my teaching career. I'm really okay with just hanging out.'

"A week later, we ran into each other at the end of a rope bridge that went across the river at the camp. We talked for a while, and just before I was going to leave to go back to my cabin, he kissed me on the lips. I said calmly, 'Goodnight. I'll see you tomorrow.' But on the inside, I was distraught. All the way back to my cabin, I thought, 'Oh, my gosh! Oh, my gosh! What has just happened!? How in the world have I led him on to think that I would want him to kiss me?'

"And then during the next break between camping sessions, at my parents' house again, as I was about halfway up the stairs to my room, David came to the bottom of the stairs and said, 'Ruby?' I said, 'Yes?' He said, 'I love you.' I said, 'Thanks,' and then ran up the stairs to my bedroom, where I burst into tears and exclaimed to myself, 'What have I done?! What have I done?!'

"I grabbed the wall phone and pulled the cord into the bathroom so I wouldn't wake up the other counselor who was in my bedroom, and called my best friend from high school. This was two in the morning. 'Heather, what do I do? I don't want to hurt his feelings. I don't even know how we got here.' We talked for a while, and she got me calmed down so I could sleep.

"Somehow in that conversation and into the next day, I got to the point of saying, 'Who cares? It's summer.' I had read romance novels in which teenagers have summer romances and then when school starts, they break up. I thought, 'Why not? Why am I resisting? Let me just have a little summer fling.'

"So I let it go. We never had a talk. Things just morphed. We started holding hands. I thought, 'Okay. Whatever. In another month, he's going back to Tanzania, and I'm going back to college at Asbury.'

At School

The end of summer came. Ruby started classes for her senior year, and David stayed at the camp to winterize it and get it ready for family camp over Labor Day weekend. "I was going to go back to the camp that weekend. During the two weeks between starting classes in August and Labor Day, I found that I missed him. I was like, 'Oh, this is not good. I'm in Kentucky. He's going to Tanzania. How would this even work?'

"After the Labor Day camp session, David spent five days at Asbury, and we hung out between my classes and at meals. When it came time for him to leave I was a mess: 'What are we going to do? If the two weeks between leaving camp and Labor Day are any indication, I'm really going to miss him.'

"We decided we would write letters three times a week and talk on the phone two times a month. Plus, we had both been invited back to the camp for the following summer. He had a job lined up in Tanzania for the coming year, and during that year he would see about going to a university in the U.S. the following year.

"I took him to the bus station in Lexington, Kentucky, so that he could get to New York City where he would get his flight back to Tanzania. We did the goodbye things—we had a picnic before going to the bus station, I gave him a little gift, and he gave me flowers and a card.

"All this while, I was telling myself, 'Summer fling. Summer fling. Summer's over, and school has started. We're done. I'm moving on. Now I can say I had a summer fling.' Yet my heart was saying, 'Oh, my gosh. What am I going to do? He's going to be gone until next summer, and I won't have a date for events during my senior year.' I panicked. And then I was irritated with myself. This was supposed to be only a summer fling. But I had let my heart get into it.

"As David was getting on the bus, I had tears flowing down my face. I got into my car and followed the bus until it got to the on ramp of the highway, with tears still streaming down my face. 'What if something happens to the bus? What if he gets on the wrong bus when he has to transfer buses?'

"It was a Friday night and nobody was around on campus. I went to my dorm room and cried and watched sappy movies and waited for him to call me from payphones at the different bus stops, using 1-800-COLLECT so I could help pay for the long distance charges. He did—at each place he called me and also right before he got onto the airplane."

Letters, Packages, and Calls

Rudy and David wrote letters three times a week for the next nine months. "I mailed the first letter the next day. All of the letters those nine months were like daily dairies. We kept paper and pen with us during the day, and whenever we had a moment we'd scratch out something—details that you don't ordinarily tell people when you're just talking to them: 'I woke up at 6:07 am, and I hit the snooze button, but I hit it only once. I wanted to hit it twice, but I needed to get up early.'

"I sent him packages. They always arrived, but they might not have all of the contents. If I sent candy or a toy for his young brother, they would be taken. When I sent a video of me playing the piano at my niece's wedding, that made it. He couldn't send me packages, though, because a postal worker somewhere or an immigration worker would take it.

"Calling was way more expensive than we had thought it would be—the internet had not yet come along in 1995. He couldn't afford to call even for five minutes with his small teacher's salary if he wanted to save money to come to a U.S. school. I had a friend near campus who could make international calls at a steep discount for a dollar a minute. I went to her house once a month on Saturday mornings, which was Saturday evenings in eastern Africa. We tried to keep our calls to fifteen minutes, which, of course, didn't work.

"David's family didn't have a phone, so he had to go to a friend's house fifteen minutes away from his house to talk. When I was missing him in between the monthly calls, I called his friend's house from my dorm room, which was $1.75 a minute. Sometimes I caught David there. When I didn't, his friend went to see whether David was home. When he was, I talked with him when I called an hour later."

At Camp Again

The two worked at the camp again the following summer. "This time, both of us were in leadership positions, which meant that we didn't have to do lane duty, which allowed us to hang out with each other more.

"When the end of summer came, we were wondering whether things could continue. David still had not gotten any scholarships to U.S. universities. He had been admitted to every university he had applied to, but without a scholarship he could not pay. We were sweating it. I knew I would be heartbroken if he could not stay in the U.S.

"On the last day of camp, when we were cleaning the entire camp, I was in the main office finishing things up. I heard an announcement that went over all the speakers in the camp asking for David to come to the office. He was, however, at the ropes course across the river, so he probably couldn't hear the announcement. I went upstairs and said, 'David is over at the ropes course. Is there something I can help with?' They said, 'Someone from Asbury University is on the phone.' I said, 'Oh, let me grab it.'

"It was one of the admission counselors: 'I'm calling for David. We have some funds that are from financial aid packages for students who have decided not to come to Asbury. So we decided to put together one more international student scholarship for someone who can start classes in two weeks—four years with full tuition and full room and board. The person has to be in the U.S. already, and the country they are from has to allow someone to change their visa without going to their home country, applying for a visa, and then coming back to the U.S., which could take weeks or months.'

"While I was writing down details, David came in. I told him about the scholarship and visa, and he said, 'Yes, I can change my visa very easily. I just have to fill out the paperwork and send it to the embassy in D.C.' He got on the phone and got all the details.

"The news spread throughout the camp. By the time of the banquet that night, which was to be a celebration of a great summer of ministry to all the kids, it turned into a celebration for David being able to go to college in the U.S. and for me and David to continue to be together."

Engagement

Ruby and David dated for the next four years while David was at Asbury University and Ruby taught elementary school nearby. "In the summer of 2000, I went to Tanzania and Uganda with him for a month. I had major culture shock. The food was not familiar. I didn't know the language. I didn't know how to get around. At the village in Uganda where his parents had lived, there was no running water or electricity. There were outside latrines and three-sided showers in which you used buckets to shower.

"Everything was so starkly different that I didn't think I could live there. We would need to break up if David wanted to live in Africa. But I was too far in to do that. There was no stopping now.

"I was also disappointed because I had thought David was going to propose to me then. But he didn't, because the engagement ring he had ordered had not come in time. We both came back to the U.S., where he was going to get a master's degree at nearby University of Kentucky.

"Several weeks after classes started that fall, I stopped by his apartment on my way home from the school I was teaching at. He wasn't home, but I let myself in, because he had given me a key, and I lay down on David's bed to sleep off a pounding headache. A couple of hours later, he came back to the apartment. I explained that I had not felt well. He said he would make supper for us. In the meantime, I had to use the bathroom.

"While I was washing my hands, he knocked on the door and said, 'I have it. Do you want it?' I said, 'Do you have what?' He said again, 'I have it. Do you want it?' I replied, 'What are you talking about? You can't talk in pronouns. You have to tell me what you're talking about.'

"He said, 'Your ring. I have your ring. Do you want it?' I was still in a dazed state after having woken up, and I said, 'What ring are you talking about?' He replied, 'Your diamond. I have your diamond.' I said, 'You're talking like you found my lost shoe or something. Is that a diamond as in an engagement ring?' He said, 'Yes.' I totally thought he was joking! No way was he serious.

"I opened the door and said, "Are you kidding me? I have a migraine headache, and I'm in the bathroom and you tell me through the door, 'Do you want it?' You have to do this right."

"I was still feeling terrible, so I went back to bed. He said, 'Well, it's right here. Do you want it?' I said, 'Yes, but you have to get on your knees and ask me properly.' So he knelt by the bed, opened up the little box that contained the ring, and said, 'Ruby, will you marry me?' I said, 'That's the way you're supposed to do it.' Then he put the ring on my finger. That was so anticlimactic that I went back to sleep while he made supper.

"I learned later that it was a hundred-dollar ring from the jewelry section at Walmart—$104 to be more exact. He didn't have the money for it, so he had to make payments, after which Walmart ordered the ring. It had come a few days before I stopped by his apartment. When he found me there, he got it from his desk and put it into his pocket, and on his way to the kitchen to make supper, just on a whim, he thought, 'I'll ask her right now whether she wants it.' He was determined to be original and not follow the norm: 'If this woman loves me in the lowest uncommon place, then she is the one for me!'

"We got married the following summer, in June of 2001."

Denise and Jon

Jon is twenty-four years older than Denise. Denise set aside that age difference because her life "is about finding love at any time, even when the past has been painful."

Background

Denise's first marriage ended in divorce after three years. "He turned out to have serious mental issues—he raged at me and was abusive. There was a lot of pain for me in that, and I went through dark times. He was very tortured, and he took his own life about ten years after we divorced.

"After a while, I met someone at an online dating site whom I fell in love with. But it didn't work out, and the grief I felt at losing that relationship was severe. I reached a point when I didn't know how much more I could take of becoming attached and then losing someone.

"Then I met someone who I saw on and off for about ten years. But I didn't feel the intense passion you have when you're falling in love. I thought maybe I was broken and couldn't have strong feelings for anyone again. My parents wanted us to get married. His mom wanted us to marry—his dad was gone—and his sister did too. But I couldn't marry someone without that magical feeling of being in love. I think that feeling is important. I tried to get it but couldn't make it come, though I cared for him and loved him as you do a friend."

At the Gym

Denise met Jon about ten years ago, when she was forty-three. "It was at the gym where I was working as a wellness coach. He was usually on an elliptical machine, and he would take off his headphones and give me his full attention when we talked. I didn't think of him as anything more than a nice guy, because he was much older than me, twenty-four years older, I later learned. I wasn't open yet to the idea that at a certain point age doesn't matter.

"One day, Jon brought in an autistic music student, because he is a music teacher. Jon was so kind and patient with him that I thought, 'What a sweet man.'

"After a few months, Jon gave me a handwritten letter and a CD of him playing piano. The letter said, 'I wish we could meet in a café in Paris, but maybe a local café will do.' Jon was separated from his wife at the time, but he was still married. I've always had a firm rule about not seeing anyone who is married. It could lead to waiting for someone to divorce and it never happening, or it could lead to ripping apart their family

"I didn't want to risk either of those things, so I called him and said I couldn't go out with him because he was married. Plus, I was seeing someone then—the ten-year, on and off person. 'I could, though, meet you in the break room downstairs,' I said. It was an awful, dingy little room with a vending machine that gave you really bad coffee and tea.

"We met there, and he bought me a seventy-five cent hot chocolate. I stood in that dinky room with him for about five minutes and drank it. We laughed because of that room we were in. Even though the letter Jon had written was romantic, I didn't think of him in that way. But I liked the kind way he treated people, and I liked it that he was very attentive to me. He would drop everything to talk to me."

The Magical Feeling

A couple of years later, Denise got up a music band. "I was going to play acoustic guitar. I had someone on bass and someone on bongos, but we needed more. I asked Jon whether he wanted to be in the band. He said sure.

"We got together and practiced. Jon has a master's degree in music, and he taught music and gave guitar lessons, so he was on a much higher level than the rest of us. I asked him whether he could help me with some chords on the guitar. On the day his divorce became final, I went to his house for a guitar lesson.

"All of a sudden, as he was helping me with the chords, I started to feel a really strong chemistry with him. It was definitely and unmistakably that magical feeling of being in love.

"We got together again, and he read to me out of *The Four Agreements* by Don Miguel. I loved hearing his voice. He touched my face, and again I felt something very strong. It was then I recognized I was falling in love, really hard. And it was happening fast. I realized there was nothing wrong with me, after all. I wasn't broken. I could still fall in love.

"These feelings were growing between us, and we started seeing each other. We took walks together at night, looking at the moon and cuddling and kissing."

Awkward

Denise had been living with the ten-year, on and off friend. "He had stayed up at night with my dad when he was dying, and I thought I should try to fall in love with him. He was a fantastic person, and he loved me. We tried living together, even though the right feelings weren't there on my end. But when I met Jon, I decided to stop lying to my friend, and to myself, and tell him the truth: 'I do love you, but I'm not in love with you. We need to stop this.'

"My friend moved out, and I helped him through the pain he experienced. He called me almost every night, crying. I felt terrible because I had never had to reject someone and cause them pain. I knew how much it hurt. This friend eventually admitted that I was right to end things, and we are very good friends now, like family.

"Although I hated to hurt this friend, I was glad I had met Jon and could feel so strongly for someone who was not only charming and supersmart, but also good, kind, and generous. I began to believe that the age difference between us didn't matter. Love is a soul thing beyond the ages of the two who are in love. Both of us are much younger in spirit than our chronological ages.

"Jon became beautiful to me. And I knew he was crazy about me. We talked about getting married within a month of getting together, though it had been two years since we had first met."

A Home with Love

Denise and Jon looked at houses. "We found one that turned out to be a great house for us. We have been in it since that unexpected whirlwind of falling in love eight years ago.

"I think back to my college years, when I was so sad because I needed the stability and love that I now have with Jon. I have always wanted to be with someone I know isn't going to leave, sharing fun things together.

"I'm not going to say that everything has been easy. You have your favorite things, you have everything set the way you like it, and the other person has the same. So you have to come together and learn how to blend.

"Not every day has been blissful. We went through a growth phase when it was work to get to know one another and to accommodate to each other. But we never gave up.

"Someone told us to think of being in a relationship as being like a growing child. Our relationship was messy and required a lot of learning in the first few years. I have to forgive Jon sometimes, and he has to forgive me sometimes. We have to decide—do we want to argue about this or do we want to have a nice day?

"In most of my relationships, I have wanted to receive love and attention, to be given stability. Now I'm finding that giving love and stability to someone else makes me happy. I finally have what I was looking for, in a phase of my life when I can appreciate it and see what love means."

3 Hurdles

"Alliyah": A Black Woman's Journey Through Academia

"Really, people, I'm just human, like you."

After graduating from college, Alliyah earned a Master of Theological Studies degree from seminary. She is an ordained pastor and is now in a Ph.D. program.

Elementary and Middle School

From the very beginning, Alliyah loved going to school. "School was the first place I found community. I went to five different elementary schools, so I was always the new kid on the block. I had a thirst for knowledge, and I wanted to belong to the community at school.

"I showed up every day to class, and I got the citizenship awards. My mom kept every single award, and anytime we moved, she brought the awards with us.

"I learned that the world would be different for me and that I would have to navigate it differently. I knew about my Blackness. Things would probably be said to me that would be unfair, untrue, and hurtful—things I now know as microaggressions.

"The first hurtful experience I had occurred in third grade when a White girl on the playground told me she couldn't play with me because I was Black. It stung, and I knew it was wrong. I went home and told my mom, who went to the school, where she advocated for me. And, of course, they tried to dispute it and say it didn't happen. But the girl classmate apologized, and she and I were reconciled. I vividly remember it all.

"That same year I was a teacher's helper who passed out papers to the class after they had been graded. I wasn't supposed to look at the grades, except once I accidentally did. Someone who was White had gotten an A for a grade of 89, but I had gotten a B for the same grade. So I told the teacher: 'This isn't right.' I got pushback because I had looked at someone else's grade, but in the end my grade was changed to an A. I learned that I had to advocate for myself, not just because I was the new kid on the block, but for justice.

"Another time in third grade, I told my teacher that my dad was from a certain predominantly Black country. The teacher said, 'That's not true. There's no such place.' I said, 'Yes there is,' and I told her where it was. I wondered why she didn't know. I knew that anti-Blackness existed.

"I had my first Black teacher in fourth grade. I still keep in touch with her. She came to my college graduation, both the commencement and the baccalaureate service, where she watched me give the main student speech. She has been taking care of me for the past twenty years. That has been so cool.

"In middle school, I intentionally thought about my being Black. I gave a presentation about being Black from the perspective of one who was young. 'Being Black,' I said, 'comes with trials, but it also comes with triumphs and beauty, along with love, hope, and redemption, plus creativity and innovation.' I also did a presentation on hip-hop and Black poetry. And I discovered that some of my Black friends who were a bit lighter than me had certain privileges that I would never have. That, I found out, is called colorism. I was always aware of my color, my dark skin, my Blackness."

High School

In one of the high schools Alliyah went to, she got bullied. "My cousins were with me at that school, and they took care of me. One of my teachers there, who was White and with whom I took Advanced Placement biology, was very encouraging to me about my Blackness and Black womanhood. He encouraged me just to be myself and not to hide any pieces of myself. My basketball coach also encouraged me to live into who I was and simply to dwell in my Blackness.

"After being at that school for a year, I transferred to another high school, which was better for my mental health.

"One thing that meant a lot to me was that the basketball team I played on sometimes played in a recreational center in the town where Zora Neale Hurston grew up. The center was right next to a church where her father was pastor. It still means a great deal to me that I was able to do that.

"In high school and earlier, I always lived with what W. E. B. Du Bois called a 'double consciousness.' In the first chapter of his *The Souls of Black Folk,* he says, 'It is a peculiar sensation, this double-consciousness, this sense of always looking at one's self through the eyes of others, of measuring one's soul by the tape of a world that looks on in amused contempt and pity. One ever feels his two-ness,—an American, a Negro; two souls, two thoughts, two unreconciled strivings; two warring ideals in one dark body, whose dogged strength alone keeps it from being torn asunder.'[1] This is a famous passage.

"I had a keen awareness of this double-consciousness in elementary school before I read about it in high school. I felt it in college, in seminary, and now am feeling it in graduate school.

"I enjoyed my Black experience. I loved everything about it. Just dwelling as a Black human being on this earth is amazing. But when people questioned my Blackness at school, I took a step back into my home experience, which was my other school of life. There I was with my parents, my cousins, my aunties and uncles, my community. I have a really strong community. It too was where I got an education.

"I've always gravitated toward Black teachers, coaches, and administrators. They knew who I was. We had good rapport, because the language was there. There wasn't any barrier, and I didn't have to explain. We could simply have a conversation.

"One of the states I grew up in allowed me to be freer than the other states I lived in because there were so many cultures there—Hispanic, Spanish, Black, Asian American. It was beautiful because of all the tribes, tongues, and nations. So I enjoyed my experience in that state a bit more than I enjoyed my experience in the other states. There was racism in that first state too—I don't want people to miss that—but it had a different flavor.

"I was a sophomore in high school when Trayvon Martin was killed just thirty minutes from where I lived then. I said to my mother, 'Mom, what are we going to do?' She just nodded her head, because she'd seen

---

1. Du Bois, *The Souls of Black Folk,* 2.

so much of it. She had watched the Rodney King beating. She was alive when Martin Luther King was assassinated. When that occurred, she was walking down a street and saw a Black man pulled out of a Volkswagon Beetle and be beaten. She was five then, so she knew about her Blackness at that early age.

"My dad didn't have to deal with racism when he was growing up, because the place where he grew up was all Black. But he knew about Whiteness and how it works, so he and my mom were adamant to teach us children about it.

"I felt my Blackness in the basketball and track teams I was on, but it wasn't something we talked about. When you are on a team, you talk about the things that bring you together for the sake of team bonding and not the things that separate you."

College

Alliyah went to a Christian college. "My parents wanted me to go to a Black church while I was in college, because they knew I was going to a predominately White institution. My mom especially was frightened for me to go to the college. Neither of them knew about the kind of racism in the region of the country where the college was located. In the region I grew up in, racism is explicit, but it is much less explicit in the region where the college is, which means that you have to navigate it differently.

"During orientation week, my parents, sister, and I went to a nearby AME church, the church that Sandra Bland had attended. She was a Black woman who had allegedly died by suicide in prison a month earlier. The church she had gone to was still in mourning, and the preacher announced an upcoming rally and protest for justice.

"My mother knew that the AME church was the church Sandra Bland had attended, and on our way there she made a comment about it. My sister glared at me, and I returned the glare, thinking about how the church would be grieving, mourning the loss of a dear sister at the hands of state-sanctioned violence.

"There was a heaviness I will never forget as we crossed the threshold of the foyer. But we were met with loving kindness from the ushers, congregants, and pastoral staff. As we sat in the velvet pews, I could only think about how Sandra Bland had sat there. I wondered how many times she prayed, sang, laughed, and cried in those pews.

"Sandra Bland's humanity came to mind. But then my thoughts were interrupted by an image of her body being slammed to the ground by Texas state trooper Brian Encinia and her death three days later.[2] I felt so near to her even though I had never met her. I held my sister's hand to comfort myself from the deep pain I felt for another Black life gone at the hands of the police. My spirit was uneasy.

"Although I enjoyed the service at the AME church, I wasn't able to keep going because I didn't have transportation to it. So I ended up going to a different church.

"If someone had told me what my college experience would have been like, I would have turned right around and gone home. It was tough. There were lots of moments of joy, to be sure, but there were lots of moments of sorrow unlike anything I had ever experienced.

"In high school, I was an athlete with many accomplishments and high self-esteem. I was confident in my abilities. But after my first year of college I started questioning my capabilities because of the White supremacy I experienced. The erosion of my self-esteem and confidence began to weigh on me. I became anxious about the future and depressed about missed opportunities. My work never felt good enough, and I was constantly searching for belonging (which I eventually found in the multicultural office at the college).

"On the plus side, I love people, and I gained lots of relationships, which I still have today, including a Black professor with whom I had five classes and who cared for me. Our interest in the Black tradition aligned. And I felt that we were both trying to figure out how to do justice, love mercy, and walk humbly.

"I also did a lot of activities: I was an event coordinator for the Black Student Union. During Black History Month, I curated Black art at the Black exposition on campus so that it could be appreciated and celebrated. I single-handedly planned and hosted a well-known Civil Rights icon from the Civil Rights Era for a lecture. I felt highly honored to have her on campus. I was grateful for the conversations and actionable steps involving social movements and racial reconciliation that took place as a result of her lecture. Also, I hosted Hip Hop dance competitions. They facilitated Black expressive culture and provided safe spaces in which our art and experience could be cultivated.

---

2. Hanna and Burnside, "Sandra Bland recorded her own arrest in 2015."

"On the negative side, White students wanted to touch my hair. They asked, 'Can I touch your hair?' And some of them touched it without even asking for my consent.

"When I joined the Black Student Union, I learned that other Black students had similar experiences of microaggressions. I became more aware of my Black womanhood and identity. I came to understand who I was becoming culturally and learned about the people who contributed to the Black American experience, such as Malcolm X, Martin Luther King, Jr., and James Baldwin. I learned about systemic oppression, mass incarceration, and voter suppression.

"James Baldwin's well-known assertion describes how I felt at that time: 'To be a Negro in this country and to be relatively conscious is to be in a state of rage almost all the time.'[3] As I became conscious of who I was as a Black person and how I and other Black people have been treated, I found myself getting angry.

"In a biology class my freshman year, I was part of a group project. The others in the group, who were all White, gave me the smallest part of the project. I asked them, 'Why are you giving me the smallest part?' They said, 'We just thought that was what you could do.' That was a form of racism—they thought that because of the color of my skin I could not do as much as everybody else. That really hurt.

"It also hurt to see so much divisiveness on campus because of the political conversations about Trump and Clinton for the 2016 presidential election. It was especially difficult to attend an all-White institution during the era of Donald Trump.

"I decided over Christmas break of my sophomore year that I wanted to be an advocate for civil rights and Black people and others who have been oppressed. I wanted to talk to as many people as possible about mass incarceration, redlining, block busting, oppression, the pay gap, and to tell people when they were saying or doing something racist.

"In one of my classes, the professor who is Black said one day that he has to dress in a full suit to get the same respect on campus as White faculty. A White guy in the class said, 'I don't believe that. No, that's not true.' I said, 'What he's saying is true. That is our daily experience.' I told him in front of the whole class about how, if I go into a store, I will automatically be followed. He said, 'Have you done the statistics?' I replied, 'Listen, this is my life. You're just glazing over it because you're a White male with privilege.

---

3. National Public Radio. "To Be in a Rage, Almost All the Time."

You don't have those issues. You're living effortlessly with respect to race. I have to pay the Black tax every day, all day.'

"In chapel one time, when a visiting Black minister was going to speak, a White student got up and walked out of chapel, saying as he did, 'Why do we always have to talk about race? There's no point. Everyone needs to pray and get over it.' I approached him and said, 'Can we get over slavery? We still have lasting effects to this day.' He said, 'I don't understand. It doesn't make sense.' I tried to talk with him, but he just walked away from me. That felt horrible. He didn't even want to listen.

"The microaggressions were not always verbal, but sometimes came through stares and glares. I felt as though there was always a suspicion.

"I think what was most difficult about college was trying to maintain mental stability. People were always trying to poke and prod, whether students, faculty, or staff—'How do you have all this strength? How do you have all this joy? Are you thankful to be here?'

"Some students challenged my academic ability. They seemed to feel threatened. 'How did you get here? Why did you choose this college where only 2.3% of students are Black?' That question was really, 'Why are you here?' I said back, 'I want to be here. I'm not here because of affirmative action or legacy scholarships. I earned my way here. I got scholarships, and this college gives a great education.' They had a narrow lens through which they viewed me. 'Really, people, I'm just human, like you.'"

Reflections

Alliyah reflects, some years after graduating from college: "I don't think the administration or even the faculty at the college understand the magnitude of the psychological damage done to us people of color at the college, the harm done to our self-esteem. They don't understand when a person of color needs to take a mental health day or to get off campus for a while.

"The White supremacist culture at the college shames and guilts you into thinking that you're inferior or that you don't belong. Imposter syndrome becomes real. A Black woman who went to the college told me that she had to take a year off after graduating just to get her mental health back. And other students I began with, particularly Black women, transferred either to an HBCU (historically Black college or university) or another school, or did something that was more mentally healthy for them.

"I still see the double consciousness that Du Bois described in my Black friends and the glare in their eyes that arises from not knowing whether they are good enough.

"So much of what I tried to do in college was to carve out safe spaces so as to grow self esteem, both for myself and for other people of color—the Hip Hop dance competitions, the Black coffee houses, bringing the Civil Rights Era activist to campus, forming friendships with people in the multicultural office, the NAACP showing up for me. I am still trying to create safe spaces for those who have been pushed to the margins, including myself.

"Someone might say, 'You didn't have to choose that college.' But that's not the point. The college is a microcosm of what it is like to be Black in America. The real question, is 'Why are you trying to make something of yourself in this White space?' Again, the White college space I was in is America. We people of color are always going to be in White spaces, trying to be visible because we are invisible to White eyes.

"The racialized stereotypes that exist at the college are an indictment of the Black body. It's dangerous to be Black in America. It's a dangerous thing. I was at a Mike Epps comedy show the other night, and he said, 'If you're over twenty-five and you're Black in America, we just gonna take a minute and clap for you.' Given the realities, he was saying, we should not have gotten this far.

"So it's not just about the college I went to. It's about American society, which continues to say, 'We don't want you. We hate you. We don't care about you. We don't love you.'

"This is not me being a victim. This is reality. It's hard to be a victor when victimization takes place at every turn. So I have to go back to my community, my kinfolk, the people at my cookout and dinner table, the people with whom I dance and laugh, all of whom I find joy with.

"In spite of the difficult things at the college, I came to care about it and wanted it to be a place where everyone was in communion with each other—Whites, Hispanics, African Americans, Asians, Asian Americans, and Indigenous people. I wanted it to be a place where we don't ignore issues of race and just hope they go away. I yearned for a time when we would love our neighbors even though they were different."

More Reflections

Alliyah is enthusiastic about education. "I love it for the community and also for the work that happens through books and professors and when lingering with classmates after class. Book projects are initiated during those lingering moments. Realizations and revelations are prompted in dialogue with others in the community of learners. I will forever be a learner.

"I don't want to idealize the academy, though, because it has issues. Sometimes you learn less in the ivory tower than in the public square. That is why I think of myself not only as a pastor who is in the academy, but also as one who is in the public square.

"Along the way, I have experienced both sorrow and celebration—sorrow when I learned how Black people have been brutalized and murdered, when I was told by a White girl in third grade that she could not play with me because I was Black, yet celebration when I got the highest grade on a writing test in sixth grade, when I was in Zora Neale Hurston's hometown, when I met the Civil Rights Era activist.

"I have been keenly aware of my Black identity in a world that is anti-Black. As a Black woman in higher education, I have sung what W. E. B. Du Bois calls sorrow songs, but I have also danced out on the dance floor. I have experienced both lament and hope."

Jenni: Escaping a Heroin Addiction

> "I woke up one day with the clear sense that I wanted a different life. . . . I wanted to feel again, laugh again, and love again."

Jenni became homeless and lost everything she had after becoming a heroin addict. Years later, she decided she wanted laughter and love again. She engineered an escape from the man who had held her captive in an empty truck and went through a detox program. She now gives motivational talks to people with mental health and substance abuse problems.

Jenni was in her late forties when we talked. The meanings of the asterisk-marked words are listed at the end.

My Best Friend

Jenni's heroin addiction started when she was about thirty-four. "Through my entire twenties, I was addicted to every pain killer you could name—morphine, Vicodin, and the all-too-famous OxyContin, a powerful prescription pain killer. Every day I was taking more than the prescribed number of eighty-milligram OxyContin pills, which were the strongest ones they made at that time. I was playing the game with all the doctors, going to each one and collecting scripts,* trading and selling them to buy OxyContin.

"At some point, I began to feel uneasy about taking so many pills. It was making me have stomach issues, among other problems. I was actually taking lethal amounts, and I wanted to get off them.

"At the time, I was a divorced mom and had three kids. My boys were almost eighteen and had left home to do their own thing, but my daughter was still living with me and was only nine. I decided to go to detox to see what it was all about. I thought, 'What could it hurt?' Detox ended up changing the rest of my life.

"In detox I met heroin addicts who said to me, 'Why would you pay fifty dollars a pill, taking all those pills, when you can just buy heroin,* which will do the same thing at a much cheaper price? In fact, you will get an even better high.' My mindset was, 'Yes, why would I?'

"So I left detox and was introduced to heroin for the first time by people I had met in detox. From that point on I had a new best friend. This friend took away all my troubles and pain. There was nothing I couldn't get through, because I had her right by my side, twenty-four hours a day, 365 days a year.

"I am very much a go-getter, and I like going all in with whatever I put my mind to. I never smoked heroin, never snorted it, never took it orally. I went straight to the needle the very first time I tried it, and it wasn't long before I became addicted to it physically, mentally, and emotionally.

"There wasn't any special reason behind using heroin except that I wanted to. I didn't come from a bad home, and I was blessed as a child. I had not yet experienced the trauma that my future had in store for me. I was your typical divorced, single mom, working and trying my best to survive."

Gaining Momentum

Jenni became more absorbed in her heroin addiction and more familiar with "the streets." She isolated herself from her friends and family. "I realized I couldn't care for my daughter properly, and I didn't want her to be around my addiction or end up going to the Arizona Department of Child Safety. So eventually I called my sister and asked her if she could come get my daughter. I also quit my job. I had worked seventeen years in construction and didn't want to tarnish my name. I tried to get into other industries, but with an addiction, that didn't happen.

"I met people on the street,* and I became good at surviving on it. I adapted to the lifestyle of what some people called 'the game.' Depending on what was going on, I slept in a house or a garage or even in the middle of the desert. One time I had some boosters* steal me a trampoline, and that's what I slept on. At that time there was no main house or trap house* where I stayed.

"Being new to the streets, I knew I was going to have to come up with a hustle.* So I did. It didn't involve a male being in charge or having to be protected by a male. I didn't have to prostitute or do any type of sexual acts. I did my own hustle, and that's how I paid for my addiction.

"In the first hustle I came up with, I went into high-end bars and solicited myself as an escort. I observed the males who came into the bars, identified the types of clothes they wore, the kinds of cars they got out of, and whether they paid with cash or credit card. I approached the men and said, 'Do you want to go to a hotel?' Of course, they said yes. And when we got to a room there, males who wore bandanas came out from the bathroom and robbed them.

"Once that hustle ran dry, I became a booster from high-end stores, like Victoria's Secret or Nordstrom, and then sold the merchandise for 50% of whatever the tag said. I was lucky that I didn't have to turn to prostitution. It was easier back then to be a booster."

Wolf in Sheep's Clothing

Jenni acquired a boyfriend who was in the game on the streets. "I knew he liked me, so I used that to get free heroin. The next thing I know, he started saying things like, 'That's my girl.' I hit him back with, 'I'm not your girl. I'm nobody's girl.' I made it very clear that my priority was with heroin. Even if there was a male in my life, heroin would always be first.

"I didn't know the extent of this fool's background, and he turned out to be a true psychopath. He gaslighted* me so much that I got Stockholm Syndrome.* Even though he was hurting me, I thought he was the only one who cared for me.

"He had gone to prison for some number of years and had become a player with some political stance while in there, and he stayed that way after he got out. A lot of people didn't mess with him because they knew his background and what he was capable of. I didn't understand the extent of his violence until I experienced it myself.

"Eventually he isolated me by taking my phones. It didn't matter how many I got. They all went missing."

Missing Person

Jenni found out much later that her parents had been looking for her for quite some time. "There were missing person flyers of me that the county sheriff's department distributed to the agencies in the city I was in. They were posted on telephone poles and in stores.

"At times, my parents were close to finding me. My mom once thought I was staying at a certain house. The police knocked on the door and asked if I was there, but the people who answered said I wasn't. Because I was an adult and there was no proof of any crimes, they left. My mom begged the police to go into the house. They explained to her that they couldn't enter a house just because she thought I was in it. But she knew I was there.

"My boyfriend told me, 'No, your parents haven't tried to call.' And then when my parents did call, he told them, 'I told her to call you,' or 'She's not here. I can't make her call you.'

"He had me believing that my family had completely written me off. But, for whatever reason, my parents knew that he was not being honest and that there was something wrong. If I had known they were looking for me, I might not have gotten so deep into my heroin addiction. Later, my father asked me, 'Do you know what it's like to call the morgues and the hospitals to see if your daughter is lying in them?' I didn't understand until much later in my recovery how my parents felt about my being gone."

Loves Me/Loves Me Not

Jenni's boyfriend, who claimed he loved her, the boyfriend who would never let anyone touch her, once hit her so hard with a clay bowl that he "blew" her eardrum and knocked her out. "I'm now deaf in my left ear because of that. The bowl busted and sliced the upper part of my ear. I had to call a friend to come over and sew that part of my ear up. While she was doing that, I had to bite a pillow, and I had to take a really big shot of heroin to mask the pain. You didn't go to the police when you were out there on the streets, and I very much feared my boyfriend. Saying I was afraid of him is an understatement.

"One time he slit a dog's throat in front of me. That, of course, instilled terror in me, which I had never felt before. Another time, when I had mouthed off to him in front of some people, he shoveled so much dirt into my mouth that I almost suffocated. People who saw him do it had to stop him.

"He was so obsessed with me that when other people tried to help me, there were heavy repercussions for them. One time he blew up the car of one of my friends because my friend had found out where I was located and had helped me. He was never going to let me go. When I tried to run, I sometimes surrendered and went right back to him if I heard he was looking for me or I knew he was coming for me.

"His obsession got to be so intense that at one point he locked me in the back of a stationary refrigerator truck and put restrictions on me. I couldn't go out when I wanted to. I couldn't take a shower when I wanted to. I couldn't have any kind of radio or digital device, because he thought I might try to contact my family. I had to use cups from Circle K to pee in.

"I had lost everything. I had pretty much only the clothes I was wearing. I had not had a job for several years. I thought my family had abandoned me, and I had no hope of ever seeing them again. The power of addiction had become so strong and the consequences of it so overbearing that I had given up on ever being saved.

"At the same time, I had all kinds of high-end stuff in the boxlike truck. He brought back expensive purses, clothes, and other things he had collected from people who could not pay their debts for drugs he had sold them. I got to pick what I wanted, and I put it into my own little area in the truck. That area of the truck was really cute. He never forgot to tell me the reason he brought me all these things was that he loved me so much.

"By this time, I was so far into my addiction, and the Stockholm Syndrome was so intense, that I accepted my situation."

Knocking on Heaven's Door

Jenni lived in the box truck for almost nine months. "Everyone on the streets knew the situation I was in, and they all tried to help me at some point. Friends tried to talk me into leaving and running away forever. His own people asked him one time, 'What are you doing to this female? This can't be going on.' He replied, 'She's going to be fine. I'll figure something out.'

"I had never been suicidal, but it got to the point at which I would be okay doing a big fat shot of heroin and never opening my eyes again. I accepted that death was knocking on my door. Sometimes, even, I prayed that I would finally answer it.

"I had a friend who died, and I overheard a conversation her kids were having about how their mom had ODed.* They didn't say anything else about their mom, just that one little phrase, which kept going through my head. I thought, 'I need to figure out how to stop using and how to get out of the situation I am in.' I didn't want to leave a legacy like that for my kids even though I had not talked with them for six-and-a-half years. And what would my parents say? Because my boyfriend was so obsessed with me, I could have contact with only a handful of people. I kept thinking, 'How the hell am I going to get out?'

"In the world we were in, males and the females who were of any importance were not supposed to be using drugs of the kind we were using. It was highly frowned on. So I thought, 'Okay. If I get him to take me to detox to get off heroin, he's going to say yes.' Then he could go to his people and say, 'This female is okay. She's not using heroin anymore.'

"I begged him for a month: 'Please let me go to detox. I want to stop using heroin. Please let me go and get clean.' I tried to make it sound as though it was going to benefit him, especially his reputation with other users and dealers.

"One night he came to the box truck, unlocked it, and said, 'Pack your stuff. You have five minutes.' It was five minutes to midnight on January 31st of 2021. I said, 'Okay,' and packed a few items into a backpack, then left."

"I Can't Go Back"

"The whole ride to the detox center I was thinking, 'This has got to be my way out. This has got to be the way I leave.' I had learned on the streets that when opportunity presented itself, take it. If you didn't, that would be on you. He walked me straight to the detox door and said, 'I will see you in thirty days.' I said, 'Okay.'

"I had previously gone through treatment five or six times. But each time I'd do a LAMA—leave against medical advice. Instead of seven days, I'd do only two, saying to myself, 'I'm out of here.'

"This time, I kept telling myself, 'I can't go back. This guy's going to kill me. I don't want to suffer anymore.' I had embraced suffering as a way of life. The feeling of happiness didn't exist. I knew I had to break the bondage my addiction had become.

"In nightmares, I replayed scenes from the horrific ordeal I had been living in for so long, such as when my hair had started falling out because he had put hair remover into my shampoo bottles, or when I had heard through the grapevine that he had been putting poison into some of the drinks and food he brought me. I didn't know whether that was true, but I'd known what he was capable of because of the violence he had already placed upon me and others.

"Everyone on the street knew what he was capable of because of the repercussions they had received for trying to help me. Some of them had been recipients of his wrath, and others had been spared. Those who had been recipients stopped trying to help me and accepted my situation, as I had. Those who had been spared stopped by the box truck to make sure I was still alive and brought me something to drink or eat.

"In detox, I made the decision not to use MAT services—medical-assisted treatment. I refused all meds. I didn't take Suboxone. I didn't take methadone. I wanted detox to stick. My life truly depended on that, because I knew either I would OD again or my boyfriend would end up killing me. Getting through detox was one of the hardest things I had ever experienced in my life, both physically and mentally. But I did it with the support of the nurses in detox. I got off heroin.

"I opted to go into a residential treatment program straight from detox. While I was going through the program, I was unclear about what exactly I was supposed to be doing about the addiction I had created and the lifestyle that was too familiar to me. It wasn't until three weeks after I started the program that I realized with some clarity that I wanted a heroin-free lifestyle. I did not want to go back to using drugs and alcohol. I wanted to feel again, laugh again, and love again.

"People have asked me, 'How did you get that clarity?' There's nothing I can come up with to explain it. I don't know whether it was because of all the trauma I had gone through or because I could actually see leaves on trees clearly when I went outside. Everything was so different, even visually. I just woke up one day with the clear sense that I wanted a different life."

Embracing Treatment

After graduating from residential treatment, Jenni decided to do a partial hospitalization program—PHP. "That's where you live in a facility that is supervised by people who also live in it. You can't leave the facility, and you have to spend a certain amount of hours every day doing a program.

"Things were going well for me, though right away I had to deal with my boyfriend. It was past the thirty days when he was expecting me, and I had not tried to contact him. He knew something was going on. So he came to the facility and attempted to get me. He sent a bunch of people to try to get me. The rehab people themselves had to get involved, and the police had to be called. He contacted my parents and anyone else who knew me on Facebook telling them he was going to hurt me. He told them all kinds of stuff that had happened during my addiction, things that parents didn't need to know. In the end, the rehab put me into a safe room.

"I had a lot of things I had to come to terms with in addition to the demons I had to slay. One of the biggest challenges was not believing in God. I am not a God-fearing woman. Part of the reason for that is that when I was praying for somebody to save me, in the end there was only me. I was the one who had to figure out how to get myself out of the hell I was living in. I was the one who had to deal with the monster of a boyfriend who had walked into my path.

"So I was having a hard time in PHP, because the twelve-step programs they used involved believing in God. In Narcotics Anonymous and Alcoholics Anonymous, you had to give your willpower over to a higher power, even if you thought of the higher power as a doorknob. That was not going to happen with me, because I believed it was my own willpower that had gotten me to where I was, up to that very day. Still, I wondered how I could stay sober without a program or fellowship.

"I started looking for a program that dealt with emotional intelligence because of my Stockholm syndrome and because of the way my mind had become so warped by the gaslighting the boyfriend had done. I thought to myself, 'There has to be something out there for people like me.' That is when I found SMART—Self-Management and Recovery Training. It's about retraining yourself to think differently, taking your negative thinking patterns and redirecting them into positive ones. It changes your emotional intelligence. Instead of saying, 'I'll try,' you say, 'I will.' And instead of labeling yourself an addict, you say you are abstaining from drugs and alcohol now. You don't label yourself in a way the public stigmatizes. I found that I could grasp this type of recovery program.

"I bugged the PHP facilitators day after day to adopt SMART, but they wouldn't do it. SMART was fairly new in the rehabs, and I think they just did not want to bother. Dealing with sixty or seventy emotionally unregulated people who were coming off of drugs and alcohol was enough for them, I'm sure.

"Finally, they gave me the green light and said, 'Fine, Jenni. If you think you can do the SMART program on your own time in addition to doing the PHP program, you can do it.' I have always gone against the grain, even as a child. Tell me I can't do something and watch me prosper. So there I was, researching every aspect of the SMART recovery program and starting a voluntary group to go through it.

"There were three people who started with me, and by the time I graduated from PHP, four months later, there were seventeen of us who had voluntarily done the SMART program. When I graduated from PHP at the rehab, they acknowledged I had taken something they didn't have and had made it into something people could believe in."

My Passion Meets My Purpose

Three years later, Jenni works for a behavioral health provider in Tucson, Arizona, where she is a recovery facilitator for the SMART recovery program. She works with individuals who have mental health and substance abuse challenges and gives numerous talks in which she tells her story to people with substance abuse and mental health problems. Her hope is that listeners will become inspired by her story. "It is intoxicating to see the inspiration on people's faces who are looking at me as I tell my story. That gives me motivation for believing that I have a chance to make an impact on humanity.

"I have also done outreach. I've brought people up from the tunnels near Tucson, where I live, and taken them to detox. A lot of the homeless people in Tucson live in the tunnels—the spaces under bridges that go over dried-up river beds, or 'washes.'

"When I talk to people, I don't use clinical terms, and I don't wear business attire. My employers would tell you, 'We let Jenni be Jenni, because she relates to people well. She is exceptional at her job.'

"Even though I had worked my way up in the seventeen-year stint with construction, I never believed it was my purpose in life. My passion for helping people recover and helping them understand their worth was my true purpose. It was to demonstrate resilience in being a survivor.

"A lot of times I hear people say, 'I can't do it. I'm a felon' or 'I did too many drugs.' My response is, 'You *can* do it. You have the ability and strength to overcome your past. If you stopped and gave yourself a minute to think about what you have experienced, you would find your teachable moment. Those challenges make you stronger. They don't have to define who you are.'

"I don't say that they can survive because I'm a success story but because people need to realize that they can experience trauma, trials, and tribulations and still recover from them."

Lost But Now Found

"Prior to recovery," Jenni says, "I was complacent. I felt dirty. Even though I had morals, the things I had to do to survive—the hustles, the boosting—were wrong. I have a sense of inner peace now, knowing I don't have to worry about that, because everything I do is with good intent and has meaning. That makes me feel that I am a better person. I am doing good things to help put some good into the world.

"Taking heroin filled a void in my heart. It masked the emotions I was hiding from and gave me a pleasant feeling about the kind of purpose I wanted then. Other drugs I used—fentanyl, cocaine, and meth—masked my emotions, too, but my particular drug of choice happened to be heroin.

"The feeling that keeps me motivated now is the self-gratification I feel when I see other people be inspired. I told my story once to a bunch of prison guys, and afterwards they all stood up and clapped. Some even had tears in their eyes. That keeps me going. It makes me feel that I can never use again.

"I keep things raw and honest in my speeches. I tell people that just because they say they are getting clean doesn't mean that everyone is going to believe them. They have to prove it by how they live. They were in active addiction for so long, and now they have to make the choice to stay clean. People can say to them, 'I'm here for you. Call me whenever you like,' but in the end it comes down to the ones who were addicted and their choices.

"When I was using, I lost my family and friends. I absconded from a court-ordered probation, I ODed a handful of times, and I had to be narcaned.* I even had CPR done on me, which cracked a rib one time. I was taken to the ER. I pulled the IVs out, and when I walked out, the first thing I wanted to do was to go get high.

"I lost my dignity, my self empowerment, my happiness, and was stripped of my spirit. Why? Because of my choices. I didn't want to sit in a group. I didn't want to get clean. My choice was to run to the street, even though I had been in and out of jail for boosting. And now that I am not using, it is still a matter of holding myself accountable.

"Most of the things I lost while in active addiction, I have back in my life again."

The Reality

Three years ago Jenni met and eventually married someone when they were in the sobriety program. "Three months ago, on August 11, 2023, I experienced the greatest pain my heart and soul have ever experienced, when my husband died from taking half a pill of fentanyl. He had been in prison for a year, and fifteen days after he got out he took that half pill. It cost him his life.

"His death stung.

"I struggle sometimes with how I can help other people when I couldn't even help my own husband. Somebody said to me, though, 'You did help your husband. He just had a moment of weakness, and you can't control every thought that comes into someone's head. He impulsively chose to act on that thought.

"He believed in me and always loved the way I helped people in recovery. I know he would never want me to go back to using. He would never want me to go down that road again. Still, it feels as though I have been left alone in this ugly world to try to figure stuff out on my own.

"Losing my husband to the very demons I am slaying everyday is intense and challenging. But I believe that things happen for a reason. I continue to work on choosing to remain sober, rebuilding my self-empowerment.

"My husband is not with me in physical form, but he is an angel watching over me, guiding me in my journey and protecting me from evil. My husband's choice was the ultimate sacrifice. Death is permanent and it can't be undone. He will forever be thirty-seven."

Glossary

Boost: steal.

Gaslighting: "Victims of gaslighting are deliberately and systematically fed false information that leads them to question what they know to be true, often about themselves." *Psychology Today,* "Gaslighting": https://www.psychologytoday.com/us/basics/gaslighting#

Heroin: "The standard street price for one bag [of heroin] ranges from $5-$20 based on factors like location and purity." Zinnia Health, "How Much Does Heroin Cost?" OxyContin is an opioid that is highly addictive. When sold legally, an 80 mg tablet of OxyContin costs $6. When sold illegally, the price is $65-$80. National Drug Intelligence Center "OxyContin Diversion and Abuse."

Hustle: an activity, especially an underhanded one, designed to secure money

Living on the street: being homeless, spending days on sidewalks and alleys and spending nights in shelters or other temporary places

Narcaned: Narcan® is the brand name of naloxone, a medicine that is an antidote to overdosing on opioid drugs. Heroin is an opioid drug.

ODed: overdosed

Scripts: prescriptions

Stockholm syndrome: See page 67 for a description of this.

Trap house: a house, especially an empty house, where illegal drugs are sold

"Robyn": Fighting Anorexia

"That was the turning point for me—when someone said, 'Will you let me help you?' and I said yes."

Eating disorders are often addicting and very difficult to escape. Intervention, voluntary or involuntary, is frequently needed. Robyn won her long battle with anorexia via a year-long treatment program and now has an anorexia-free life. She was in her early thirties when we talked.

Beginnings

Robyn's eating disorder started early. "In first and second grade, I became concerned about my body and began weighing myself. By the time I was in fourth grade, I had a great deal of shame toward my body. I had a strong desire to be thin.

"In middle school, I had some pretty severe anxiety and depression, but it never got dealt with: 'You're a good kid. You come from a loving family, so you're just fine. Keep pushing on.' I was never a problem at school, so most people didn't see my thinness as a problem.

"The disorder became more active when I was fourteen or fifteen, and when I was sixteen and seventeen, it got bad. I spiraled down. Within six months, I had lost thirty pounds. I was skin and bones, down to nothing—ninety pounds, my lowest of lows.

"What provoked the spiral was that I had to miss out on a basketball season because of a bone tumor in my leg and knee surgery. That was when I had my first major bout of depression. I went inward, and everything went off the charts—the food restricting, the obsessive weighing and exercising, the self-hate. That was all I could focus on. I couldn't pay attention to what my friends were doing or anything else that was happening around me. My weight became a complete fixation.

"Some of my severe depression was rooted in the fact that I constantly compared myself to my older sister. I tried to measure up to her, but I never could: 'I'm never going to be like her. Never going to be worthy. Never going to be good enough.' But I desperately wanted to be good enough.

"At the time, I didn't know I had a problem. I wasn't consciously aware that I was restricting my food and that I was obsessive."

Worse

Robyn's older sister found out that she had a problem with her eating. "One day as I was about to leave for soccer practice with my sister, she said, 'If you don't tell Mom and Dad, I'm going to.'

"So I wrote a letter to my parents and told them I had an eating disorder. I folded it up and laid it beside my mom, who was taking a nap. I walked out the door and went to soccer practice.

"My mom called me at soccer practice and yelled at me. My parents' way of handling my problem was to get me in trouble for having it. When that happened, I shut down even more and became totally closed off. My behaviors got worse. That's when I got down to ninety pounds.

"My parents put me into a treatment program. While my friends were enjoying life, dating, and doing things, I spent only a few hours each day at school and then my mom drove me to the treatment program.

"I got better. Then I got bad again. In my senior year of high school, I turned to self-harm—cutting and burning myself. My eating was no better.

"My soccer and field hockey coach caught on to my eating disorder. She became the one person who was always there for me, my go-to person for everything. I told her about the cutting and other stuff. One afternoon I said to her, 'I'm done. I don't want to keep doing life.'

"She called my parents, who picked me up and took me to a psychiatric facility for self-harm, eating disorder, and suicide watch. I had multiple bouts of pretty severe suicidal episodes, times when I felt I couldn't keep going. I never made any attempts, though, and I was genuinely trying to fight the depression and self-harm. That was during my senior year of high school and all through Christmas break."

Molested

While all these things were going on, Robyn was being sexually molested by a neighbor. "It lasted five or six years, until I was seventeen. At first I didn't recognize what was happening, because there was a slow process of being groomed. Then it happened more often until it became a regular thing.

"Over and over, he told me what I now see were lies: 'No one is going to want you. You are unlovable. You will never be good enough.' The constant repetition made me believe these assertions. I told them to myself, day after day.

"He stopped molesting me at one point because he didn't want someone who weighed ninety pounds and was just a skeleton. When I got healthier, the molesting started up again. I began to believe it would be better to be unhealthy so as to stop what he was doing to me.

"I hated my body. I felt so much shame toward it because of what he used it for. I wanted to hide. I wanted to disappear.

"I knew it was all wrong, but I had so much shame that I couldn't tell anyone what was happening. I just couldn't.

"My family now knows about the molesting, but we don't talk about it. Nor about my eating disorder. I think that is both a cultural thing and a family thing. I also now think the silence at the time of the eating disorder and the sexual molestation contributed to their continuation."

More Lies

In college, Robyn continued to experience ups and downs while doing therapy. "I started believing that the ongoing battle with anorexia and bulimia was going to be my life and that I was never going to get better. My family would just have to accept it.

"The most deep-rooted lies involving my eating disorder were the same ones I came to believe because of being molested: that I was unlovable, not worthy, not good enough. At the time, I wasn't aware of this similarity. And I didn't notice that the shame and self-hate in the one reinforced the shame and hate in the other. In both cases, I had lost the desire to get healthy. I believed that no one was ever going to love me.

"I almost didn't want people to love me or like me. I didn't want them to see the other side of myself. I myself didn't want to see that side. I was nearly to the point at which I didn't want to love myself.

"I continued to compare myself with my sister. She had everything together, and she didn't struggle with eating. I felt that I had to strive to measure up to her standards. But I never could. She is a wonderful person, but she was always criticizing me then. At one point she called me "Thunder Thighs," a derogatory phrase for people who have extra large thighs. I had legs that were good for playing soccer, but they were not extra large. Still, I kept replaying in my mind the negative things she said to me.

"People didn't know what to do. They were like, 'Just eat, and you'll be better.' But I couldn't just eat. And I couldn't tell them what was really happening—the lies I believed, the not eating, the molesting that was feeding the eating disorder. It was all a mess."

Fighting Treatment

By the time Robyn had graduated from college, she had been to six or seven treatment centers. "I still had not been able to overcome my eating disorder. I didn't know who I was. In college I at least had a little more sense of identity, but as soon as college ended, I had to become an adult. For two years, I was merely the anorexic believe-it girl who couldn't get it together.

"All the lies came right back. I used laxatives and diuretics. I exercised, purged, lied, didn't eat, and hid what was going on. I got myself into another downward spiral. I did not get to my lowest weight then, but I was probably less than a hundred pounds. My body was not in a good spot healthwise. I was twenty-three, and I couldn't function.

"I found a treatment center that my parents wanted me to go to. I wanted to go too. At the same time, I did not want to go. But I went.

"I did not get better. I did not want to get better. I fought it and fought it. Insurance was paying thousands of dollars a day for me to be there, and I was refusing even to want to change.

"My psychiatrist and one of the program directors there called my parents and said, 'Your daughter is getting worse. Her heart is not well, her kidneys aren't well, her blood work is terrible. You need to come here immediately.'

"I did not know that they had called my parents. When they showed up, I thought, 'No, no, no, no, no!

"My family all wrote me letters about why I needed to get better. Some of them were meaningful, including my dad's. But my sister's letter hit me hard. She said, 'I know how desperately you want to be an aunt to your nephew.' (He had been born a few weeks before I left for the treatment center.) 'However, if you continue the way you are, you are not welcome in his life, because I've watched you slowly kill yourself for six, eight, years. And I will not let my son watch you die.'

"I realized then the impact I had made on my sister. She had, indeed, watched me slowly kill myself. I did definitely want to be an aunt. I knew I needed help, but I still wasn't there yet.

"My parents left. I had the letters. And I was in distress."

The Dietician and the Nurse

Change came when the dietician at the treatment center took an interest in Robyn. "She pulled me into her office and said, 'Robyn, you have so much to live for, and you can recover. I want you to give me two weeks, just two weeks, of trying it my way. I want you to let go and let me help you. Can you trust me for two weeks? If you hate what we're doing, you can go back to your eating disorder. It will still be there.'

"I thought about it, then went back to her office, where I broke down and said, 'Fine. I'll give you two weeks.'

"They had nurses be with me every moment of the day and night—while I was sleeping, even when I went to the bathroom and was showering. I was never alone.

"I was angry at first—angry that they were following me everywhere and angry with myself for having gotten myself in that situation. I was frustrated that I couldn't do anything without having eyes on me. I was sad that I was hurting so badly that I was slowly killing myself and sad that it took so many people to help me to see a glimmer of light.

"After going through these uncomfortable emotions, I surrendered. I laid down my condition and put it into someone else's hands. I became grateful for the nurses who sat with me, followed me, and talked with me. They had hope for me, and because of that, I felt supported.

"All that was the turning point for me—when someone said, 'Will you let me help you?' and I said yes.

"I was in that treatment center for almost a year—for my birthday, Christmas, Easter. Then I transferred to a day hospital in a different city. At one point I was going to that hospital three days a week. Then it was two days, and then weekly counseling. After that, I went back home and did an evening program. Altogether, it was sixteen months of constant, intensive treatment."

A Life-Changing Job

Robyn got a job at a local school working with special needs students. "I loved doing that. And because I was healthy, I was able to start running again. Then I was asked to be a coach for an organization at the school for third through sixth grade girls that encourages positive body image and self-esteem while training the girls for a five-K run. So I started coaching. I have been doing that for nearly ten years now and have not had to go back to treatment.

"Each fall I coach ten and eleven-year-olds, and in the spring I coach the younger girls. Right now, in the fall, I have girls who are struggling with body image and comparison. I talk to them about positive self-talk and how to catch themselves before negative self-talk becomes a spiral. They know that I too have struggled with body image and self-esteem.

"There is so much power in stories. Other people's stories inspired me to get better. Now I am able to tell my story to girls who need an older friend.

"One of my girls has an eating disorder, and she and I talk one-on-one from time to time. She'll ask me questions, such as, 'How do I fuel myself enough when I run?' Her parents are very aware of her eating disorder, and I have gotten to build a relationship with them. They know my story.

"Last week, I texted the girl's mom about a compulsive pattern I was seeing with the girl. The mom texted back saying that they were seeing the same thing at home: 'Glad we're on the same page.' Her mom and dad have asked me to continue mentoring their daughter.

"I love having conversations with the older girls. I have become someone they can talk to in the same way I had a coach I could talk to when I had difficulties in high school.

"I don't think the girls know how much they are helping me. They all think I am the one who is coaching them. But their impact on me has greatly aided in my continued recovery. When I am struggling with anxiety or depression, even now, I say to myself, 'I can't get back into my eating disorder, because I wouldn't be able to coach.' And I love coaching. All my girls are wonderful. They're crazy and goofy, but they're a joy to be with."

A New Life

Robyn's life has changed in a number of ways. "I now have a good relationship with my sister. I hated the letter she wrote to me more than ten years ago, but at the same time I am grateful for it. I would never have wanted my nephew or niece—my nephew now has a sister—to see their aunt in the state I was in then or watch me slowly kill myself. That is not the example I want to set for anyone.

"My sister's two children are my everything. As soon as I got out of treatment, I was at their house every other weekend. Now that they live in another state, I see them every other month. This coming Friday morning, I am going to fly out and take them to a football game in the afternoon. I love it that I am making memories with them.

"I no longer feel unlovable. When I didn't feel lovable and didn't have a purpose, I didn't care much about getting better: 'I can get better. But for what?' Now that I feel lovable and have a purpose, I want to keep on living.

"There are days, though, when I think, 'This is too hard' or 'I can't deal with this right now' or 'I just want to die.' I'm not suicidal, but sometimes I am so overwhelmed by stress or anxiety and depression that I want to escape.

"When I was in the midst of the eating disorder, I felt very lonely. Neither my sister nor any of her friends or my friends struggled with an eating disorder. I felt that I did not belong and that no one understood me.

"Now I can be a support for those who are walking through the same things so that they don't feel overwhelmed or lonely. That keeps me going. I feel as though I am on a wonderful journey. It all is my way of seeing how God has used my recovery so that I can inspire and encourage young girls.

"I run a lot, usually every morning with friends. I did my first Ironman last year. That's a triathlon in which you swim 2.4 miles, bicycle 112 miles, and do a full marathon, 26.2 miles, back to back. Doing things like this is another motivator to continue to stay healthy.

"If I had not changed when I was at the long-term treatment center, there's a good chance I would have died. Your body can withstand not eating for only so long before it begins to shut down. At least five people I knew at the center have died in the last three or four years. I get sad every time I hear about another death.

"I have learned that my identity does not come from what someone does to me. When I was being molested, I let the molester have control over me. I have gotten that control back and am my own person now.

"I want people to know that there is hope even though it takes a lot of work. If someone else can shine their light, then you can see that light at the end of the tunnel. And if you get there, you can say, 'Wow! All the hard work was worth it.'"

"Ariana": Confronting My ADHD

"I still keep looking in disbelief at what I have become."

Throughout her grade school, high school, and college years, Ariana thought that her inability to do well-structured studying was due to lack of discipline. She had to give up her dream of going to graduate school. After receiving a diagnosis of ADHD some years after graduating from college and starting on medication for ADHD, her life became much different. She and I talked when she was in her late twenties.

According to the National Institute of Mental Health, Attention-Deficit/Hyperactivity Disorder "is marked by an ongoing pattern of inattention and/or hyperactivity-impulsivity that interferes with functioning or development. . . . For a person to receive a diagnosis of ADHD, the symptoms of inattention and/or hyperactivity-impulsivity must be chronic or long-lasting, impair the person's functioning, and cause the person to fall behind typical development for their age."[1]

Early Life and High School

When Ariana was being evaluated for ADHD in her midtwenties, she recalled a number of past events that were pertinent to ADHD. "As I reflected on my childhood, it became clearer and clearer to me that I struggled to concentrate and pay attention in elementary school. I remember the imaginative games going on in my head and the doodles I drew on my

---

1. National Institute of Mental Health. "Attention-Deficit/Hyperactivity Disorder."

paper. I was in my own little world, but I didn't recognize that that was not normal. And I wasn't worried about it.

"In high school, I became interested in academic subjects, especially in the humanities. Doing well in school became important to me. But being a diligent student did not come easily. I was a huge procrastinator. I couldn't organize my time so that I could sit down and do what I needed to do when I needed to do it. I often got up at five or six in the morning to do the lion's share of my homework the morning it was due.

"At the time, this felt as though it was a lack of discipline. I did not see that it had to do with an inability to pay attention to things or to focus on what I was doing. So I perceived myself as a bad student due to lack of discipline and willpower. I felt guilty about it all. Grade wise, though, I wasn't a bad student, because I got As and B+s. I have often thought that if I had spent more time on schoolwork and had not turned in so many late assignments, I would have been an A student.

"I always had the hope that eventually I would get the right habits and summon the right discipline to be a good student: 'Next year I will straighten out my study habits,' I told myself every school year."

In College

In college, Ariana started thinking about going to graduate school. "I was getting good feedback from my professors and had reason to believe I had what it took to do well in graduate school. I was able to understand difficult texts. At other times, though, I read the same sentence over and over with no comprehension. 'Maybe this is above my level,' I thought. 'Maybe I am deceiving myself into thinking I can do well enough for graduate school.'

"I thought for a time that I might be crippled with imposter syndrome. Other students talked about imposter syndrome a lot. For me it was the idea that others perceived me as more intelligent than what I deserved: 'I'm not really as good as all that. My peers are more competent and intelligent than I am. I'm just pretending to be smart.' I definitely felt that some of the time. But sometimes I turned out a really good paper, which made me feel that I actually was capable of doing good enough work for graduate school.

"It never became clear to me either way. I was confused. And I was still procrastinating, because I couldn't force myself to focus on assignments until the adrenaline of an impending deadline kicked in.

"I noticed all these things the most when I was sitting down to do homework. I blocked out a good amount of time to do it. I went to the library, sat in one of the quiet study carrels, where there were no distractions, and put the text in front of me that I had to read or the document I was supposed to write. But it wouldn't happen. I kept thinking of other things I wanted to do or things I wanted to think about.

"It seemed to me, again, that it was a lack of discipline that made me unable to do what I should have been doing. Or it was due to a weak will. I got distracted. I went on Facebook or read something unrelated to what I should have been reading or sat there thinking about something else. I couldn't will my mind to focus on what it didn't want to focus on."

Becoming Aware

At some point during college, Ariana started to think that a lack of discipline or a weak will wasn't key to what was going on with her. "I thought that my brain might work differently. There might be ways in which I could not do what other people could do.

"Also, it occurred to me that my problem was something a psychologist might be able to help me with. At the same time, I was trying to diagnose it myself. So I kept chickening out from actually going to a counselor. I did a lot of research on my own.

"I thought at one point that I might have some kind of perfectionism that was tied to obsessive compulsive disorder. But the things I read about them didn't add up. I conjectured at another point that I might have some kind of crippling anxiety, but that didn't line up either. I dismissed all the possibilities and quit trying to find out what I had."

Giving Up My Dream

Until Ariana's last semester, she was planning on applying to graduate school. "That was my dream. That was what I most wanted to do. For a time it felt as though I had a choice between going for that dream and consequently having a stressful, chaotic, and unhealthy life or not going to grad school and being depressed because I could not do what I most wanted to do. But that choice dissipated during my last semester of college when I finally realized that I couldn't do grad school. I just could not do it.

"I had gotten a decent grade point average, but my study habits were chaotic. I got up early to do assignments, as I had done in high school. Sometimes I turned in papers that I knew were subpar. Or I didn't make a deadline and then was penalized. It seemed less and less sustainable to think I could keep doing these things in grad school. Besides being stressful and unhealthy, it would include a good deal of anxiety.

"It hurt to give up the one dream I had for my life. But I couldn't figure out how to have the right study habits or the right kind of routine to make it work. I had a faint hope that I would get it together someday, but I was not very optimistic about that."

Feeling Like Garbage

After college, Ariana moved in with her parents to work and to try to find herself. "I thought it would be much less stressful to have a nonacademic life. But I struggled in many of the same ways I struggled in an academic environment. I couldn't keep up even with lowered demands. If I had a list of things I needed to do, I merely sat thinking, 'I should be doing that. I should be doing that.' I couldn't push myself to do anything, even for simple things like washing the dishes or making a phone call to set up an appointment.

"It was a bizarre to feel so helpless. Most people don't experience that, at least not on a regular basis. If they know something is important, they can push themselves to stand up and walk over and do the thing, even if they don't feel like doing it. But I couldn't do that.

"I thought, 'This isn't normal. I need to find a therapist.' So I did for a few months. It turned out to be an extremely painful experience.

"The therapist suggested trying depression medication and then anxiety medication. But I knew that the depression and anxiety were not essential to what was going on but were their results. So even though I was acutely unhappy, I knew that taking medications for them was not something I wanted to try. I knew people who were depressed and anxious, and I could tell that my depression and anxiety were different.

"I was depressed and anxious because I couldn't do the things that were personally fulfilling to me. When I was in certain social situations, my mind sometimes went blank when I wanted to say something. I lost my train of thought in the middle of conversations. When I sat down and tried to read something academic, my mind was flooded with other thoughts and I couldn't concentrate.

"I described these to the therapist. I dredged up all my struggles and dissatisfactions. And after each therapy session, I was an emotional wreck. Therapy made me feel like garbage.

"The therapist was a general therapist and may not have known the symptoms of ADHD. Or maybe she didn't recognize them because ADHD looks different in different people. She wasn't able to help me, so I stopped seeing her. But I kept looking on my own."

Researching

After a year or two of researching online, Ariana started to catch on that she might have ADHD. "It took a long time to figure this out, even after I was reading about ADHD. So many of the descriptions of ADHD did not seem to match up with my experiences. Part of that, I think, was because most of the descriptions were from a third-person perspective. They were by outsiders describing what people who have ADHD look like to someone who doesn't have it. And those didn't ring true for me.

"Also, I discovered that there are three kinds of ADHD. There is hyperactive ADHD, inattentive ADHD, and a combination in which people show signs of both the first two kinds. Boys generally have the hyperactive symptoms, and girls generally have the inattentive kind.

"Boys get diagnosed more easily than girls, because they are disruptive in the back of the classroom. They throw paper airplanes around the classroom or something like that. So people realize that something is off with them.

"Girls have a much higher rate of not being diagnosed, because girls with ADHD are often sitting still and quiet in the back of the classroom off in their own little worlds, not being disruptive, but not paying attention either. So they fly under the radar, especially when, like me, they get decent grades.

"A lot of what I found when I looked up ADHD had to do with young boys. But I finally started finding descriptions of ADHD experiences that were like mine, the kind that girls often had. And having the right vocabulary helped a great deal—words that I had not applied to my own experiences, such as 'focus' and 'attention,' plus some psychological terminology.

It seemed more and more clear to me what was going on. I was pretty much convinced that I had inattentive ADHD before I sought diagnosis.

"I had to go through a long process of being interviewed about my childhood experiences, and I had to reflect back on things that were less obvious to me. It took several months before I got an official diagnosis. But pretty quickly after that I started on medication. I was lucky that the first prescription they tried on me worked. Over two years later, I am still on the same dosage of the same medication."

A New Life

Ariana had read that some people who took ADHD medicine felt a big difference right away. "But experientially I didn't notice a difference. I didn't feel more focused or organized. What I did notice was that I was able to navigate my life differently.

"Without medication, there was a spectrum. At one end, I could not sustain the effort and concentration needed to read and write. I was at that end of the spectrum most of the time. At the other end, I could concentrate on reading books and writing papers in short bursts. That, however, was never enough to live a fulfilling life in the way I wanted.

"With medication, I could more consistently work on the better side of the spectrum. I could focus and concentrate on reading and writing complex papers over long periods of time, the very things I needed to do for graduate school.

"After years of discouragement, I was finally able to pick up an academic book and read more than a few pages at a time. I went to the library and practiced taking notes. In college, my notes were on unorganized loose sheets of paper. I didn't have notebooks to organize my notes. It had never even occurred to me to organize my thoughts when reading an academic book.

"Later, I worked on my writing sample for graduate school applications. I set aside a few hours each day to sit down at a table with my laptop and make the changes I had flushed out. I found that I could do that. I could work between whatever hours I set for myself. And I discovered that that was what working was really like.

"My default experience in the past had been so unlike that. If something else popped into my head that I wanted to do, I ended up doing that instead. So I gave up on what I had originally set myself to do. And even if

I didn't go and do the other thing, I sat there battling with my will trying to force myself to concentrate on the thing I had first wanted to do. That, of course, took up the time I had set for myself to work on something.

"It was harder then to push a thought to the back of my mind. If I was trying to focus on a project, my own thoughts would distract me, and I couldn't easily push them away. But after taking medication, I was able to direct my attention in a way I wasn't able to do before. I could organize my thoughts, and I could have more control over my life.

"I was also able to set goals for myself and follow through on them in a way that I couldn't consistently do before. I could tell myself that at a certain time, I was going to get up and wash the dishes or make a phone call and then actually do that more often than not. Without medication, I was paralyzed. I could not make myself do something, even if I had decided to do it.

"All of my new experiences, I discovered, were connected to being able to focus my attention, including those in social contexts. In conversations, I had struggled with the impulse to interrupt someone I was talking with because it was hard to bracket a thought that came to mind and wait until the other person had stopped talking. I don't struggle with that as much now, though I am still working on it. The medication hasn't cured everything, but it has given me the ability to work on doing better.

"My academic life, though, has been like night and day. I got all As in my first semester at a decently prestigious graduate program. Every few weeks of that semester, I stepped back from what I was doing and stared in disbelief. All through high school and college I had been disappointed at not having gotten myself together. I had repeatedly given up hope that I could ever go to graduate school. And then gradually I became disillusioned with that hope and thought it would never happen.

"Even after I started taking medication, I thought that academic life would be only a possibility until I actually did it. Now that I have done it, I am pretty sure I can keep doing it."

Finding Meaning

"I was miserable during the years after college," Ariana said. "I had very few friends who shared any kind of academic interest with me. I was not doing things I was good at and that I felt were meaningful. I was working at dead-end, minimum wage, part-time jobs because it was too draining to maintain a full-time job I didn't find interesting.

"Now I have a tight-knit social circle of people who I have a lot in common with. I'm surrounded by brilliant people who I am keeping up with. I am feeling competent and confident, at least in academic situations. I still keep looking in disbelief at what I have become. And it has been wonderful to make sense of my childhood self, the one who was sitting in the back of the classroom in her own little world. I can understand things about myself I never understood before. Everything has been fitting together."

Michael: Recovering from a Stroke

"I have become more aware that I am going to die."

Michael suddenly found himself lying on the driveway in front of his house. At first, he did not know he had a stroke. When he found out that he did, the thought occurred to him that he might die that day. He was in his early sixties when we talked.[1]

On the Driveway

Michael was forty-six when the stroke occurred. "I was probably the healthiest I had ever been. I had been teaching college for the previous nineteen years and was training every day for a half marathon. In fact, about a week before the stroke, a heart scan showed that my heart and arteries looked good.

"But, also, a week before the stroke, I had been working out in the backyard, tearing down an old shed that had become rotten and was starting to fall down. I was pulling on a chain that hooked to a piece of the shed that had come loose, and I fell backwards against a wheelbarrow. It didn't hurt, though I had twisted my neck. I got up and was just fine. No pain. Nothing indicating that there was a problem.

"Exactly a week later, I was doing the same work again out on the driveway, hauling some of the shed debris over to a dumpster I had rented. I was standing there—I didn't feel anything, didn't have a headache even—when

---

1. 7.8 million adults in the U.S. have had a stroke, and it is the fifth leading cause of death. Centers for Disease Control.

suddenly I was lying on the ground and didn't know why. I had not felt my legs give way or felt myself fall. I was abruptly on the ground.

"I felt good. I didn't have any pain or any sense that something was wrong. In fact, I had a really strong sense of well-being. I was certain that everything was okay.

"I thought, 'Maybe I'm a little tired and dehydrated. I need to rest for a while.' So I lay there, calmly, feeling absolutely certain that I was okay and that all I needed was for someone to help me get up.

"I had tried to get up, but all I could do was roll over in one direction. I didn't realize my left side was paralyzed and useless. There was a little weedy tree that had started to grow in the driveway that I was able to reach with my right arm. I tried to pull myself up with it, but one arm was not enough.

"Much later, I realized I had had something called anosognosia, which is the inability to be aware of your limitations or disabilities. It comes with some kinds of psychological and physical trauma, but especially with strokes in the right side of the brain, which is what I had.[2]

"I was half paralyzed and did not know it. I couldn't even look at my left side and say, 'My left arm and hand aren't doing anything to help me get up.'

"There was no one around. The neighbors had been outside earlier, but they weren't then. My wife, Patti, was at work. My phone was in my shirt pocket, and I was able to reach it with my right arm. I tried to call Patti. But I couldn't figure out how to do it. The phone's screen looked funny.

"I did manage finally to call her by pushing buttons where I knew they were. I left a voicemail message that I thought was asking her to call our neighbors to ask them to come over and help me get up. But she said that when she got the message, it was garbled and she couldn't understand what I was saying.

"I think I spent about an hour on the driveway. I was certain I would be okay if only I could get up. Patti came home. She was going to call the ambulance, but I said, 'No. no. Just help me up. That's all I need. You don't need to call anyone first.'

"She tried but couldn't lift me, because I'm too big for her to pick up. And I couldn't help her. I kept flopping back down.

---

2. "Anosognosia is a neurological condition in which the patient is unaware of their neurological deficit or psychiatric condition. It is associated with mental illness, dementia, and structural brain lesion, as is seen in right hemisphere stroke patients." National Institute of Health, "Anosognosia."

"After a bit, she glanced at the left side of my face and instantly became shocked and terrified. I knew then that I had had a stroke, because she had seen that the left side of my face was drooping.

"I went from an absolute certain, 'I'm fine. I only need to get up,' to, 'Oh, no. I've had a stroke.' And I suddenly realized my life was in danger and that it had been ever since I had fallen down. I needed to have an ambulance."

In the Ambulance

It came quickly. "When the EMTs came over to put me onto a stretcher, they said, 'Yeah. It looks like you've had a small stroke.' That began to sink in. I thought, 'I may die today.'

"I asked, 'Do you have that magic stroke drug—tPA?'[3]

"One of the EMT's replied, 'We're not allowed to carry it in the ambulance. But I'm sure they're getting it ready for you at the hospital.'

"After it occurred to me that I might die, I thought, 'I guess I'll find out whether my Christian faith is true, which says that I will be meeting Jesus after I die.' I didn't feel absolutely sure that I would, though I felt confident about it. So I wasn't afraid of dying. And I was glad when I realized that that was my reaction to the real prospect of death.

"I had developed a discipline that whenever I was in a situation in which things became different from what I was hoping or expecting, I thought, 'I wonder what God has in mind for this.' So all the way to the hospital, I kept going over and over that. I expected that whatever happened, it would be something God would use for my good."

At the Hospital

In the emergency room, Michael's head was in a great deal of pain. "The people there kept asking me to cough up phlegm, because even my muscles for swallowing had become partly paralyzed, which happens with a

---

3. Tissue plasminogen activator. "When administered quickly after stroke onset (within three hours, as approved by the FDA), tPA helps to restore blood flow to brain regions affected by a stroke, thereby limiting the risk of damage and functional impairment." National Institute of Neurological Disorders and Stoke, "Tissue Plasminogen Activator."

left-side paralysis. You have to get up the fluid before you choke or develop pneumonia.

"I gradually got stable enough to go to the intensive care unit, and I thought things were looking better. But in the morning, I started vomiting uncontrollably. They said that that's a sign my brain was swelling. So they called Patti and told her to come, because it was a turn for the worse. They didn't know whether I was going to make it.

"That's when the surgeon said, 'We need to do a craniotomy.' In that, you cut out part of the skull to allow some of the pressure to be released, because the brain swells after a stroke and there's no room for it to do that. It starts to crush itself. That's what kills people after a stroke or a concussion.

"My wife and I agreed to the craniotomy. I went under anesthesia, and they took out a two-by-three inch piece of my skull about three inches above my right ear, nearest to the place where the swelling was worse. They put it into a Ziploc bag and then into a freezer.

"The huge swelling on that side of my head looked very strange. But they said it was only fluid: 'It's not your brain sticking out.' I also had to be fitted for a helmet to put over the swelling, because if I ever bumped it, the shock would go straight to the brain."

Coping with Vulnerability and Dependence

Immediately after Michael had the craniotomy, he felt an acute sense of vulnerability. "I felt weak and small, like a young child.

"The hospital people explained to me that everyone who has a craniotomy feels that way until the piece of the skull is put back: 'At an unconscious level, your body knows you are vulnerable. If something hits your brain, you could die. When your skull is complete again, you will feel back to normal.'

"At some point after the surgery, I needed to go to the bathroom for a bowel movement. It took four or five nurses and two orderlies to pick me up and put me onto the commode near my bed. The nurses went out of the room, and the two orderlies, young men, were still standing there. One said, 'Are you okay?' I said, 'Yes.' He handed me a roll of toilet paper, after which the two walked out. I turned and tried to wipe myself when I was done. But I tipped over, and the commode and I fell to the floor.

"I had caught myself with my right arm, so I didn't hit the floor hard. I was able to reach the call button, and the nurses came in, cleaned me up, and got me back into bed.

"Falling off the commode was extremely humiliating. I definitely did not want to admit that I couldn't take care of myself. I was a forty-six-year-old man, and I knew how to wipe my own butt. But I had to recognize that I was not a competent, independent adult anymore. I was like a little child in some ways.

"That was hard to admit, not only because of the anosognosia, which made me feel okay, but also because of cultural expectations. Part of growing up as a male in our culture is that you have to learn how to be independent. You have to push yourself not to need anybody. You have to go above and beyond.

"So in the regular hospital and the rehabilitation hospital, there were times when I wanted to push myself. I fiercely wanted to do things my body could not do and which were dangerous to me.

"Another time I was in my room in a wheelchair with a belt around my waist in case I fell asleep or something. I decided to go to the bathroom by myself. I thought, 'I'm a man. I can do this.' I unbuckled myself and stood up, took a step, and fell with a crash. I made enough noise that the nurses heard me and came to get me. My physical therapist was very upset with me about that.

"After several weeks, they said it was time to put back the piece of my skull that had been removed. Before I went under, they showed me the cold piece of bone in the Ziploc bag. When I came out of the surgery, I felt dramatically different. I felt whole again. I felt that I was going to make it and that everything would be okay."

On Dying Well

Michael learned several things from his stroke. "I have become more aware that I am going to die. I'm not afraid of it as much as I used to be. At some level, I am afraid, because I'm human. But what I want is to be more afraid of an unlived life. I don't want to get to the end and realize I could have lived better. I do not want to have to admit that I could have been more present and more aware.

"I know people who have regrets and become angry and controlling as they get closer to death. But the ones who die well are the ones who have been humbled by life. They no longer think they are in charge and can make everything the way they want it to be. They no longer fight against being disabled.

"One of the nurses in the hospital who helped me was someone who lived near my house. She asked, 'Is it okay for me to help you?' I said, 'Yes. This is a community. You can be part of it. You can be one of the ones who helps me sit on a commode.'

"I want to be more willing to be helped. I want to recognize that I need to be helped. Being so vulnerable in the hospital and tipping over on a commode showed me that that is how it is going to be for me again, if I live long enough. When that happens, one of the gifts I can give people is graciously to receive their help and be thankful for it. I don't want to resist or feel ashamed that I need help. I want to become more of the kind of person who can live with limitations and disability without being angry or upset."

Me and My Body

"I am aware now," Michael continued, "that there's no such thing as me and my body. There's just me. If something happens to any part of my body or brain, it changes who I am. My body is not a separate thing. I am not simply taking care of my body when I do things such as eating right or exercising. I'm taking care of me.

"This dramatically new conception of myself is a more holistic conception of what people are. That is what I felt firsthand when I was in the hospital.

"Adopting this new conception of myself has also changed how I think of heaven. When I was growing up in church, I got the notion that when we go to heaven, we won't have our bodies anymore. We'll just be floating spirits, whatever they are.

"But now I believe we will have bodies in heaven. This is what resurrection means in the Bible and the Apostle's Creed.[4] I don't know whether we will have the same molecules or whether God will put together a new body. The important thing is that we will have real, concrete bodies, not something abstract and mystical.

"The same is true, I believe, of Jesus. Easter, which is coming up soon, is a celebration of Jesus coming back to life with a body. And his having had

---

4. I Corinthians 15. From the Apostle's Creed: "I believe in the resurrection of the body and the life everlasting."

a body means he understands being weak and vulnerable. That makes a difference to me, because I have been weak and vulnerable."

Certainty

Michael now is suspicious of the feeling of certainty. "That suspicion started less than a year after the stroke. From time to time, I felt anger well up inside me when I couldn't do something I used to be able to do. After a while, I realized that the anger was really directed at the certainty I felt at being okay when I was lying on the ground.

"If I had not had that feeling of certainty, I would have been able to see that my left side wasn't working. I would not have wasted precious time in which I could have been treated. An ambulance could have come much sooner, and I wouldn't be disabled as much as I am today.

"A neurologist who has studied the feeling of certainty has shown that it is an emotional brain state.[5] When I was certain that nothing was wrong with me as I lay on the driveway, it wasn't a conclusion I had come to but was a brain state that had been artificially inflicted on me.

"For a time I was angry at God: 'Why did you let the stroke inflict a lie on me, telling me I was fine when I wasn't?'

"Since then, I have been on a quest to search out and destroy certainties in my life. I have been realizing how many things I have thought were certainly true that I found out later were totally untrue. I no longer trust those certainties.

"I am especially revisiting what I picked up from church when I was growing up, things I was told I had to believe with certainty. I do not want to feel certain about my faith merely because somebody told me I needed to feel certain about it.

"Even though I don't believe in certainty anymore, I do believe in confidence. It comes from evidence, reasoning, and facts, unlike the sense of certainty. It can also be questioned, whereas the feeling of certainty can't.

"My stroke has prompted me to look at things honestly and to examine them truthfully so that I can become confident about them, not emotionally certain about them. I do not want emotional brain states to be the basis for making decisions in my life."

---

5. Burton. Abstract of Burton, *On Being Certain*.

Rebecca: Surviving the Suicide Disease

"Every day I write a gratitude list, everything I am grateful for that day, the fact that I'm not in a wheelchair, that I have a place to stay, that I'm still alive. I'm literally stunned that I'm still here."

Rebecca had been battling symptoms of multiple sclerosis and trigeminal neuralgia for a number of years prior to 2020, when she finally sought treatment for them. Trigeminal neuralgia is a rare nerve disease that causes sudden episodes of severe facial pain.[1] That pain got so intense for Rebecca that it was all she could do simply to survive. She was in her late fifties when we talked.

The Diagnosis

"Trigeminal neuralgia is called the suicide disease," Rebecca said, "because as the pain increases, more pain medications are prescribed, which causes dizziness, drowsiness, loss of balance, and very negative, often suicidal, thoughts. I had acute pain, large amounts of pain medications, and suicidal impulses, but am glad I did not succumb to those impulses.

---

1. "Trigeminal neuralgia (try-JEM-ih-nul nu-RAL-juh) is a condition that causes intense pain similar to an electric shock on one side of the face. It affects the trigeminal nerve, which carries signals from the face to the brain. Even light touch from brushing your teeth or putting on makeup may trigger a jolt of pain. Trigeminal neuralgia can be long-lasting. It's known as a chronic pain condition." Mayo Clinic "Trigeminal Neuralgia."

"For ten years my legs had been getting numb, my balance had worsened, and I had experienced unusual fatigue when it got hot. Then in early 2020, I began experiencing other strange things. My right arm occasionally went numb, then seized up. I had episodes of pain on the right side of my face, and sometimes it felt as though it was being squeezed.

"A neighbor urged me to call my doctor because she thought I might be having stroke symptoms. So during the first week of March, 2020, I tried calling the neurologist I had visited six months earlier, but couldn't get through. Finally, on the Friday of that week, I did get through, and the neurologist told me to get to the nearest hospital right away for tests.

"Despite the fact that things were shutting down because of the onset of Covid-19, the hospital staff listened to me and ran the needed tests. The doctors diagnosed me with multiple sclerosis and trigeminal neuralgia. As hard as it was to hear that I had these, it was actually a relief to have names for what I had been experiencing. I was super grateful to the hospital people for working on my case amidst all the Covid activity."

The Nightmare Begins

For two and a half years after having the hospital tests in 2020, Rebecca had trigeminal nerve pain in her right jaw. "But it was not severe. That changed in September of 2022. The pain became more like an electric shock than a tingling. It started at my right cheekbone and shot down my face. It started getting really bad in October and November. The day after Thanksgiving I had to go to the emergency room, where I was given steroids for the pain intraveneously. The following week I ended up in the emergency room four more times.

"In December I went to see a new doctor, who said she could give me an injection every month for $50.00 a month. When the doctor's assistant wanted me to sign forms, I said, 'Let me think about it.' I couldn't afford that amount.

"In January of 2023 I went to an acupuncturist. It didn't help, although the acupuncturist was super kind.

"In February the pain ramped up, and the pain meds too, which magnified the side effects—dizziness, drowsiness, loss of balance, and mood swings.

"My multiple sclerosis had also been getting worse. My left leg 'dropped,' which means that I was not able to lift it as well, and that made it more difficult to walk without falling. On February 8, after much research and the generosity of friends, I picked up an electronic L300 leg device. I got it programmed in the middle of March, which helped me raise my left leg so that I could walk better.

"In March the facial pain from the trigeminal neuralgia became unbearable. It shot up to the top of my head and down through my lips and the right side of my jaw. I couldn't brush my teeth, eat anything, or even talk or laugh without pain. I got horrible negative thoughts. And I made more emergency room visits.

"When I went to the emergency room on April 1, my new neurologist got concerned and admitted me to the hospital. The next day an MRI and an EKG showed that a large blood vessel was crushing the trigeminal nerve on the right side of my face.

"The neurologist wanted me to see a surgeon. After I got out of the hospital, I did and got an appointment for surgery for May 11. But the neurologist was afraid that I was getting poisoned by all the medicine I was taking. So he urged the surgeon to move the date up, which he did, by three weeks, to April 26. I was elated.

"During all this time, I had four or five major falls, which got me back to the emergency room each time. One of the falls was onto my tailbone. On April 16, I hit my head and jaw hard on a desk. The next day I experienced the worst facial pain ever, at level ten, and the day after that I had a very bad fall onto my right hip and arm. I had to be taken to the emergency room by ambulance for that. My hip turned purple with hematoma, which occurs when an injury causes blood to pool under the skin.

"On April 19 I was admitted to the hospital in the city where I live, then transferred to the hospital in another city the next day, where I stayed until my surgery for trigeminal neuralgia six days later, on April 26, 2023.

"Also, as I said, in March I had really strong negative thoughts. During my fifty-seven years, I have never been suicidal or even thought of suicide. But when I was on eight different medications, I got so depressed one time that I told my therapist I just wanted the pain to be over. I wanted everything to stop because it was so horrendous. I didn't want to do anything.

"That was extremely hard to deal with because it was not my personality to give up. Even though I had been having symptoms of multiple sclerosis, I took care of my elderly parents for ten long years."

After Surgery

The surgery Rebecca had, microvascular decompression, was said to be the most likely to get rid of the pain and to prevent it from recurring. "The surgeon made an incision behind my right ear, drilled a small hole in the skull, and moved the blood vessel that was compressing the trigeminal nerve. The surgeon then put padding between the blood vessel and the nerve.

"My facial pain left immediately after the surgery. Six days later I was transported by ambulance to the hospital in Bartlesville for inpatient rehabilitation. I had been in bed for some weeks, so I needed physical therapy to help me walk again. I also had to have speech therapy. And I had to recover from all the medications I had been taking—some in pills and some given intraveneously: carbemezapine, prednisone, pregabalin, lyrica, solomedrol, extended phenytoin, oxycarbemezepine, and ambiom.

"While I was in rehab, I had several meltdowns—I sobbed and sobbed because I couldn't remember where I was from or what my family members' names were. One time when I was sobbing, the doctor put his arm around me and said, 'Oh, Rebecca. It's almost like you had a little stroke with everything you've gone through—the medications, the falls, the surgery.' Then he said, 'Just so you know, it's going to take some time.' I never had a doctor comfort me like that.

"I spent more than two weeks in rehab and was discharged on the morning of May 18. I was immediately readmitted so that I could get an infusion of Ocrevus for my multiple sclerosis. At the end of the day, I was taken to a friend's house in Bartlesville. It has a wheelchair ramp, which I needed because I had to use a rolling walker or a cane when I walked.

"Unfortunately, surgery for trigeminal neuralgia is not always a hundred percent successful. One morning six months later facial pain struck again as I was eating breakfast. I wanted to whip my cereal bowl at the wall, cereal and all. I sobbed and sobbed. 'No way can this be happening again.'

"It was, however, not nearly as severe as it was at its worst. My neurologist gave me pain medication, at first to be used as needed, then a double dose twice a day. That is what I was taking for nearly a year after the surgery. The pain can be at zero, then suddenly run through my cheek and shoot up to level three. If it were to go up to eight out of ten, I would have to go back to the emergency room. Fortunately, I have had to do that only once since having surgery.

"I also had to deal with continuing pain from my falls. I had several fractures along my spine from one of my falls, and in January, 2024, I had a kyphoplasty to help with that.² I also got a steroid shot in February of 2024. But the pains ramped up again in April, and I had to go back to the emergency room of the hospital.

Radiation

It was not until Rebecca had a radiation treatment that her pain left. "The day after that April visit to the emergency room, my neurologist started me back on the face pain medication I had taken last year. I asked him about a radiation treatment called CyberKnife that he had mentioned at a previous appointment. He referred me to a doctor in Tulsa for the treatment, and I went to see her three months later, on July 11. She explained that with radiation the nerve in my face would be numbed, which meant that for the rest of my life I would no longer feel any pain.

"When she said that, I started crying.

"I had the radiation treatment two-and-a-half months later, on September 27, 2024. Before then, I was in the emergency room and urgent care four times because of the facial pain. Plus, I was in and out of the infusion center at the hospital for steroids to ease the pain. And I was on a number of pain medications.

"For a week after the radiation treatment, I was in almost no pain. But then the pains started up again—flashes of pain in my cheek or major flares of pain on my whole head. I was given more pain medications. But the pain continued, and I couldn't function well. I couldn't do things with my friends. It was taking me longer to get up in the morning and get moving. I couldn't even celebrate Christmas with the people I was staying with. I was drowsy, woozy, and prone to falling.

"Finally, my friends, the Blakmons, were getting so concerned that they called the radiation treatment doctor and made an appointment for me for January 6, 2025.

"Dr. Heaton spent ten minutes reading through everything I had typed up about the things that had happened to me since the radiation treatment on September 27. Then she said, 'Well, Rebecca, I need to tell you a couple of things. First of all, it takes about nine months for the radiation treatment to become fully effective. Second, the pain medications and steroids are actually delaying your healing process.'

2. "Kyphoplasty is a minimally invasive procedure to treat compression fractures in your spine." Cleveland Clinic, "Kyphoplasty."

"It turned out that she didn't know that I was taking so many pain medications and steroids, because she and my neurologist had not been communicating with each other. They were in two different towns, working out of two different offices and hospitals.

"That day I felt hope again for the first time in months.

"It took a month and a half to get off the pain medications. That was five months ago. I have felt no face pain. I can eat and chew. I can brush my teeth morning and night. I can laugh. I can smile. I have been able to drive. One of the employees at a pharmacy who had been seeing me through the whole journey saw me recently and exclaimed, 'You look fantastic! You are looking wonderful!' She ran up and hugged me."

What Kept Me Going

A number of things kept Rebecca going when she was in the midst of extreme pain. "The friends with whom I was living took care of me in the hospital. They helped me get to the bathroom. They prayed with me. The whole church where I and my friends went prayed for me.

"I can't afford private insurance, so I am on Medicaid, which is called SoonerCare in the state I live in. Without it, I would have been lost. It has paid for all of my appointments and procedures from day one, some of which were thousands of dollars. Every time I got a bill or a statement, I started sobbing, knowing it would be taken care of.

"I think gratitude has also kept me going. At the follow-up appointments with the neurologist and the surgeon during the months after my surgery, they asked me, 'How are you?' I said, 'I'm still here, and I'm getting my life back.' I took their hands and bawled. I hugged them and said, 'Thank you. Thank you.' It is the same with all the other healthcare people at the hospital—the nurses, the techs, the paramedics, even the cleaning people. They are heroes in my mind. So are the people in the church I go to, who have done so much for me, especially the friend with whom I was living.

"Every day I write a gratitude list, everything I am grateful for that day, the fact that I'm not in a wheelchair, that I have a place to stay, that I'm still alive. I'm literally stunned that I'm still here.

"Also, I am a God survivor. My faith has been a central part of my life since I was young, and it sustained me through even the level ten pain when all I wanted was to give up."

"I am grateful to Velma Powell for allowing me to stay with her until a bed was found at a nearby assisted living facility; Cyndi and Joe; Fran and Chuck; the pastor and people at the Bible Church of Bartlesville, Oklahoma; Dr. Tyler Auschwitz, my surgeon in Tulsa; Dr. Jason King, my neurologist; Lisa Hoyt, my therapist; all my friends from Libertyville, Illinois, and Bartlesville, Oklahoma; the nurse who suggested I tell this story; and our gracious and loving God above. All of these have played a role in saving my life."

4 Transitions

Michelle: Transitioning to a Woman

"I've never been more comfortable with myself."

Growing up male with gender dysphoria was definitely not easy for Michelle. She was not able to accept the fact that she identified with being female until several years after she married. She was in her early thirties when we talked.

Childhood

Michelle grew up in a small rural town in north central Wisconsin called Antigo. "It's not super secluded, though the nearest town of any real size is at least forty-five minutes away. You saw only a few other people and a whole lot of trees and dirt that potatoes grew in.

"From a very young age, I felt that something was not right. But I didn't have the vocabulary to put my finger on it. I do know that I was delicate and that I was constantly on the losing side of whatever battle was being fought. In kindergarten, I was diagnosed with a particularly severe case of ADHD, which caused further struggles.

"Another thing I know is that I was always a lot more comfortable being friends with girls. My best friend in elementary school was a girl until she moved away. She was the only person in school who was nice to me.

"I also noticed that my demeanor, my bodily movements, were naturally more like that of a young girl. And there were other girl things I was naturally drawn to.

"Here was this boy-appearing kid, the smallest person in the class, who acted girly. He lived in rural northern Wisconsin where being tough was a virtue. If he was not tough, that was embarrassing. And he could get bullied.

"I learned to avoid certain things because I didn't want to be bullied. My favorite TV shows involved girls, such as Powder Puff Girls. I had a weird feeling when I watched it and felt a great deal of shame. I had no idea why I had these reactions. But I stopped watching it because I was teased when I did so. For other things, too, such as my feminine bodily movements, I said to myself, 'Don't do that. It's girly. You're going to get teased.' That kind of avoidance informed a lot of my childhood. I didn't realize until very recently that that's not the way most children think. They just do things."

Puberty

When Michelle hit puberty, she noticed herself changing in a direction that distressed her. "I looked at girls who were changing and found that my brain was not responding in the way I anticipated, that is, in the way I saw typical teenage boys responding to teenage girls. I responded with an odd sense of jealousy instead. That was a very confusing time for me. I asked myself, 'Why am I naturally drawn to feminine things? Why do I move girly?'

"When the internet became more available, I learned that I was not alone. Suddenly I had a context for what I was feeling.

"I started wearing women's clothing, always at home, though once at school when there was Opposite Day. Antigo is not a safe place for the queer community. In high school, there were a couple of gay kids, but they knew it was not safe to be known as gay, so they tried their best to hide that part of themselves.

"At first, I told myself wearing women's clothing was something of a hobby, like something normal boys might occasionally do. But over the next couple of years, I slowly realized that my interest in femininity wasn't just a hobby. It wasn't just a small part of my life. I was finding more and more that who I was when presenting in a more feminine fashion was me. I finally admitted to myself that it was who I am."

Becoming a Christian

In the midst of these changes, Michelle became a Christian, a born again believer. "I experienced God for the first time in my life. I made a definite decision to give my life to Christ.

"The church I was affiliated with was staunchly against even the idea of transgenderism. I met someone in the church who became my mentor. He was, and still is, the closest thing I had to a brother at the time and has been an instrumental part of my life. I told him, very shamefully, about my cross-dressing and transgenderism. During one conversation, he said, 'I think God may be calling you to give that up.' (He has since become very supportive of me.)

"As a new Christian, I had started chopping off parts of myself: 'This is sinful. That is sinful.' And that is what I did with my transgenderism. I decided that God was calling me to something else, in fact, to Christian ministry. So one night I gathered up my women's clothing, my makeup, shoes, wigs, and everything else I had accrued, and threw it all away. It had played such an emotional role in my life that I had held onto it. But I bagged it up and got rid of it.

"That is what is known as 'purging' in the transgender community. You throw everything away. For close to two years, I remained steadfast in that because I believed God was calling me not to transition. I resisted the urge to engage in presenting as a woman or to give any brain space to thoughts about who I was inside. I tried not to be jealous of the women around me or to think about who I wanted to be.

"But like anything else that is an integral part of yourself, my gender discomfort would not stay away. The struggles came back. The unhappiness with my body and with being perceived as male and with everything that came with that perception returned. The internal struggle was awful. I became angry and depressed.

"At the same time, I was convinced that God was calling me to Christian ministry, which I prepared for at the Christian college I went to and which meant that I would have to be male-presenting. I had an innate conviction that God was asking me to be male-presenting even though it came with a great deal of suffering and distress. This was my internal experience the whole time I was in college.

"Because I take the Bible seriously, I spent a lot of time in college seeing what the Bible said on LGBTQ issues. I used every tool at my disposal, every methodology that was taught in the Bible classes I took and what little bit of Greek I was able to figure out from my year of Greek classes.

"I didn't do this so that I could make the Bible say what I wanted it to say, that is, to justify my inner drive toward being a woman. For me, it was a done deal that God was calling me to a lifetime of suffering—to put down my transgenderism—so that I could have a life of ministry among Christians.

"At first I studied what the Bible said about LGBTQ issues very begrudgingly. I was super conservative, because I had grown up in a super conservative town and believed that even being interested in what the Bible had to say about those issues was sinful and dangerous."

Shaken Loose

After Michelle graduated from college, she got a position working in a church. "I thought I had all the answers: 'I've got a biblical studies degree. I know what I'm talking about. I can read a small amount of Greek. I'm better than everybody.' It was both a haughtiness and a hardness: 'I know what's right because I've studied certain things.'

"I got a wake up call really quick, because, in my job at the church, I wasn't dealing with students who were ready to get into fights at lunch over whether Calvinism is true. I was dealing with people who were living actual lives, who were suffering, who felt different and unlovable. I had thought I had all the power in the world, given to me by God, to fight these things. But I found myself becoming bewildered and overwhelmed.

"What broke through my hard edges was that one of the volunteers I supervised told me that she was bisexual and in a relationship with a woman. She could not sign the 'lifestyle expectations agreement' that people who worked with the church were supposed to sign. Yet she was excited to be working at the church. I didn't know what to do. I sat still while she cried in front of me.

"That knocked something loose in me. I got back into studying what the Bible said about homosexuality and other LGBTQ issues. I talked to spiritual leaders, read books, and prayed. I came to the conclusion that I didn't know whether being gay or transgender was wrong. It was not the black and white issue I had been made to believe it was. I thought, 'If I have to choose between love and acceptance, or judgment and exclusion, given the uncertainty about the matter, I am going to go with love and acceptance.

"All of this occurred within the context of my settled belief that I was called to be male-presenting forever. None of what I was thinking about had anything to do with my own inner reality. I didn't know what I didn't know."

A Jolt

Michelle went on like this for several years until 2018, when the church she was working at closed. "The closure was traumatizing. I had been thriving. I loved my job. I saw a wonderful, long-term future. My job seemed secure. I was happy with it, with my ministry, and my church community. Actually, it was more than a job. It was my entire life. I had helped build that church community from its inception some years earlier.

"It was even more jarring because it occurred about two weeks before I was to get married. I had found a marvelous woman at the church, and all of our friends at the church were going to be at the wedding. Then suddenly the church was not there anymore. I was left sitting in my living room applying for jobs and dealing with being on the other side of security in a way I had never felt before.

"I still was male-presenting. But during the next six months, the trauma of losing my job and my church plus getting married while being freshly unemployed knocked something loose in my brain and brought my gender struggles to the forefront."

Letting Go

Michelle decided to see a therapist. "We examined everything. At first, it was, 'I think I just like wearing women's clothes.' Then it was, 'I think I'm bi-gender,' which is a way of saying that you feel that you are two genders at once. Then my inclination toward being transgender reached the point at which it could not be ignored. It felt as though God was allowing me to begin accepting myself as transgender.

"I found a new church to work at. But I had a growing unhappiness because of my increasingly strong feelings about being transgender. And the feeling I had earlier, that I was doing what God was asking me to do even though it involved suffering, left. It was replaced with a feeling of freedom—the feeling that I needed to let go of the security I felt when being male-presenting.

"My wife, Aly, knew everything. About six months after we had started dating, I told her about my desire to present as a woman. At that point, that was what I convinced myself was the extent of it. Actually, that is what I was hoping it just was, because the idea of also being transgender was too scary. And telling her was probably the scariest thing I have ever done. I thought she would break up with me. But she didn't. She responded with a ton of patience and understanding.

"Aly even taught me how to use makeup and to coordinate outfits and get dressed like a normal woman. And she was the one who helped me accept the fact that I was transgender.

"What prompted this acceptance was a huge argument with her three years after we had been married. I can't remember what it was about, but she had seen my growing unhappiness and mental deterioration, which was a deep depression. I had even started thinking of suicide as a possible option down the road. I could see that that's where I ultimately would end up if I did not acknowledge the feminine part of myself.

Aly said, 'You need to stop lying to yourself. You're transgender, and you aren't happy as a man. You need to admit that you're happy as a woman.'

"That broke me, and I burst out crying. I really, truly, began to let go of what I had been holding onto for so long—the lie that I was a man. The pain that lie brought me had helped me be compassionate toward others, but it was time now to let it go."

A Decisive Event

Another event helped put this acceptance into action. "About this time—two years ago, in 2021—I was invited to apply for a ministry position at a different church. It would have been an awesome job, but I was crushed all the way through the application process. If I got the job, I would have had to set aside my plan to transition. I would have had to put my acceptance of being transgender on hold.

"During the final interview, I was asked to describe the hardest thing I had ever had to do in ministry. I told them about the woman who had told me she was bisexual and who I had almost kicked off my team for dating a woman. And now, I said in the interview, 'This woman serves faithfully in the church we were at.'

"Then I told the people who were interviewing me that if I got the job at their church, which had an anti-gay policy, I would submit to the authority of the church on LGBTQ issues even though it would be an internal struggle for me. For the next hour and a half, they tried to get me to say that being gay was wrong. 'Tell us that and you've got the job.' I said, 'I can't in good faith lie to you.'

"I didn't get the job.

"Applying for that job felt as though it was an Abraham-Isaac test (Genesis 22:1-18). Was I willing to follow God's lead to take a new job even though it meant I would have had to give up the new feelings of freedom, happiness, and relief that I had never felt before, feelings that had come from acceptance of being transgender? Was I willing completely and permanently to deny who I was created inside to be by taking the job? I was swinging the knife down on the transgender life I had started to plan for myself. And God stopped me by denying me the job. I had passed the test—I was ready to follow God's calling even though it meant suffering by continuing to present as male.

"The fact that I didn't get the job cemented in me the resolve to transition."

Transitioning

Michelle started going to her doctor and getting referrals to specialists. "The last day I worked at the church I had been at for over a year was in December of 2021, and the next day was my first day of transitioning on feminine hormones. It was fulfilling to go through puberty a second time as my body adjusted to female levels of estrogen.

"A lot of the transition was waiting—waiting for my hair to grow longer, waiting for my facial features to soften up, waiting for my body shape, including my side profile, to change. There were also leaps forward, such as the eight-hour facial surgery I had this past summer, in 2023, to smooth out parts of my face that had developed in a male way. The surgeons peeled away parts of my face and made adjustments so that it would be softer and more feminine.

"The recovery period from that surgery was long, and the first three days of it were the worst three days of my life. But the surgery was totally worth it.

"Some of my masculine features didn't change as a result of taking estrogen. For example, my voice is still deep, which drives me absolutely insane. There is a rumbling from deep in the abyss that comes out of my throat every time I open my mouth.

"At the same time, I am much more comfortable with myself. The first day I was on estrogen, I immediately felt better. It was like wanting a drink of water when all that is available is soda, and then at last you get a drink of water, or watching a show on an old-style television that has static, and then watching the show without static on cable television. This sort of immediate relief isn't everyone's experience, but I'm glad it was mine because it comforted many doubts I still had.

"Another way to describe my transition is to say that the disconnect between what I was feeling about myself and what my body looked like had disappeared. That disconnect brought about the gender dysphoria I had been experiencing. Dysphoria is defined as 'a state of unease or general dissatisfaction with life.' In my case, it was a dissatisfaction with my masculine body: it didn't look right, it didn't sound right, the behavior wasn't right.

"I experienced the disconnect whenever I saw pictures people took of me having a good time. All I could see were the masculine things—the brow ridge, the broad shoulders, the extremely dimpled chin. Pictures that should have been joyful brought me distress. I know it may sound ridiculous, but that is what I felt. Now I can look at pictures of myself without hating them. There is more harmony between what I feel about myself and what my body looks like. I am a lot happier."

Michelle and Aly

What was it like for Aly to have someone she saw as her husband become a woman? "My transitioning was also a transition for Aly. She is in mourning for losing the husband she thought she had when she married me. She is grieving for no longer being married to the person I was with respect to gender.

"At the same time, Aly encouraged me to transition because she could see that if I did not, my mental decline would continue, which would jeopardize our family.

There was never any dishonesty or hiding on my part. I shared with her everything that was going on with myself. And she was willing to admit that I was really a woman inside before I was willing to admit it to myself. She fully saw all that was going on.

"Still, Aly is grieving. She needs time to process what has happened, and I need to encourage her to take whatever time she needs. I need to pay attention to what she is feeling. She is also worried I might die because of my transition. Murder rates are much higher for trans people than for the general population.[1]

"In spite of the big change, we are still best friends. My personality has not changed. There is a lot of hope and positivity. We both love our two girls. One is three and a half, and the other is almost two. The two-year-old was born right after I started transitioning. We have been talking about having another child because our girls are so joyful. There's nothing marriage-ending going on. I'm feeling positive about it all, and Aly is too. In all fairness, though, some things are hard, and we are working on them. But, overall, we have a beautiful life that we're happy with.

"Our three-and-a-half-year-old, who knew me before I transitioned, has taken the transition easily. When I show her pictures of me before I transitioned, she says, 'I don't like pictures of you like that. I like you now. I love having two mommies.' We have done our best not to let my gender stuff influence her."

Living as a Woman

Reaction to Michelle's transition has been almost uniformly positive. "I had been expecting nothing but hardship and suffering. But I have gotten almost universal acceptance from family and friends. Aly and I are in a wonderful church community that is very encouraging and supportive. They are not worried at all that I am a trans woman. In fact, there are times when they see my unique experience as being healthy for them because they get to learn about other people's experiences. My transitioning has helped us find the best church community we've ever been a part of. That has been enormously satisfying.

"On the downside, I have lost a couple of people who were important to me, one of whom was my best friend for a long time. I have been using the women's restroom for the last two years and once someone said something negative about it. And sometimes somebody gives me a weird look. They know what is going on, and they don't see me as a woman.

---

1. Moeder, "Number of trans homicides doubled over 4 years." abcNews. See also "Transgender people over four times more likely than cisgender people to be victims of violent crime." UCLA School of Law.

"I realize there are going to be people who won't accept me as a woman. That will be hard. I could sit here and say that I'm tough enough to let that roll off me. Sometimes I am. But other times it is definitely unpleasant.

"Overall, it feels as though Aly and I are on the right path. I've never been more comfortable with myself. I have a feeling of freedom and high potential for the future. We feel secure in our church and community. What we are experiencing is beautiful."

Amy: From a Refugee Camp to the United States

"In a refugee camp . . . , you can't dream of becoming a doctor or lawyer or business owner some day. You are stuck in a jungle, living in a small house."

Amy describes what it was like to live in the refugee camp in which she was born. At one point, she had dreams of doing more with her life than what was possible in the camp. She applied to go to the U.S., where she arrived when she was fifteen. She was in her early twenties when we talked.

In a Refugee Camp

Amy's parents and grandparents fled Myanmar, formerly known as Burma, in the early 1990s because of "armed conflicts and/or horrendous human rights abuse and persecution by the Burmese military. . . . Thousands of villages, especially in the Karen and Karenni States, were burned to the ground, including houses, religious buildings, schools, belongings, and sometimes even domestic animals."[1] Amy's parents and grandparents

---

1. "In many areas [of Burma], it became the norm for the villagers to live in a constant fear of the Burmese military coming to their village, terrorizing the villagers, stealing their food, forcing villagers to become porters and mine sweepers, raping ethnic women, and torturing and killing anyone suspected of having a connection to the ethnic armed opposition." Burma Link, "Refugee Camps."

settled in Umphiem Refugee Camp in Thailand near the Thai-Myanmar border, where Amy was born.[2]

"My parents divorced when I was two, and they left the refugee camp so that they could find jobs in Bangkok, a large city in Thailand that is further from the border. My grandparents raised me, and my parents supported me financially along with the others I lived with. My parents never came back to the camp, which I regarded as my home.

"The camp was like a village. It contained bamboo houses that were built by the refugees. When my grandparents came, there were fewer than twenty houses, and when I was little there were about a hundred. Today there are about a thousand houses in the camp.

"The bamboo houses had just one large room. A part of that room was used for the kitchen, and another small part was a Buddhist space, because my grandparents were Buddhist. There were six of us—me, my sister, my two grandparents, and my auntie and uncle. My grandparents slept in their Buddhist space, and the rest of us slept in a different part of the large room.

"The bathroom was outside. It was waterless. But there was a community water pipe where we got our water, and there was a shower there where we showered. There was no privacy at it. The water pipe came from a stream at a nearby mountain, as the camp was located in a mountainous region of Thailand.

"We also got water from the banana trees that grew near the camp. There is more water in the ground near banana trees, so deep holes were dug near the trees, and clear, cold water came up into the holes. Sometimes people used buckets to get the water out of the holes, but mainly underground pipes brought the water to the camp.

"It was jungle living in the camp when I was there—no electricity, no phone, no car, no TV. Each family had been given a small plot of land that was enough to build a house on. Every month, the United Nations Refugee Agency, the UNHCR, gave each family rice, beans, and lamp oil, plus salt and pepper.[3] We survived on that plus the fruits and vegetables we grew in the gardens next to our houses.

"Because we were in the mountains, it was cold and windy, and we weren't always warm. In the U.S., houses have drywall that keeps the wind

---

2. Wikipedia. "Umpiem Mai Refugee Camp."

3. United Nations High Commission for Refugees (UNHCR): www.unhcr.org. The U.S. website is at www.unhcr.org/us/.

and the cold out. But in a bamboo house, the roofs are made of leaves, and the walls of bamboo. There are lots of little holes in the walls.

"At night, we slept together in a line on the floor, cuddling each other to keep warm. We had enough blankets and pillows, but we still got cold at times. Our houses were six or seven feet above the ground, on poles, so sometimes we made ourselves warm by making a fire under the house. At least our sides or backs were warm when we slept. We were very careful with the fires so that the houses would not burn down."[4]

Dreams of Doing Something with My Life

Living in a refugee camp with her grandparents was peaceful and happy, Amy said. "The only thing is that there was no better future. You can't dream of becoming a doctor or lawyer or business owner some day. You are stuck in a jungle, living in a small house. You go to school until the ninth grade, and then you're done. You are restricted to the camp, planting bamboo trees and fruit to survive each day. You don't get to do what you want with your life.

"When I was in middle school, about twelve, people came from other parts of Thailand and Myanmar to teach at the camp for a year. They asked us what we wanted to be when we grew up. No one had ever asked us that. I had thought that when I grew up I would just be helping my family financially, because that was the Asian tradition. My grandparents took care of me, and when I was older I would be taking care of them.

"Those teachers prompted me to start thinking about what else I could do. I wanted to know what it was like to live in a big city. I wanted to learn about lots of things and pursue a career. I wanted to become something more than simply a survivor in a refugee camp. That's when I decided I wanted to go to the United States.

"It took a long time to get approved to go to the U.S. I had to go through interviews. I had to have health exams to assure them I didn't have health problems or some disease that would spread to the whole world. They had to be sure I wasn't an informant for the Myanmar military or some other villainous human. Everything had to be clear.

"My grandparents went to the U.S. first and left me in Thailand with my auntie. I was scheduled to go to the U.S. with my older sister, but

---

4. For pictures of refugee houses built on poles see Wikipedia, "Mae La Refugee Camp," and the link for Burma Link, "Refugee Camps."

two months before we were to go, she found out she was pregnant by her boyfriend. So she was not allowed to go. I was very sad, because I thought I would no longer be able to go.

"At an interview, the U.S. people asked, 'Why do you want to go to the U.S. so badly? Tell us the reason we should let you go with your aunt instead of your sister.' I said I didn't see any future living in a refugee camp. There would be no growth. I wouldn't be able to own a house some day. I would only be living in a jungle, planning for my next meal.

"I was approved to go to the U.S. with my auntie. That was when I was fifteen. When I got here, I lived with my grandmother, as my grandfather had died earlier."

In the United States

Even though living in the U.S. has been stressful for Amy, it has been better than living in the refugee camp. "I was overwhelmed at first. Daytime and nighttime were flipped, so for a time I slept during the day and stayed up at night. In the refugee camp, it was quiet and calm, but in the U.S. it is noisy because of all the cars and televisions. At 6:00 pm in Thailand, everyone is in their own home enjoying supper with their family. In the U.S., people are at the park or going places in the early evening. In the camp we had only little oil lamps which we used mostly indoors, whereas in the U.S. there are lots of lights on, inside and outside, after it gets dark.

"I didn't know any English, not a single word. In Thailand the only two languages we studied were Burmese and Karen.[5]

"I was put into the tenth grade. I don't know why, maybe because of my age. After I was dropped off at the high school, I didn't know where to enter it because it was so large. After I figured out how to get in, I didn't know where I should go. I couldn't ask anyone for help, because I didn't know anyone who spoke my language.

"Finally, I said to someone who looked Karen, 'Do you speak Karen?' When he said he did, I asked, 'Can you help me get to class?' He asked one of his friends to help me. She took me to an office where I got my schedule. But she left right away to run to her class. All I had was a sheet of paper, which I couldn't read. And I couldn't ask anyone else to help because all the students had gone to their classes. Then I saw a number on the paper:

---

5. Wikipedia. "Karenic Languages."

AMY: FROM A REFUGEE CAMP TO THE UNITED STATES

'Maybe that is the number of the room I have to go to.' I followed the map of the school and finally made it to class, late.

"I was late to classes the whole first week. The school was so big that I had a hard time finding my way around. I didn't know where the cafeteria was, and I didn't know how to ask permission to use the restroom.

"I gradually learned English by listening to my teachers. I also took English Language Development classes. I learned best when the teachers showed examples instead of just talking and talking. In my last year of high school, I took a choir class, which helped me learn faster because I was speaking words and not just listening to them.

"I went to college after graduating from high school and graduated from it early because I had gotten college credit for classes when I was in high school."

Working

"When I was in the refugee camp," Amy said, "my dream was to have a peaceful and financially stable life, making enough money not to worry about my daily living expenses. And now that I have the opportunity to make my dream come true, I have to work for it. I'm not going to say that working has been easy. It has not.

"In high school, I worked as a dishwasher in a Thai restaurant, because I couldn't speak English well enough to be a cashier or server. I had to run straight to the bus stop right after school so that I could make it to the restaurant on time. I got paid only seven or eight dollars an hour, but I worked six days a week so that I could have enough money to send to my mom, who had moved to the refugee camp in Thailand.

"After high school, I knew enough English so that I could work as the cashier at the restaurant. I also did customer service, picking up the phone and talking to people. I loved doing that. That is when I decided I wanted to become an international flight attendant or hotel manager. I chose to major in hospitality and tourism in college.

"After I graduated from college last year, one of my professors reached out to me to say that she could help me get a job as an international flight attendant. But when I applied, I failed the swimming test, because I can't swim. At first I thought, 'Oh, maybe I can learn to swim.' But I am terrified of water. So then I became the owner of the business that manages the restaurant I was working at.

"I was not looking to run a business. I was thinking only about traveling around the world as a flight attendant. But my boss at the restaurant said, 'Hey, Amy. Do you remember when I asked you whether you wanted to manage the restaurant some day?'

"I said, 'I do remember that. I was sixteen then, shortly after I arrived in the U.S.'

"She said, 'I have decided to offer to sell you the business that runs the restaurant now.'

"When she said that, I said, 'Is that for real? I thought your relative wanted to run the restaurant.' She replied, 'No, I don't want to sell the business to them. I want to keep my promise to you.'

"I said, 'Give me some time to think about it. It would be challenging, because I don't have any experience running my own business.'

"I thought about my mom, who had come to the U.S. when I was in college and had tried to get a job. She had applied at a number of places, including a warehouse and Amazon, but they all denied her because she couldn't read or write English. I thought about the rest of my family, my uncle, my auntie, and my other aunt, none of whom could speak, read, or write English. We were all struggling financially. I thought, 'Why not run the restaurant and then have my family work at it?'

"That's when I decided to buy the business that manages the restaurant. I would have them all work at it so that they would not have to worry about applying at other places. It would be a family restaurant. That was eight months ago, about four months after I had turned twenty-two.

"Also, I bought a house with a relative three years ago, when I was twenty. "That was to bring my family together. When we first arrived in the U.S., we all lived in different apartments, which was expensive. But now we all live together in the house—my grandma, mom, aunt, uncle, three sisters, and two cousins. Lots of people! Not like what Americans do. We have a family dinner time, and we have our own yard to play in. I have one other sister, who is older than me and who is still in Thailand. I'm not sure when she can come to the U.S.

"I like keeping myself busy, and I love being productive. So I work a lot. I want to be a good role model for my younger sisters, showing them that when they grow up they can work hard for themselves and their families."

I'd Rather Be in the U.S.

"My very first memory of the refugee camp," Amy recalls, "is waking up in the morning, seeing my grandpa sit in front of the house listening to the news on his radio and my grandma cooking in the kitchen. It was a peaceful life. I liked the people in the camp, who were very humble and grateful for what they had.

"But I am glad I came to the U.S. If I had stayed in the refugee camp, I probably would have ended up married, with kids, staying home and doing nothing. By coming to the U.S., I have had a chance to go to school and learn more languages. I can experience being my own boss in the business I run. I live in a house I co-own, work in a restaurant I manage, and help my own people who came from the refugee camp and who are struggling with English. It has all been a wonderful journey for me."

Jonas: Growing Up Amish

"What had provided comfort before came to feel like a prison."

Jonas grew up in an Amish community in rural Kentucky with four sisters and eight brothers, all of whom are still Amish. Here he describes some of the distinctive features of Amish life plus the distress he went through that prompted him to leave. He was in his early forties when we talked.

A Tight Community

Living in an Amish community, Jonas said, is like being inside a bubble. "It is a distinct and separate world. For one thing, everything among the Amish is very much community-based in the sense that you look out for each other. I never knew of any homeless Amish. I did know of a number of people who for various reasons fell on hard times, and the community took up offerings and provided for the families. A box was sent out and passed from family to family, and each family put in what they could. When the box was full, it was given to the family in need.

"One of my sisters had two babies that were born prematurely, and she had to spend quite a while in the hospital for each one. The Amish do not have health insurance, so there was a substantial hospital bill, about a million dollars. The community worked with the hospital to get the bill reduced as much as possible for paying out of pocket, which made the bill a good deal under a million dollars. Then they took out loans to pay the hospital. For the next year and a half, they did community fundraisers, and within a year and a half, they had the loans paid off. My sister contributed very little. It was a community effort that surrounded her and her family and cared for them.

"Another time a brother's house burned down. He and his wife woke up and the house was in flames. They grabbed the kids, and his wife grabbed an armload of clothes. That was the only thing they saved. Amish people from thirteen different communities came together and built a brand new house for them in four weeks, from the ground up, with furniture, all ready to go.

"Church life too binds the community together. You have to attend church. Not attending is not an option. The lines are drawn geographically, and whatever geographical community you are in, that's the church you attend. The only way to avoid a particular church is to move to a different community. To be Amish is to attend a church service.

"Keeping the communal structure is very important to the Amish. The community actually becomes more important than the individual, more important even than family structure. The communal governing system, which resides in the local church governing body, is where you find your identity. You don't have an individual identity—your identity comes from being in the community."

Stepping Outside the Rules

Community life also plays out in negative ways, Jonas said. "There are always people watching, making sure that you are staying within the community's rules. Whoever sees you step outside them will usually go tell the preacher or deacons or someone from the church governing body. So you always have the sense that you are being watched and that you have to act in a certain way or you will be expelled.

"There is a procedure if you go outside the rules. Someone visits you and talks to you. If you admit the offense, then, depending on what it is, you confess it before the church at the next church service. Then there is public forgiveness, which means that the offense has been addressed and you can go on as part of the community.

"Sometimes, though, you are excommunicated. You still stay in the community, but you are expected to have a very strict, obedient life during the excommunication time. They call it a trial period. For some, the trial period is two weeks, while for others it is longer, up to six months. After the trial period, you are reinstated into the church membership."

Comfort and Struggle

Jonas had mixed feelings about Amish community life. "I grew up having a strong sense of community, and I took a lot of comfort in being part of the community. It gave me a sense of security. I had the feeling of belonging to a large family where you know you are cared for and supported. I felt known.

"In addition, Amish life is very much slower than the larger, fast-paced life that is always looking for the next big thing. For a time, that too felt good.

"If I had continued to want to be part of the Amish community, I would have found it extremely difficult to leave. But in my teenage years, I drifted away from Amish life and no longer wanted to be part of the community. It felt very imposing, very restrictive. I was not allowed to be myself. I felt that I could not have an identity as an individual, because the community structure was so strong and pervasive. What had provided comfort before came to feel like a prison."

Questions

When Jonas was twelve to fourteen years old, he started wrestling with the contradictions he perceived in Amish life, especially in the dual worldview the Amish held to. "In a dual worldview, what is right and good for the Amish doesn't necessarily mean that it is good and right for those who are not Amish, and the reverse—what is right and good for the non-Amish does not mean that it is good and right for the Amish. It is like holding two opposite truths—what is true for me doesn't necessarily translate into what is true for you, because you are not Amish. As you grow up in the Amish community, you learn to hold a dual worldview. You learn the worldview that you are expected to function on and the worldview that the outside world functions on.

"A big example of a dual worldview is whether it is okay to use modern conveniences, such as electricity or vehicles, or okay to have a radio or television or any number of things. The Amish say that it is wrong for them to own these things. But it is perfectly okay for outsiders to own them, because the outsiders were never part of the system. And they say that both Amish and non-Amish can be Christians and be following God to the fullest extent in spite of these differences. But for me, that didn't make sense. If it's right for somebody else, why wouldn't it be applied to me too?

"Another contradiction was being able to use something that you didn't own. The Amish say that it is wrong to drive a car or anything with a motor but that it is totally acceptable to sit in the passenger seat of a taxi. But I couldn't comprehend the difference between renting and owning, or between riding in a car versus driving it.

"A plain black buggy was supposed to keep one from being prideful, yet I saw people taking a lot of pride in how shiny black their buggy was, or how new and clean it was. Placing restrictions on what we could own didn't seem to help, so why did we have the restrictions?

"Even though most Amish are aware of these contradictions, they accept them and learn to live with them. I couldn't do that. I started asking questions. 'Why do we do something this way? Where did that come from? How could something be right for one person, but not for everyone?' I wanted to understand. I was trying to make sense of it all.

"I wasn't just asking myself. I asked other Amish people too. They usually downplayed the contradictions by saying, 'I'm not smart enough to understand all this, but I trust that our forefathers knew what they were doing. This is just the way we've always done it, and we need to keep the traditions.'

"That answer did not work for me. Consistency and logic are pretty big things for me. And I could not make any sense of the contradictions in the dual worldview. It all left me very confused."

Losing Faith

Jonas lost faith, in two ways. "As I saw more of the inconsistencies in the Amish way of life, and the more I got inadequate answers to my questions, I lost faith in the Amish system. I thought, 'If I can't make sense of the things that are so obvious to me, why should I trust the Amish with other things, such as spiritual matters?'

"I became agnostic—I lost faith in the existence of a God. I lost respect for the Amish religion and did not want to have anything to do with it or any other religion. That was a large part of what contributed to the feeling that being in the community was restrictive and oppressive.

"To be in an Amish community, though, you have to be very religious. So I practiced the religion only to stay in the community. I got baptized in the Amish church at the age of seventeen. When an Amish person is baptized, the bishop pours water on the head of the person being baptized, who is kneeling. I remember being on my knees, having just made the vow to remain in the Amish church for the rest of my life, and as the water was running down over my head, thinking, 'God, you know I don't mean this, and the first chance I get, I'm leaving.'

"The duality of practicing a religion that I didn't believe in left me feeling very fragmented. I felt like a complete fraud."

Leaving

Jonas knew that he could not be true to himself if he stayed in the Amish community. "I could not truthfully and honestly live the Amish way. I would be going against myself. I would be living a lie. I wanted to leave because I wanted to be completely myself.

"If I did leave, though, I would be turning my back on everything I had been taught. And if there did happen to be a God, I was willingly and automatically condemning myself to the worst kind of hell. The whole Amish religion is based on attaining salvation in the afterlife, and even though you can never know with any level of confidence that you will have salvation, you definitely know you won't get it if you leave the Amish community, especially after being baptized into the Amish church.

"Leaving meant abandoning my family, friends, community, and any hope of salvation along with my very identity. The weight of the decision tormented me day and night. I started having bad stomach problems, and I was severely depressed and suicidal for several years.

"Finally, I realized that the only hope of finding any meaning and purpose in life was to leave. I knew I wouldn't find them among the Amish. I didn't know whether I would ever find them, but I knew where I could not find them.

"I left at the age of twenty-three.

"It was on a Sunday, when everyone was expected to go to church. I was still living at home, so I told my parents that I had a headache, and I stayed home. While everyone was gone, I wrote a note and left it for my parents. Then I walked out the door with only the clothes I was wearing. Nothing else.

"At the time, I felt that this was the only way I could have left. I wish I could have done it differently. I wish I could have sat down with my parents and told them I had to leave and why I was doing it. But I knew they would have been extremely upset and very distraught. I didn't think I could handle their emotions or the emotions I would have because of their reaction. And, of course, it would have been impossible to have anything like a going away party.

"Leaving the Amish was one of the most difficult things I have ever done in my life. I walked away from everything I knew and into everything I didn't know. But it was my only hope of ever feeling unified. I had to try to find my identity somewhere else."

Excommunicated

Jonas was excommunicated. "One of the Amish pastors came and talked to me at the new place I was living and tried to get me to go back. About a month later he came again and said that if I didn't return, I would be excommunicated. On the following Sunday, the church voted to excommunicate me.

"I still am excommunicated. If I ever wanted to be accepted back into the Amish community, I would have to go back and live a trial period. Then they could choose to remove the excommunication or not."

Beginning a New Life

Jonas began a new life. "I had been working on a non-Amish dairy farm only a few miles from where I was living with my parents. The boss there knew I was considering leaving my Amish community, and he was a big advocate for it because then I could drive a vehicle and do other things. When I left the community, I lived in one of the tenant houses on his farm.

"I felt very raw, very numb, for a while, especially the first three months. I was very anxious. During the day, I was okay because I did what was expected of me at the farm. But during the night I was left to my own thoughts. The stomach problems that had started a couple of years earlier got worse. I went to a doctor, who said that I had ulcers that were causing internal bleeding so bad that I was very close to needing emergency surgery. That shows the stress I was carrying after I left."

Searching for Meaning and Purpose

Between twenty-three, when Jonas left the Amish, and twenty-six, he underwent a slow process of transformation. "When I left, I thought that if I found happiness, I would find meaning and purpose. So I pursued the things that American culture said would produce happiness. I watched television shows and listened to music to try to figure out what the culture said was valuable. Then I pursued those things. But what I thought would provide happiness never did. Each of the things I tried made me feel more empty than before. When I tried latching onto something, it was just like grabbing air. Nothing I grasped for was there.

"I did this for about a year. At the end of that year, I came to the conclusion that life is full of pain and misery. And if there is nothing after this life, why not end the misery early?

"I visualized life like a snow globe. When I was born, I entered the snow globe on one side, and life consisted of traveling to the other side. When I got to the other side, it would be back to nothingness.

"I was utterly hopeless.

"I started grasping at anything I knew, especially worldviews. The two worldviews I knew were naturalism and a creation worldview. I started comparing them, and gradually I found that the creation worldview could give me answers that the naturalistic worldview could not.

"For one thing, the creation worldview could tell me why something exists instead of nothing, whereas naturalism could only tell me that something does exist.

"For another, naturalism could not explain the intelligence in how things functioned. One day, as I was working on the farm, getting grain out of a grain bin, I saw an acorn hanging out on the limb of a big oak tree. I thought, 'All the information needed to grow another tree is in that seed.' I could not figure out how the tree could put the information into a seed to reproduce itself. I could not make sense of that.

"The more I saw things like that all around me, the more it seemed that if atheistic evolution were true, it would be the most intelligent thing that exists. But that is exactly what evolution says it is not. So, again, the creation worldview could explain something that naturalism could not.

"The third big point was morality. I didn't have a problem cutting down weeds or smashing annoying bugs. But I felt that it was wrong to hurt another person. I asked, 'Where does that come from?' If all life forms evolved out of the same substance, then all life forms should have equal value. But I believed that they did not.

"Each of these individually, but especially when put together, made me think that a creation worldview could explain things that a naturalistic worldview could not explain. The only logical explanation was that there had to be a God, something outside the natural world that put things into motion.

"At some point while I was thinking about these things, I found a Bible that someone had left at the tenant house I was staying in. If anyone would have offered me a Bible, I would not have taken it. I would not even have touched it, because I had become very antireligious. But since no one knew that I was looking at it, I opened it and started reading.

"About that time I was talking with an atheist who made the passing comment that she wondered whether Jesus actually lived. That struck me as an important question, especially since I had lived among people who based their whole lives around this person. So I started reading through the gospel stories and became convinced that he did live, that he died, and that he came back to life and ascended to heaven while being alive.

"My first thought about the resurrection of Jesus was that it must have been spiritual, not physical. But he ate physical food. I thought, 'Wow! Spirits don't eat physical food. So Jesus must have been physically alive.'

"The ascension struck me too. I thought, 'If he was physically alive when he ascended to heaven, he must still exist today.' That shocked me.

"Another thing I took as concrete evidence that Jesus existed was based on the calendar we use. I looked up what B.C. and A.D. meant and concluded that for the calendar to have been based on a belief about when Jesus was said to exist must mean that he actually existed.

"Putting all these things together, I realized that this was the truth I had been pursuing. It made the most sense of the world I lived in, which is what I had been looking for my entire life.

"I also came to the conclusion that Jesus had died for everyone, and if that was the case, he had died for me. I thought, 'If I were the only person to discover this, and I chose to walk away from it, that would make everything he had lived for, died for, and suffered meaningless.' That was a lot of weight on me that I had not asked for."

Kneeling

Jonas wrestled with these things. "At the end, I thought, 'If I walk away from this, then I walk back into nothingness.' That's when I chose to surrender myself to whatever this new truth I had found meant. 'I will give myself over to this reality, and whatever happens will be far better than going back into nothingness.' So I did.

"I knelt beside my bed and prayed to God for the first time in I don't know how long. I asked God for forgiveness. I didn't know whether God would forgive me. I didn't know whether God would accept me. I felt that there was no hope for me. At the same time, I thought, 'Here is this truth I've found, and if I have any shred of hope, it is in this.'

"I said to God, 'I really need to know that you can forgive me. I'll just stay here on my knees until you let me know.' I prayed and prayed. I don't know how long I knelt there. It could have been a few minutes. It could have been a few hours.

"All of a sudden, a sound like wind rushing into the room came upon me. It felt as though the wind wrapped itself around me, and it felt as if I was lifted off the floor.

"Instantly, I became a completely different person. A tremendous relief came over me. I had finally found peace. I wept and wept and wept. The bedsheet was wet with tears.

"I went to bed that night thinking I would wake up the next morning and things would be just like before. The constant struggle to find something meaningful would still be there. But when I woke up the next morning, the peace was still present. And it has not left since. That is the moment when everything in me changed. I found the identity I had been looking for."

Visiting My Parents

Jonas now has contact with his parents. "I have developed a better relationship with them now than when I was Amish. They have welcomed my wife, Abigail, and our two kids in as family, even though Abigail was never Amish.

"The excommunication I am under comes with shunning. Excommunication is the act of being removed from church membership, and shunning is avoiding a person who has been excommunicated. It is intended to shame the person into repentance and humiliation so that they return to the church. Shunning varies by individual and community.

"My parents have asked that I not drive a vehicle on their property. So when I go to visit them, I park at a neighbor's place or beside the road and walk the rest of the way. They are not allowed to sit at the same table and eat with me, so they set a separate table for me. Also, they are not allowed to receive any gift from me, or have any monetary transaction with me, or even listen to my beliefs. But I and my wife and children still visit with them as much as we can, and they welcome us as much as they can while respecting the shunning."

Bobby: Am I Really Gay?

"When I stopped having problems with being gay, no one else had a problem with it either."

Bobby describes how he wrestled with being gay for several decades until he finally accepted it in his midthirties. His grappling with being gay was made more intense because the church he went to highly disapproved of being gay. Bobby was in his midsixties when we talked.

Early Memories

Bobby went to church from the time he was an infant. "I started out in the nursery with the babies. When I was four or five, I knew I was different from the other boys, though I didn't have the vocabulary to talk about it. I was afraid of adult men, and I was afraid of other boys. I was much more comfortable in the company of women, and I identified more with them. I clung to my mother a great deal.

"I remember thinking that things would have been much easier if I had been a girl, because I perceived the world as a female might. But I never wanted to swap gender—that never occurred to me.

"At that point in my life, I didn't know what sexuality was. I didn't know what sex was. I didn't know people had sex, and I didn't know where babies came from. But I did know that I was very different from most of the people I knew.

"I learned that my sense of being different was something I should cover up. That was never verbalized to me, but I had downloaded the perception that I couldn't tell anyone—'I've got to keep this secret. It is shameful, and I will be rejected if I let it be known, even to my parents.' So I never told anyone about feeling different.

"When I started school, I was suddenly thrown into recess out on the playground. I had zero ability in that area. It was too painful to try to cultivate what was needed to mix with the others. They all knew I couldn't connect with them, and that reinforced my sense that I was quite different from the other boys. I was miserable.

"My mother single-parented me and my older sister during the week, because my dad traveled Monday through Friday. This was before there were cell phones, so once my father was gone, he was gone. He sometimes called at night, around bedtime, but he was not available for day-to-day things. There was no everyday touching base with him.

"My mother was a very nervous, anxious, high-strung woman who didn't handle change or surprises well. Actually, she didn't handle anything very well. It was apparent that my sister and I had to be the adults and needed to take care of her. We could not ruffle any feathers or cause any trouble, because she was already on the edge. If anything else went wrong, she would go straight over the edge and then my sister and I would be by ourselves. There was no quick, available help. We lived a four-hour trip away from the rest of the family.

"Overlapping with these experiences, there was the fact that I grew up in a very fundamentalist, Christian home. My mother was comforted by fundamentalist Christianity, because it was the only thing she had. She loved that she could open the Bible and find an answer to any circumstance in her life. The blueprint was there, and she never had to make any sort of evaluation or decision on her own.

"That's how she raised us. If there was a question, you go to the Bible and find out what it says and then you do that. This was coupled with the 'fine print,' which said that if you did that, there would never be any trouble. There would never be any anxiety. God would mop up after everything and it would be bluebirds and butterflies for the rest of your life. However, we never got to the birds and butterflies phase.

"So when my dad came home on Friday evenings, my mother had a list as long as her arm of the things that had gone wrong and how she had to handle them all herself and how she felt so helpless with two kids who had driven her crazy and whom she resented, and she would never have married my dad had she known it was going to be that way.

"She couldn't see that the only reason we had a life was because my dad paid for everything. She just felt that she had been abandoned and that he had let her down.

"I got the message really quickly that grown men are terrible. They cause sadness. They cause fear, plus conflict and trouble. My dad would be home maybe an hour and he and my mom would start into arguments because he didn't want to come home to a family he hadn't seen all week and then hear her complain. They argued all weekend, and then he got on a plane and left. I thought, 'Okay, marriage must be really difficult.'

"I wasn't aware of straight and gay then, just adult men. I thought that adult men must be the lowest form of humanity. I was very attached to my mother and very estranged from my dad. I never developed any sort of bond with him. I was on my mother's side when there were arguments—'How dare you sail in on weekends and upset the apple cart like this? How dare you agitate my mother when she is doing her best? You have no idea how weak and fragile she is.'

"I was like her little husband. She leaned on me for anything a male should do way before I was old enough or able to do it.

"I knew I was going to grow up to be an adult man. I had looked at myself in a mirror and had seen that I had the anatomy that would make me develop into a man. There was no avoiding it. But I wasn't going to grow up to be that kind of man. I would find a way to be different. I would be something else, I vowed, because what I knew about being a man was that it was full of trouble and betrayal and sadness and conflict. It did nothing but create an environment of calamity, and I didn't want to do that to anybody. I thought these things when I was only eight or nine."

Going to Church

Going to church was a way for Bobby to escape home calamity. "I loved the music at church, which I could reproduce at a very young age. I loved to sing and I loved to play the piano. So I escaped into music.

"When I hit puberty, it became very apparent that I was a sexual creature, because my body started doing things. But I was never pulled to girls. I was always pulled to boys. And as I said earlier, we learned in church that we only needed to go to the Bible for every answer and every guidepost in life. When I went to the Bible for sexual things, though, I got a very daunting, very unfriendly, and very unapproving account about what was happening to me.

"It was the clobber passages where I got this, which are used by well-meaning people of faith to beat up on people whom they don't approve of or don't understand. It's not that they want to be mean. It's that they don't understand. And they are afraid of me. They are afraid for my very soul.

"In all this mix, when I was nine or ten, I had a very real salvation experience face-to-face with Jesus. I accepted Jesus as my Lord and Savior. I walked the aisle, and I went through the counseling and got baptized in front of the church. They presented me with a Bible with my name on it. I still have it.

"This was not something I just thought I should do. It was real. I had a genuine conversion in which I wanted Jesus to be my savior. It still is real, and he still is my savior.

"This experience set up a push and a pull in me, because I believed that if I was a Christian, I could not be gay, and that if I was gay, I could not be a Christian. I could not blend these two together.

"I picked up from my church that I couldn't say anything about my being gay. So I never told anyone there about it. I had only an internal dialogue between me and God. There was absolutely no person on the face of the earth to whom I could talk about what I was experiencing.

"At school, though, I heard other kids talk about being gay. They had not grown up in the squashed, fundamentalist environment I had grown up in, one that was very contained, with thick walls around it. I had a thick wall around myself—the kids at school were unsafe, and I was afraid to socialize with them. They were evil, and something evil would get onto me if I mixed with them."

Dealing with Being Gay

Bobby tried reconciling being gay with being a Christian. "The way I did that was to think that the feelings inside me were not real. Or if they were real, they were something God would take away from me. And when God did that, I would be the Christian I wanted to be.

"In the meantime, I had girlfriends. But they were not romantic relationships. There was nothing physical about them. I didn't have my first kiss until I was twenty-four. But I thought, 'I don't get it. What is the big deal about that?'

"My prayer life during this time changed. It became, 'God, fix me. Apparently something went wrong in the wiring inside me. You are the only one who can go in and see where that is and rewire it and make it work.'

"Someone told me that I was a pen that was supposed to write black, but that somehow there was blue ink inside me instead. What I needed was for God to drain the blue ink out and put the black ink in. I just needed to make myself available for that and then God would do it.

"I had faith that that was going to happen. I prayed and prayed and prayed and prayed. But the gay feelings didn't go away. That made me think that I must not really have gotten saved when I first invited Jesus into my life. At the church I was going to there was an invitation at the end of the services to go forward and rededicate your life to Christ. So I went forward multiple times. I thought I had not done it right the first time.

"Nothing changed. I still had the gay feelings."

Engaged

Bobby graduated from college. "After graduating, I met a captivating, talented, witty young woman. She was funny and entertaining. I hung out with her because I got a kick out of her, and she got a kick out of me. We were both smart, but we were catty with it, and when we were together we were extra catty.

"I thought I could probably spend my life with her because she was so much fun. So I asked her to marry me, and she said she would. There wasn't anything physical about our relationship, though, and I had no physical attraction to her.

"Not long after this, she met the man whom she married. I knew right away when I saw them together that that was going to happen. It hurt because I couldn't spend time with her anymore. But I understood, because I was not going to be able to give her what she wanted. She and her husband have four children, and they have had a very happy life. I don't resent that at all.

"That ended my experience with women and my desire to get married. I wasn't motivated to try again, especially because what I saw in my family as I was growing up was nothing I wanted. It would be so much easier just stay single."

An Affair

Bobby decided to go to another church after the engagement broke off. "I didn't want to be in the same church that the woman to whom I had been engaged and her husband went to. It was simpler for me to let them have that world.

"At the new church I went to, I caught the eye of one of the men there. I started getting a lot of attention from him, and he invited me to lunch and dinner at his house. I met his wife and children. Then he took me on a cruise and bought clothes for me. We became very, very close.

"It soon became apparent to me that I had feelings for him, feelings that I had never had before. I liked the attention he gave me, and I felt singled out and special. I did not know at the time that he had a track record of singling out young men, fluffing them up and grooming them for doing physical things.

"One day the man's wife went out of town for a night, and he invited me over. Things got physical. I didn't know what to do with that. It was my first time, and it was very confusing to me. I knew, though, that I had to hide it. He said afterwards, 'We have to take this to our graves.'

"He stayed at the church for a number of years, and every time anything happened between us he said, 'You have to take this to the grave.' I thought, 'Well, okay. I'll take it to my grave.' I stayed in that limbo position with him as long as he stayed at the church.

"Whenever we had interactions at the church, he was horrible to me. He was insulting and demeaning so that no one would ever think that anything bad was going on between us.

"People asked me, 'Why do you take that? Why don't you defend yourself?' I said, 'Oh well, it's just him, you know.' I made excuses for him, because I wanted the relationship to continue even though I knew it would never go anywhere, that is, that we would never get married and be public with our relationship.

"Eventually he got called to another church and our relationship was abruptly cut off. One day it was there, and the next it wasn't. My life broke."

A Transformation

"Even though I knew that what had been going on was wrong, I liked it. I thought, 'What do I do with that?' I still prayed constantly for God to take away my feelings for men. But they wouldn't go. They just would not go.

"I had gone back to school for a master's degree in counseling, because I believed God was calling me to be a counselor. I became a counselor. And God, in his crazy sense of humor, kept bringing gay men to me who wanted to be fixed. I couldn't fix them, because I couldn't fix myself. They were asking me to help them do something I couldn't do for myself. I kept seeing myself sitting opposite me in the counseling room.

"By now I was in my thirties. It was a very discouraging time in my life. I was trying to piece everything together, and I could not. There were times when I thought it would be such a relief to kill myself, to die and go to heaven and end the constant, twenty-four seven conflict. Something had to give.

"One evening in my mid-thirties, it all came to a head. I went into my room, closed the door, and collapsed. I cried and cried. I wailed, crying out to God: 'You can do anything, God. You made me, and you can fix me. I need to be fixed. I just need to be fixed. God, change me. Why won't you change me? Why won't you change me? You are the only one who can do that. Why won't you?'

"I heard a voice as clear as any voice I have ever heard. I heard it with my spirit ears, not my physical ears, but it was a definite voice. It was not my own voice, and it was not simply my thoughts.

"It said, 'I'm not changing you, because you don't need to change.'

"And just like that, all the black stuff in me poured out. I felt peace for the first time in a very long time. I felt accepted and loved for who I am. I felt clean. I let go of the struggle that very night, just let go of it."

Leaving Church

As a result of this evening experience, Bobby left church. "I backed out of church altogether. But I was still spiritual, and I looked for some place to connect with others. I found groups of philosophical people with whom I could be cerebrally spiritual. We talked about loving one another and making the planet a better place. But there was no structured church worship."

Finding a Gay Partner and Returning to Church

Bobby decided to try to meet someone who was also gay. "I thought, 'I will be open about who I am and see what happens. If I meet someone, then I'll meet someone. And if I don't, then I won't.' Nothing happened, though, because to meet gay people you had to go where they were. And I didn't go to the places they inhabited. Plus, it was before the internet. I was in another limbo phase for a long time.

"The year I turned forty-two I made a New Year's resolution—I was going to get a computer and get online to see who I could find. I met Don in March. We hit it off right away.

"He said, 'I belong to a church that is gay friendly. You would really like it there, and I want you to come to church with me.' I replied, 'I really don't want to go to church.' He responded, 'I want you to come to church with me. Trust me. You'll like it there.'

"I went, not really wanting to. But I fell in love with the church. It was everything I loved about church. About fifty percent of the people in it were gay, and the rest were very inclusive understanding. Everyone was welcome at the church. The music wasn't astounding, but I was back in the world I loved, except this time as my authentic self. My spirit woke up again.

"The theological part in the church was that God made you this way, and God loves you as much as he loves anyone else. For the first time, I was able to reconcile my being gay with being a Christian. I could say, without contradiction, that I was a gay Christian man. I was okay.

"My life finally came back together. The shame left me. If I had to go back to my parents' circle of friends or go back to their church for a special occasion, I could put up a shield. But I knew it was something I could put up and take down. And I knew why I was putting it up. So it was tolerable."

Dealing with Parents

Bobby's parents had not been welcoming to gay people. "My mother knew I was gay. But she wasn't going to talk about it. She got cancer and died in June of 2011. It was lingering and painful, and she had an awful end. On Mother's Day, a little over a month before she died, she called me up and said, 'I've come to the conclusion that God is not going to heal me, which I have been praying for. The reason he's not going to heal me is that you do not live a lifestyle that pleases him.'

"I made an excuse and hung up. And that was the last conversation I had with her before she died. That's how we ended our earthly relationship.

"At some point before she died, I was talking with my father. I could hear my mother working on him in the background: 'We've got to be a unified front. You've got to confront him and make him change. You've got to talk to your son,' and so on. He kept saying, 'No, I'm not going to do that.'

"After my mother died, I told my father that Don and I were going to get married, which we did, in August of 2021, after being partners for twenty years. My father's only comment was, 'I can't stop you from doing that, but I'm grateful you didn't do it while your mother was alive, because it would have killed her.'

"My dad remarried, and the woman he married saw things differently. She was able to convince my dad to accept me. Before he died, in June of 2022, we had some honest talks."

Being Open

Bobby has now been living an open life. "I am happy with who I am. I'm happy with my husband, and I'm happy with his family. They are very accepting. I don't really know anyone who's not. If they're not, they don't hang around in my life very much.

"That evening experience in my mid-thirties was pivotal. It began a process that lasted several years. I dropped the self-deprecation and self-criticism I had been doing. It stopped mattering to me what others thought about me. My meeting Don and forming a family with him finished the process.

"I discovered that we humans are transmitters. Whatever I'm thinking or feeling about myself is somehow silently transmitted to other people. They pick up on it and give it back to me. So when I stopped criticizing myself and being down on myself, the cord was cut and it didn't matter to others that I was gay. It was like a magic wand—suddenly no one cared about it.

"When I was a child, I was ashamed of myself. I felt that I deserved nothing and that I was less than everyone else. It is no wonder that I was bullied, because I was transmitting to others that I was worthless—I didn't deserve to be here, I'm not as good as you are. I was inviting the bullying in an unspoken way.

"Then when I wanted to have a relationship but believed that I didn't deserve it and couldn't have it, I became the other man in an affair with a married man, who was completely unavailable. That was nothing but painful to me, because that is all I thought I could have.

"When I met Don and realized I could have something else, I let myself have it. Our wedding was such a celebration. The people at it were genuinely thrilled for us.[1]

"The biggest takeaway from my current experience is that when I stopped having problems with being gay, no one else had a problem with it either."

---

1. Don died on May 5, 2023, just fourteen days after Bobby and I talked. He had developed increasingly debilitating Parkinson's Disease.

Kendall: The Audacity of Speaking Out—A Woman's Story

"I wanted an experience that would jolt me out of the cave of fear and anxiety and timidity I had been trapped in."

Kendall was confident and outspoken as a young child. But that was squashed by a sixth-grade teacher, and she became quiet and submissive. In what follows, Kendall describes how she has become outspoken again. She was twenty-seven when we talked, halfway through her second year of law school.

Spunky and Outspoken

Kendall's earliest memories are of being on the playground during kindergarten and early grade school. "I had a take-charge personality—I usually suggested and led the make-believe games. I thought of myself as the main protagonist in any game we played. I especially liked stories in which I was the heroine, the one who saved the day. When we played Middle Ages, I might be a princess, but a princess-knight who could sword fight.

"My favorite thing was when I got a group of kids together and we were all the heroes in our own ways. Everyone had their own spotlight. I was always spunky and active and outspoken and played with both girls and boys."

Kendall's parents encouraged this confident outspokenness. "They never tried to put me into a box by telling me I could only play with girls. They certainly never told me that I needed to be timid and quiet or sit still and not voice my thoughts. They encouraged me to use my voice to assert boundaries, to stand up for others, speak my opinions, and take my space as an individual in the world. They encouraged me to be active and not just an onlooker.

"I always felt that my parents were proud of me not only as a daughter but as a person. They taught me that doing what was right was more important than looking right. And being a bystander was as bad as being a perpetrator.

"All of these things stuck with me. I wanted my life to be bigger than myself and to serve a purpose for others. I felt that I could do that if I set myself to it."

Scolded

Kendall's peers and teachers, though, did not always appreciate her outspokenness. "Some kids said I was weird or bossy or tomboyish. When I was caught talking to a male classmate when I wasn't supposed to be talking, I was scolded harshly though the boy wasn't. When I played games with boy classmates, I was berated for the same behavior that the boys were permitted to engage in—roughhousing or playing tag too hard. I got into trouble when I pushed them after they had pushed me.

"One time at the dinner table when I was seven or eight, my father told me that I had his permission to slap any boy who kissed me without my permission. My first thought was, 'Wow! What if that actually happened?' Inexplicably, it did happen a couple of days later. I was on the playground, and a boy classmate came up and kissed me on the cheek. So I hauled off and slapped him. I was promptly pulled off the playground. When I tried to explain that I had been kissed without my consent and that I had my father's permission to slap him, I was reprimanded."

Kendall's confidence took a beating. Each time she got in trouble she felt embarrassed and ashamed and rejected.

"In sixth grade one day, the Spanish teacher had to be elsewhere in the school for a time, and my Spanish class had a fun no-work day. A boy classmate threw a paper ball at me, and I tossed it back at him. Just as I did, the teacher walked into the classroom. He was angry. 'You guys were loud, you were obnoxious. That was not how you're supposed to behave.' And he called me out: 'I am especially disappointed in you, Kendall.' I just withered in that moment.

"My girl classmates were praised more by my teachers and liked better by the teachers than I was. They were all quiet and put together. They didn't get dirty. They weren't messy. They never got into trouble. I felt different from them."

A Decision

Kendall decided that she needed to be quiet. "That scolding incident in sixth grade prompted me to feel sharply the tension between my natural desire to speak out and the sense that speaking out was not desirable for a girl or woman. I started to hide the part of myself that was more audacious and outspoken and bold and impolite. I tried to be nice and timid and quiet like the girl classmates. I took on a different personality and adapted to what I thought was more acceptable.

"I still had, though, the desire to advocate for people who had been wronged. In high school, I worked for a human rights education center and brought speakers to my high school. I wrote a couple of essays and did projects with the center. I also did projects with organizations in Africa."

"At one point, I wanted to join the debate team. But an English teacher said to me, 'Do you want to argue for things that you don't believe in? Is that really who you are?' I thought, 'Oh, she's right. I shouldn't do that.'

"Overall, I wasn't being true to who I really was. I had taken on the persona of being quiet and timid and trying not to make waves. I wanted to be liked. And I wanted to be perceived favorably."

Recreating Herself

Kendall decided to join ROTC (Reserve Officer Training Core) in college, partly because she needed money to pay for school and partly because she wanted to re-create herself. "I wanted to go in a different direction, and I thought, 'Yes, this is my time.' I didn't wholly understand what being in ROTC entailed, but I was excited about it. I wanted, at least subconsciously, an experience that would jolt me out of the cave of fear and anxiety and timidity I had been trapped in. I wanted to speak out instead of shrinking myself, suppressing my opinions, and staying safe in myself.

"I was one of only three female cadets in the ROTC program. I knew that if I spoke out, I would be perceived as overreacting or be dismissed, while male cadets enjoyed the presumption of innocence. At the same time, I felt a push to be able to protect myself, to protect my family, to learn how to protect others, to fight back against the bad guys, so to speak, like being a hero in one of my childhood games. So I decided to join the army after college."

Kendall was appointed Lieutenant—Lieutenant Jones—and assigned to be a platoon leader immediately after graduating. "The challenge I faced was learning how to be a leader of twenty to thirty mostly men. This was the first time in the real world that I had to look at myself and decide, 'Who am I going to be?' I was still fighting my desire to hang on to my adopted, false persona—to be quiet and never speak out, to sit in the corner, be very introverted and timid.

"I'd been told during my college days that men needed to be outspoken, authoritative, and have a command presence. So I tried to be these things with the platoon I was in charge of after college. But when I was authoritative and commanding, using my big girl voice, I was treated as though I was being bossy or demanding or rude. That was confusing, because I was doing the same things my male peers were doing. I felt that my leadership and command presence were awkward and clumsy. I didn't feel that I was strong and influential. I didn't feel that I was the right combination of accessible, relatable, and likable, but also tough.

"What I had to do was to decide that if I was going to be a successful platoon leader, I would have to let go of my concern for what people thought about my leadership presence as a woman. I needed to start using my voice again. That is what I did. I accepted the fact that doing so was who I really am."

At one point, Kendall's platoon was sent to Ethiopia for a month to build good relations with the Ethiopian National Defense Force. "We were to teach them how we did things, and they were to teach us how they did things. I talked with high level Ethiopian officers, because I was the point of contact with my platoon. By this time, I had let go of any concern about how I looked or how I was perceived.

"I was one of four or five women among hundreds of U.S. soldiers, and was one of only two women who were out in the field, doing exercises, carrying weapons, teaching tactics, and learning tactics from the Ethiopian National Defense Force. Though all of the Ethiopian officers were male, I got along great with them. They were very friendly, and I loved working with them.

"One day, the U.S. officer who was in charge of all the soldiers there, a colonel, pulled me aside and asked, 'Are you doing okay?' I said, 'What do mean?' He said, 'Well, there's all these men, these Ethiopian men. Are you feeling intimidated?' And I said, 'No! Absolutely not!'

"He did not appreciate that I could handle things by myself and failed to understand that when women were given space to speak, there could be a beautiful partnership that was not gendered. I felt okay using my own voice. Not even Ethiopian officers who had never worked with women were going to keep me from accomplishing what I needed to."

Alone in Court

Another major transformational experience for Kendall involved dealing with a stalker. "My college experience was not a gentle transition into discovering my fully actualized self. In my sophomore year I started being stalked by a fellow ROTC cadet. He followed me around campus, emailed me, called me, made advances toward me, and in general never left me alone. I became alarmed—I feared for my safety, sometimes even for my life.

"The stalking escalated to the point that I had to decide whether to share what was going on and fight against it, or just sink under the pressure of feeling that I would simply be causing drama. I did not want to be perceived as dramatic, as over the top, calling attention to myself. I did not want to put myself out there unnecessarily, and I didn't like the thought that people would be judging me for what I was doing. I did not want people to know about the stalking at all.

"I decided to get a court order of protection. I didn't qualify for legal aid, though, so I had to do the legal work alone. And I had to present my case to a judge alone. I was scared, afraid that I would not be able to manage things on my own.

"The courtroom was paneled with dark wood. It felt like a dark and dingy dungeon. Besides the defense attorney and the stalker, there was a very stern judge, who was an older white man. He was deciding 'order of protection—no order of protection' cases for women who said that they had been abused by their significant others. They were in and out in five minutes. It felt as though the judge was dealing with them dismissively. Just routine stuff.

"I was careful about how I dressed that day. I didn't want to look as though I wanted to be stalked by this man who wouldn't leave me alone. I was afraid of being 'that girl,' someone who has been too nice, flirtacious, giving off vibes that had encouraged this man to show interest and who had misperceived his advances as more than what they actually were. So I put on my most modest looking dress. I wanted to project that I was innocent, that I didn't ask for it.

"I did not have a chair, so I stood before the judge—all five-foot three of me. It took about five hours of arguing, standing before that very educated man who could tell me that I was wrong. It was harrowing. I felt intimidated. I wondered whether women and oppressed people went through this every day.

"Thankfully, my dad was in the small audience, watching it all. Afterwards, he said that it was one of the hardest things he had ever had to see.

"In a way, I was glad for the courtroom experience. It reawakened a passion for using my voice. It forced me to realize I had to be different from what I had become. I learned that I didn't want simply to float through life without speaking out just because I was a woman. My outspokenness was revived.

"When the stalker tried to discredit me by saying, 'You're just trying to call attention to yourself. There is no way you are actually afraid. You are "that girl,"' I had to dig into my inner resources and stand up to him and say, 'No. This is how I feel. This is what is really going on.' I had to do it firmly, defiantly, and with conviction. I had to bury the desire to be timid and quiet and unnoticed.

"Essentially, I had to grapple with whether I would speak against my stalker, whose wealthy parents were alumni of the college, and make waves, or give in to my fear.

"I made waves. I lost some friends. A few people judged me. I made enemies. By speaking against the stalker, I learned that using my voice can be polarizing. I had to make peace with that fact.

"The courtroom experience also reawakened in me the passion to help people who could not help themselves, people without a voice. I wanted to use my privileged station in life and my experiences to help those who were not able to speak for themselves. For a very specific period of my life, I was like them. I did not have money for an attorney. I did not have time in between studying and life obligations to do what I had to do to make the stalker go away.

"The judge granted an order of protection. The stalker was booted out of the college. Over the next few years, however, he followed me to three different states, trying to find me. That resulted in his arrest and prosecution for interstate stalking, a federal felony. He was convicted and spent more than a year in prison."

Law School

A third set of experiences that changed Kendall was being in law school. "My decision to go to law school," she said, "was not one I arrived at on my own. My husband was very supportive of my needing to find my voice. My parents said, 'You have the experience with the stalker, you've been in the army. You would be good in law school.'

"At first, I brushed it off. 'No, I just want a quiet life—do my time in the army, then stay home and be quiet.' But the more I thought about it, the more I became convinced that going to law school made sense. It would fit in with the early childhood times when I was energetic or couldn't sit still at my classroom desk or stop talking in class.

"It would also fit in with the strong penchant for justice I have long had, with my wanting to speak out against what I perceived to be injustice and not be concerned with how it looked to do the right thing.

"During my first year of law school I decided that I would be very quiet. Because I took mostly science classes in college, I didn't write more than two essays a year. Law school requires a great deal of writing, so I felt very unequipped.

"The second year I decided that I was going to raise my hand at least three times in every class, something I have always felt uncomfortable doing as a woman. I would do it, I decided, even if I felt stupid or like a know-it-all. So I did.

"Sometimes I had the fleeting thought that my classmates might be thinking I was too bold, too conceited, or too arrogant, things my male classmates didn't have to worry about, and things I knew women were often perceived as being. But the more I spoke in class, the more I realized I didn't really care how I was perceived.

"Being in law school has unlocked the part of my personality I had squashed for so long. It has helped me pursue my bent for justice. I have let go of a lot of the self-consciousness I had earlier.

"In law school they tell you that you need to be a zealous advocate and that you can't do that without being passionate about your client, your cause, or your case. And this passion is needed to be bold in speaking up for justice.

"As a woman, I need to be liked, and I need to be uncontroversial. But I have liked myself so much more since I started to embrace boldness. The parts of my personality that I had buried have been resurrected. I finally feel at peace with who I am and with what I am becoming."

Andrew: The Making of an American Rock Musician

"I love moments when I and my listeners are connected. These energize me."

After making his way through a long period of family tension, Andrew now creates and performs American Rock, which includes classic rock, alternative rock, country, and alternative blues. He has a steady schedule of solo and full-band shows throughout the Midwest, which are listed on his website at andrewscottdenlinger.com. The lyrics to his songs speak of heartache, love, friendship, and death. He was thirty-nine when we talked.

Beginnings

Music was deeply part of Andrew's life from the time he was very young. "My mom played viola in an orchestra, which I listened to when I went with her to rehearsals. My dad was pastor of a small church, and he was the piano player for evening services. My two sisters were accomplished piano players.

"At my aunt and uncle's, on holidays, we sang hymns and old standards. In church, I learned harmony from my mom, who showed me the different parts in the songs we sang. I sang the alto line with her. My family told me that I could sing on pitch by the time I was two.

"When I was four or five, my parents started me on violin and piano lessons. I practiced one instrument one day and the other instrument the next. I was a very excited kid, so I had a lot of fun with them."

Tension

When Andrew was seven, his exposure to rock and roll music provoked tension between him and his parents. "Before that time, I listened to everything my parents and sisters listened to. We went to a fundamentalist Bible church, and everything we did fit into a very conservative mold, including the music we listened to: a lot of classical, religious, and southern gospel music—the Gaithers and the Cathedrals. Rock and roll and pop music felt very 'off the table.'

"Both my sisters were in college by the time I was seven, in second grade, and they were making their own choices without interference from our parents. One of them had DC Talk's 'Free At Last' album, and though Christian, their mix of rap, hip-hop, rock music was exactly the type of music I was not allowed to listen to. I got my hands on her cassette, and I was immediately drawn to the lyrics and style of those songs.

"That started conversations between me and my parents. They thought that kind of music was wrong. My church thought it was wrong. I wanted to know why.

"In my third, fourth, and fifth grades, my parents and I went through the albums they believed were acceptable. Michael Smith's 'Go West Young Man' may have gotten the 'okay,' but it was still pushing their boundary because of the lead guitar playing in it. It felt to me that making those sounds with that instrument was inherently wrong. But I loved it. Our intellectual disagreements became heated debates over time.

"My tastes continued to push my parents' limits. I got a CD player when I was ten and a subscription at Columbia House Record Club. You could pay a penny and get a whole bunch of albums, then more month by month, by mail.

"The first CD I ever bought was at a Christian bookstore. It was an album by Carman, a contemporary Christian music singer, which was the most rocking thing I'd ever heard. I loved it because of its syncopated drumbeat. It sounded like the secular music I couldn't listen to, except that it had a Christian message.

"By the time I got into my early teens, I had been exposed to a variety of music genres that didn't fit well into my parents' approved categories. I got into the hardcore music scene. One of the first albums I listened to and connected with in that genre was by Klank, an American industrial-metal band. It was eye-opening for me because it was so dark. The singer, who is also called 'Klank,' sang about childhood abuse, addiction, the struggle of life—about being a mess. I resonated with that as a young teenager. It articulated feelings I couldn't always express. I specifically remember how uncomfortable the aggression in those songs made my dad feel.

"Hardcore vocals have a lot of rawness, which is always very emotional. The emotions need not be negative, though. I've been to hardcore shows and punk rock shows that have a very positive vibe. But they are always intense. Maybe 'high intensity music' is a good way to describe the hardcore genre. I took in so much 'new' music during that time. I felt, and still feel at times, that I had to catch up on everything I had not been exposed to. I listened to metal bands like Ozzy, Metallica, and Pantera and to rock and punk bands like The Offspring, Soundgarden, Nirvana, and Bush.

"Over the years, the music I listened to included a lot of screaming. My parents didn't understand screaming, so there was a big disconnect between them and it. Yes, screaming can be angry, and it can be dark. But it can also be positive. I feel like it is the ultimate expression of what you can do with your voice. It's leaving nothing behind. It is beautiful, though not in a classical way. There's not always a melody with screaming, but it always embodies strong passion.

"I absolutely loved music. I recorded stuff off the radio, my friends let me borrow their CDs, and I started going to shows. The first big concert I went to was at a Christian rally with the Newsboys, a Christian pop rock band. I became a big fan of Audio Adrenaline and Living Sacrifice, Christian rock and metal bands, respectively.

"All of this was adding to the tension between me and my parents. And it was becoming more of a tension point within me as well, because I was still putting in a large amount of energy into playing classical violin and piano. Although I loved rock and roll, I was not playing it. The music I played was my parents' music. I have come to love classical and gospel music now, but at the time it felt forced for me to play it.

"Also, in my early teens, I started getting extraordinarily intense stage fright. I hated recitals or performing at church. One time, about fifteen, I was to play a song on the piano from memory in church because I was to play it at a recital soon. About halfway through, I lost it. I tried to get to the end, but couldn't. I vividly remember how horrible I felt about myself.

"I did not want to do any more performing. If you had asked me then about becoming a playing and paid musician when I grew up, I would not have wanted any part of it."

A Shift

This sentiment did not last long. "When I was a freshman in high school, my parents gave me a bass guitar for Christmas. The person at the guitar shop told my mom there needed to be more bass players in the world, because everybody was buying regular guitars but no one really knew how to play the bass.

"There was a spark in me from day one. I remember lying on the couch that Christmas break with the guitar on my chest, not even plugged in, feeling the vibrations as I picked out the notes of the songs I heard on a CD. Almost immediately I started writing songs, which I had never done before. I became the bassist in a metal band that I formed with three friends from school, and I invited my parents to the first show we performed.

"When we got home, they sat me down and told me I was playing the music of the devil. I ran out of the house. I didn't have anywhere to go, but I did not want to be in the house. Eventually I came back home, but our issues were not resolved.

"The band was invited to play a public show in the small town in Illinois where we lived. My dad told me that I couldn't do it because he was a pastor in the town and what would people think?—'He isn't doing his job, raising his family right.' I was glad, though, to have a deacon on the church board who stood up for me. We played outside, downtown, right next to the historical dome there and in front of an assisted care facility. The people in it were older than my parents, and they must have thought the band was crazy.

"That band lasted three months. After it disbanded, I quickly joined a pop rock band."

Reapproaching Music

Andrew went through other shifts when he was a senior in high school. "The music department must have seen some of the natural instincts I had for music. They gave me the opportunity to have a free period by myself in a room with a piano.

"The first things I played were three songs from church that I knew—'Turn Your Eyes Upon Jesus,' Bill and Gloria Gaither's 'There's Something About That Name,' and Keith Green's 'There Is a Redeemer.' The lyrics of the songs were where my faith was: they were simple and heartfelt.

"Up until this point, I had always played from sheet music, but I figured out how to play those three songs without reading the music for them. And from that point on, I played without sheet music nearly all the time. When I perform now, I want to be in the moment, fully present with my guitar and the audience, without something between me and them.

"Also, when I was alone in that room, I figured out how to play in different keys. I moved my hands around on the keyboard of the piano until I could play the songs in every key.

"One day, in the study hall during the previous period, I wrote out the lyrics for a song. It was about death and someone's last moments with a dying person.

"Right after that period was over, I went into the room with the piano, grabbed my guitar, which I had put in there, and picked out a pretty guitar tune. During the next forty-five minutes, the song was done. It was a magical moment. It was one of those 'songwriter' moments in which you almost feel as though someone else wrote the song and you were just the pen.

"The song stuck, both the lyrics and the music. Many years later, I recorded it and included it as the closer on a hard rock album, and I am honored to have sung it at two different funerals."

In-Between Years

Andrew had a scholarship for football in college plus a partial scholarship to play the violin in the college's orchestra and to receive private lessons. "I loved my violin lessons, and I loved my teacher. The orchestra director's passion for music and his openness deeply encouraged me. Because of a conflict between football and the music department, though, I had to stop playing in the orchestra. I put my violin away and didn't touch it for years.

"I joined a band with some of the football players, where I was the lead singer and screamer. I stayed with that band for a time after graduating from college. We were great at creating music and dreaming about possibilities, but we didn't know how to make connections or make money. Things ended up falling flat.

"After that band dissolved, I wrote music and sang for friends at house parties or around bonfires. When I was twenty-three, I got a job at a church as worship director. I played piano there and sang, plus played acoustic and electric guitar, and bass, when needed. It was there that I learned to play the drums, doing my best to fill in when our drummer couldn't make it. I am still with that church, and my position at it has expanded to other creative roles.

"In 2009, three years after college, I stumbled into a large loft apartment in Chicago's Lakeview neighborhood. One of the people who lived there had an incredible studio set up in the space and gave me a super cheap rate to record. I recorded fourteen songs with members from my previous band, but did not release the album until 2016. I had the ill-conceived notion that you had to gain momentum before you should release an album.

"As with the earlier band, I didn't know how to make money. In some of the places I played, I get a cut of the door, but I was able to get my friends to come out to shows only so long. I did some shows for free and got paid very little for others. I was naïve, not knowing how to create interest in what I was doing.

"In 2013, I shut down the band I was in then, because we were just spinning our wheels. A year later, though, I got a call from a friend asking whether I wanted to be in a country band. I said I would."

On Tour

The band Andrew joined was run by country music artist, Nick Lynch. "For the next eight years, until 2022, I toured the country with that band, playing bass. At our height, we played about 150 shows a year. We toured the New England area, Louisiana, Colorado, and once were on a talk and entertainment television show, Windy City Live, in Chicago.

"We did a lot of covers. I used to look down on playing covers, but soon came to realize that good songs have worth no matter when or in what genre they are played—when all the intangibles are right, we players can be fully engaged with them, and listeners can connect with them in the moment.

"The biggest thing for me about touring was seeing how the business of making music was done. After a few years of creative silence, I started recording."

Releasing Songs

Andrew started releasing singles. "In May of 2021, I released my first single, and in August of that year, a second one. This past February, in 2023, I released my fourth one. These are digital releases on all of the streaming services, including Spotify. It used to be that radio was the big place where people could hear music. But that has changed. Now it is playlists online.

"So I had to figure out how to get myself listed on various playlists, then be consistent about putting out new songs. I put out a lyric video for every song I released to let people know what I was singing about. I made my art visible in every space and place possible.

"I had waited for so long trying to find out how to bring listeners to my music. Eventually I learned the importance of bringing the music to the world. It was always going to be up to me to do the work.

"After eight years with the Nick Lynch Band, I started doing shows on my own. Last year, in 2022, I did about fifty solo shows and another ten with my band."

My Message

Andrew's shows, he says, are a way he shares his overall message. "My overall message is that people are loved. I end most of my shows saying, 'Thank you very much for being here! My name is Andrew Scott Denlinger. Goodnight. I appreciate you. You are loved.'

"My songs talk about my journey, wrestling with my faith, my addictions, and my own mess. I also sing about what I see in others."

Making Music

Andrew's parents are now proud of what he is doing. "They have come to understand that God works in genres they might not like and in different ways with different people. They would love for me to play violin more, but are excited that I am pursuing music.

"Recently I have made enough money to start a small business and support my family with the shows I have been doing. I would love to tour hard during summers but right now am mostly doing weekend shows throughout the Midwest, some solo and some with the full band, some in Illinois, where I live, and some elsewhere. As long as I'm not getting stagnant and I see the path climbing higher, I am not going to stop.

"What keeps me going is creating music. I love moments when I and my listeners are connected. These energize me. And over the years I've learned a few things: how to market, make a profit, and expand what I do.

Plus, I like feedback from listeners, both in the live shows and through stories of how a song or recording has impacted them.

"I'll tell you what I love about a song. When it encapsulates what I'm feeling, that's great. When it says something I didn't know I was feeling, that's even better. And when a song carries me to a better place, whether it's processing something from my past that allows me to live better now, or whether it gives me a vision for where I can be going, that, most of all, is a special thing.

"These are why I create and perform music. They motivate me both when I am playing in church and when I am playing in bars and restaurants and clubs."

"Claudia": A Month and a Half in a Cult

"If I see someone with narcissistic traits, I run for the hills."

After graduating from college, Claudia went to work for a mission organization in Mexico that turned out to be different from what she had been led to believe. She began to have disturbing experiences, and when they finally became too much, she packed up and left. We talked several years after that.

Looking for Work

After graduating from college, Claudia wanted to work with a Christian NGO that worked to alleviate poverty. "I looked for places in Mexico where I could do that kind of work. I had been there before with a program sponsored by the Christian college I went to. So I met with someone who could connect me to an organization in Mexico where I could work at alleviating poverty for a living.

"She showed me a glossy brochure that had statistics about how a certain organization in Mexico was reducing poverty. 'This group is doing the real work,' she said. That authenticity grabbed me. I took her word for it, because I wanted to be one of the real ones who is actually making a difference, doing meaningful work.

"The next step was to send my resume and then be interviewed. I met with a large, pot-bellied white man who was very confident of himself and thought he was funny. I laughed along with him. I knew that if I was nice to the man's ego, it could go well for me. It was just one of the steps I had to go through, I thought. He also struck me as the kind of older man who is over friendly to younger women. He was flattering toward me, which felt weird. But I rolled with it, and the interview went well.

"'The woman you would be working with is a powerhouse. She is a hard worker and gets a lot done,' he said. I thought, 'Great! My boss would be a woman. That will be interesting.'

"I had two more interviews, and on Christmas Eve they told me that I had gotten the job."

Starting Work

Claudia went to a small town in Mexico. "Through a connection, I had found a room to rent in a woman's house. My boss had told me that I would have two weeks to get set up and adjusted before starting work. It ended up being two hours.

"First, there was a week of training. Then there was another week of ten-hour days with intense sessions on the theology of the leader. I was put in with pastors from nearby poor neighborhoods. We were kept in a room in the hot sun with only instant coffee and limes to keep us awake. When I had to leave the room because I was feeling dizzy and nauseous, I was scolded by my boss.

"The leader of that week's sessions was the leader of the organization. He was charismatic, and everyone adored him. One of my coworkers said, 'Isn't it wonderful that we get to do this ten-hour training for five days with this man who has two master's degrees? What a blessing! How lucky we are that he chooses to spend time with us.' She insisted that I agree and also praise the leader.

"Everyone there, I discovered, was obsessed with the leader. That reminded me of pastor-centric churches where the pastor was overbearing and confident about everything.

"My boss told me that she and her husband had decided to become missionaries in this organization before they had gotten married. 'We completely trust the leader's vision,' she said. Their whole marriage seemed to be based on working for the organization."

Disturbing Experiences

Claudia had a number of disturbing experiences. "Everyone in the organization lived in the same neighborhood, and they did everything together. They all went to salsa classes and bars together. I was invited to go with them. That felt friendly at first. But later it felt as though they wouldn't leave me alone—they constantly asked me to spend free time with them. My world got smaller and smaller.

"After the two weeks of orientation and then a week of indoctrination, I worked all day—twelve hours each day. I left my apartment before any stores were open, and I went back after it was pitch black. I couldn't leave the apartment when it was dark, because it was in a dangerous neighborhood. So I couldn't always buy food at a grocery store or restaurant. There were times when I went to bed hungry.

"I had been told before I arrived at the organization that they would always take me to my apartment in a car, but once I moved in I had to beg for rides so as to avoid using buses and combis, which were unsafe.

"I like to think I'm a tough person, because I've done hard things before. I've slept on the ground, and my family lived through terrorist attacks in another country. Still, when I literally couldn't eat, I began to realize how bad it was to be at the organization.

"Sometimes the woman from whom I rented the apartment fed me. We talked and shared a lot, which was really nice. It became a respite from what was happening at work."

More Disturbing Experiences

The disturbing experiences began to pile up. "One of the males I worked with wanted to take selfies with me and give me hugs. I had spent enough time in Mexico to know that this was not a normal amount of affection for Mexicans, especially between women and men. It felt creepy. It was definitely not your basic, 'Oh, hi.'

"One day another male coworker looked me up and down in a disgusting way and said, 'You look nice today.' It wasn't what he said that bothered me, but the way he said it. It was gross.

"My boss was right there when that happened. Later she said, 'That's not okay. I'm going to talk to him.' I asked her several times whether she had talked to him. But she never did. He even made inappropriate comments to her.

"During one of the early weeks I was there, we hosted donors, most of whom came from the United States. They were nice older couples. They came up to me and asked, 'Are you okay?' I said, 'Yes. Sure.' But I was not okay at all.

"By this time, I had starting noticing things. Plus, the room I was staying in at the organization's building during the week the donors were there was a storage room. Everybody knew where it was, and the door to the room was rickety so the lock on it was not very good. There was no privacy and no boundaries. Everyone came and went at all times. The creepy, male coworker who wanted selfies left his stuff in the room, and he went to it at odd hours to get his stuff.

"One night during that week, after working eleven to eleven, I was eating leftovers I had found in the fridge with that coworker, just us two. The room I slept in was right behind me. He started bragging to me about how much girls enjoyed sleeping with him. I started to freak out, because he was much bigger and taller than I am. I finished eating, put away my plate, got into the room, and locked the door, which, as I said earlier, did not seem to give much security because the door was so wobbly.

"I truly thought that that was the time I would get assaulted. That is how it happens. And people would blame me because it was midnight and I was alone with the coworker. Thankfully, nothing happened.

"Another time I was scolded for talking to the cook. I had been told that I should be helping with the breakfast that had been served to the donors, and I was in the kitchen helping the kitchen staff clean dishes, talking to the cook as I was working. My boss's husband came in and said, 'What are you doing? Talking to the kitchen staff? Get out there. You're supposed to be helping with the translation sets.' So I rushed to the translation sets and found that there wasn't anything for me to do."

Leaving

Claudia left a month and a half after she arrived. "I talked to a couple of my friends from college, telling them about all the freakiness of what I had been experiencing and about how scared I had become of the people I worked with and how I did not trust them one bit. They both had worked with Latin

American NGO's, and they said, 'That's not normal. Get out of there! Don't include it on your resume. Just forget the experience ever happened.'

"I called my boss and said I had to go. She was shocked, but I said that it was because the pandemic had just started and because I didn't have health insurance in Mexico. I told her I was feeling sick, and my mom was worried.

"I packed in three hours. The next morning I went out for breakfast with the woman I lived with. Then I took an Uber to the airport and flew back home to the States."

Restoration

At home, Claudia spent a lot of time in the garden. "I went to Home Depot and bought compost and seed. With my parents' permission, I tore out a lot of their landscaping. I dug out roots and took away trash I had dug up. I planted squash, corn, and amarine, a flower. I worked myself hard. I swung whatever I was working with—a shovel, hoe, or rake. That was how I got out my anger about the wrongness of how I had been treated. There were a million little things that had made me feel small and unworthy.

"If anyone were to ask, 'Did you say anything to the people in Mexico?' I would say, 'Yes, I did.' I explained to my boss my concerns about the organization. I asked her whether she would recommend that a friend of hers work at the place. She said she wouldn't. I talked to my boss's boss. I told him about being harassed and about everything else. He did nothing.

"I've worked as an intern with brilliant lawyers at the Department of Justice, and they never made me feel small because I was an intern. They were just the opposite—encouraging and respectful. But with the organization in Mexico, there was no amount of proving I could do to show that I was worthy.

"My parents had taught me to obey people in authority. But I had enough of a rebellious spirit in me by the time I started working with the organization to realize that I didn't deserve what was going on."

A Cult

A number of things prompted Claudia to conclude that she had been part of a cult. "People at the organization were observing me and talking about me. There were multiple times when I realized that they were sharing information about conversations I had with different people. They definitely seemed to be checking up on me.

"They wanted to know about my personal life. Both my boss and the leader's assistant kept digging in about my personal life—are you seeing anyone, are you thinking of getting married, how is your relationship with your family—much more than is normal with coworkers.

"The leader's assistant asked me what I 'really thought' about the organization. It turned out that she was testing my loyalty to the organization.

"They didn't like it when I had conversations with the donors during the week they were at the organization. I was told, 'You should be working right now,' even though I had just checked with my boss about what to do.

"There was never any downtime. I had to be constantly working though there were no clear expectations of what I should be doing. If I was doing one thing, I was told that I should be doing something else, but when I got to the other place, there was nothing to do.

"You couldn't treat work there like a regular job. It had to be your life. My boss said, 'We work really hard and we play really hard.' All I wanted to do was to do a good job.

"They wanted me to spend all my free time with them. It was either spend all your time outside of work with them or you had no free time outside of work because you worked too much.

"Before I joined the organization, I was told that I would be coordinator for short-term mission trips. They did not give me a description of what I was to do for this, did not train me for it, and did not tell me what their expectations were. I was told many times that I would simply have to read my boss's mind to see what I was supposed to be doing.

"My position was downgraded after I had been in the organization for a month. I believe that my asking questions figured in the decision to downgrade my position. Critical thinking there was definitely discouraged.

"One of the most important things was that the director was a total narcissist. He needed his ego stroked all day long. He needed everybody to be hanging onto his every word and know that he was brilliant. 'Oh, brilliant, wonderful, wonderful! Please talk to us more, man with two master's degrees.'

"I learned after I left that the director used to work with a missions agency that he broke away from so as to start the one I joined. He had been restrained by that agency and started a new one so that he could implement his own ideas.

"I also learned some time after I left that the organization no longer existed. It had crumbled apart because the money manager was embezzling funds from it. The director had known about that but refused to believe the manager would do that kind of thing. Plus, the director himself had been having affairs with multiple women, one of whom worked at the organization. Later, his wife divorced him and got custody of their son."

Suspicious

The whole experience left Claudia with suspicion. "I became suspicious of churches after I left. I have trouble trusting people in church spaces now. I am alert for narcissism. If I see someone with narcissistic traits, I run for the hills.

"I find myself shadow boxing a lot, such as when someone says, 'Oh, there's this wonderful charity, or this wonderful NGO, or this wonderful pastor,' or when someone says that some religious organization is going to transform the world.

"I listen to my intuition now, because when I was with the cult, my intuition told me something was wrong. I could have rationalized away everything the organization did, but in the end I listened to my intuition, because it was right.

"It is so easy to make transformation of the world about your own ego, especially for covert narcissists. They are sneaky, because they say that they are going to die for a grand vision, whereas in reality they are shallow and insincere. I can sometimes see things like that in flashes, when someone, just for a moment, lets down their guard."

"Matthew": Becoming Disillusioned with Teaching

> "In place of ideas and curiosity and the beautiful blooming of young people discovering life, I felt as though I was dying in front of them."

Matthew decided to become a teacher some years after he graduated from college. He earned a master's degree in teaching and started teaching, both with a great deal of enthusiasm and devotion. But when the pandemic hit in 2020, things changed so much that he could not continue. He was in his early thirties when we talked.

Becoming a Teacher

Matthew's road to teaching began four or five years after he finished college. "I had studied writing when I was in college, but didn't know what I wanted to do with it. I worked as a barista for a while. Then I spent several years doing various marketing jobs. I did copywriting, I wrote blog posts for businesses, and for a time I was a brand manager.

"After spending a few years in the world of marketing, I got jaded with it. I didn't believe that more things needed to be sold. So I left marketing and started working at a bookstore.

"When I was in college, one of my professors had us read Marilynne Robinson's novel, *Gilead*. I wasn't ready for it at the time, but when I read it again after college, I fell in love with it. Then when a friend who also worked at the bookstore told me about Robinson's new collection of essays, *What Are We Doing Here?: Essays,* I read it too.

"That book expresses Robinson's frustration with the way the humanities were treated by government institutions and businesses, even by the educational system itself. She advocated for the beauty of reading and writing, and wrote eloquently about deeply human things.

"I resonated with what she said and decided I wanted to enter into the struggle to help the humanities find a home in the twenty-first century. I wanted to fight their constant exclusion from our day-to-day lives. So I applied for a master's degree in teaching and left my job at the bookstore."

On Fire for Teaching

Matthew became passionate for teaching. "I took my studies seriously. We students did student teaching at the same time we were doing classwork, and I went to the classes I was teaching with a lot of enthusiasm. I loved it all.

"I especially loved seeing young people engage seriously with books and poetry, then write seriously. I was teaching freshmen. I don't know whether I had some special group of kids, but they dove into everything all the way. It was a beautiful time.

"When I finished the program, which was two summers in addition to an academic year, I worked as a substitute teacher, beginning January, 2020. I was doing that when the pandemic hit."

The Pandemic

Matthew noticed an immediate difference. "It was as though the students thought doing school from home via Zoom was a joke: 'We don't really have to do this stuff.' They phoned in their responses to the assignments. Their responses were breezy. The assignments were breezy too, because changing to at-home school happened so fast that we teachers didn't know what to have kids do.

"I got a full-time position, starting in the fall of 2020, at the same high school I had gone to. I taught the standard English class for sophomores and juniors, plus another class called Literacy Workshop. That class was for freshman students who were in need of more help to acclimate to high school English. It was something of a remedial class. A number of students in that class had been left behind or for one reason or another had gotten lost in the educational system.

"Often they were disinterested in school. They had given up on it, maybe because they felt that it had given up on them or that there was no place for them in the world of education. That meant that fewer than half of them were showing up to the Zoom classes.

"In my other classes, students showed up but often were doing something else. Actually, I didn't know what they were doing, because they didn't have their screens on. They were just black. It quickly became the norm for students to have their screens off. Usually only one or two students, sometimes even three, consistently had their screens on. That was nice, because I wasn't just talking to myself. Someone was nodding their head and engaging with the class.

"Some teachers tried to put in a policy that you had to have your screen on during class. But a case was made that requiring students to have screens on was not equitable, because it might reveal a home life that students were not eager to reveal. That was seen as an invasion of privacy. So we teachers had to stop requiring students to have their screens on.

"The outcome was that students could get away with doing anything during Zoom sessions, because there was no way of knowing who had a legitimate reason not to have their screen on and who didn't. Even asking the question was seen as insensitive."

Complications

The matter of the screens was the beginning of Matthew's disillusionment with the American educational system. "What online teaching introduced was a complete and utter lack of expectations for students. The norm became that if students handed something in, they would pass the class. Prior to the pandemic, of course, that was not the case.

"There were also arguments about whether a grade was an equitable way of measuring the work students did. Was it taking into account all the things in students' lives that they brought to the work up to the moment they handed in an assignment? If not, then basing grades solely on the quality of their work was not appropriate. Suddenly we teachers had to reduce our expectations for whether students even did an assignment.

"During the second semester of that first year of teaching, in the spring of 2021, we switched from a completely virtual system to a hybrid system.

In the virtual system, classes were held on Zoom. In the hybrid system, half of the students in a particular class were at school and the other half was at home. Every other day they switched places. Wednesday was an off day.

"To do classes this way, we had a camera in the classroom that streamed to the students who were at home. The idea was that students who were at home would be listening in and engaging with the class that was happening in person.

"It was, however, nearly impossible to teach both to an audience you could see and to an audience you could not see. I think a lot of people believe that teaching is like giving a TED talk or something. I just get up there and do my thing, and you'd get the same result no matter whether you're in person or at home.

"But anyone who has taught knows that teaching is physical, that is, happens in a space. The students who were at home ended up not doing anything. They told me as much: 'It was a hybrid day. I had my computer on but was doing something else.' I replied that I still expected them to do something. But doing class online was such a miserable experience for them that they didn't care.

"The students were totally fine telling me they weren't doing anything while at home because they knew, and I knew, that the at-home in-person system wasn't working. It was, in fact, not working to such an extent that participating in it could make things worse for them. Why submit yourself to such an awful online experience more than you had to?

"In reality, students were getting only two days of being taught during the week, the days that they had to show up in person. And, again, there was an incredible reduction in what we teachers could hold students accountable for. It was all a mess."

In-Person Teaching

The next school year, 2021–2022, was completely in-person. "I was looking forward to it a great deal. All the problems we had earlier were going to go away because students would be embodied again. They would no longer be able to check out.

"For the first week or two, students seemed to have the same sentiment. Unfortunately, that changed. A full year of virtual and hybrid learning, and a lot of home time, along with the reduction in expectations, had changed the psychology of the students. That change was so dramatic that

"MATTHEW": BECOMING DISILLUSIONED WITH TEACHING

even though we were back in person, things were never going to be the way they had been before.

"Imagine being a freshman the year school became virtual. You would have missed getting a pep rally when you first came to school plus all the things that induct you into the high school environment—you would have to know where your locker is, learn where your classes are, adapt to being surrounded by humans in varying stages of puberty. There was the whole psychology of entering into high school you would have missed. And when you became a sophomore after spending a year at home, you would still be an eighth grader psychologically.

"We teachers thought, 'Surely, those freshmen would get the classic high school experience when they did school in person as sophomores.' But no. The whole system had become off kilter. As sophomores, they had lost crucial periods of interaction. And they had gotten something entirely different during the virtual year.

"What they had gotten was a lack of structure, a lack of expectations, plus dramatically increased amounts of time which they had spent on their phones and computers connecting with the rest of humanity. They had been shaped by the internet in that year of lockdown in ways no students had ever been shaped before. What they went through was huge.

"I wanted to teach my students books and writing when they came back to school. I wanted to read their writing. I wanted to read about what students were interested in and how they expressed themselves. But it was very rare that I got an earnest effort from a student.

"My response to their learning loss required a high level of interpersonal connection. But I had 140 students per semester. I was trying to teach them all how to read and write, which are intensive and demanding things to learn how to do. I would be lucky if I could have the required connection with fifteen students total.

"With 140 students, they were turning into data pieces. I'd look at the grades I was giving them and hope I could remember what I had experienced when reading their assignments. But I couldn't hold all that information in my head.

"In addition, I had to respond to the trauma students had experienced from the incredible amount of societal upheaval that had occurred during the lockdown.

"I was swamped."

A Tussle With the School Administration

"During that first in-person school year, 2021–2022," Will said, "the administration of the school I was teaching at told us English teachers, without consulting the English Department, that we could no longer tell a whole class to read *Of Mice and Men* by John Steinbeck. This was because it has sixteen instances of the n-word in it. The administration was worried about the impact the book would have on our Black students, who were already struggling.

"We English teachers got upset about this. No matter the rationale, it was a book ban. The administration told us that the new policy was not a book ban. We could still have the book in the school library, and students could opt to read it if they wanted to. But it couldn't be taught. In the mind of an English teacher, though, all literature can be taught, no matter how horrific it is.

"We fought against the policy. We had a big meeting, but the administration didn't listen to us. We provided sophisticated arguments why they shouldn't be able to make the policy without consulting us. They didn't care. When that became evident, I realized the administration did not see education the way I did.

"They thought of Steinbeck's *Of Mice and Men* as 'problematic.' In reality, it poses a difficult problem that would have been very interesting to suss out with students. It says a lot of very important things about race and poverty and class and class warfare. It uses the n-word in ways that the n-word was used at the time the book was written, in 1937. What do we do with all this? I wanted to engage students with that challenge. This is what I regarded as the whole duty of teaching.

"I think the school administration was scared of complexity—and also scared of making mistakes, scared of doing something that could invite negative public scrutiny.

"I was ashamed of them, because I saw what they did as complete and utter cowardice. I realized that they would not protect me if I were to make a mistake in my classroom, a mistake made in an effort to have hard conversations. Hard conversations would inevitably end in a mess. You can't avoid a mess in the classroom. That's part of learning. Teachers are going to make mistakes. Students are going to make mistakes. At some point, we all will unintentionally hurt each other.

"MATTHEW": BECOMING DISILLUSIONED WITH TEACHING

"It is like any relationship or anything else we do. It can't all be beauty and truth and goodness. Sometimes in the pursuit of these, we step on our own feet.

"I would have liked to know that my administration understood that, understood that we were all a bunch of humans and that we were doing our darnedest and that we had to talk about the hard stuff. We had to talk about it even if we didn't know how to talk about it. We had to give it our best shot. But the administration didn't want us teachers to have those conversations.

"The same thing was occurring in the United States. People didn't know how to have conversations about hard things. You were only allowed to present your stance, and then someone else presented their stance. And then you said, 'You stupid bigot. I don't like that, and I'm not going to listen to you.' Then the conversation stopped.

"It became scary knowing that my administration would not support me in having hard conversations. This and the other stresses of having to figure out how to care for students individually when I had so many and trying to figure out how to reinvigorate the educational system so as to revitalize the love of learning among young people who had become jaded and did not believe they needed to know a lot of what I was teaching, on top of the societal pressures not to have the conversations or not to have them in a way that was so clean as not to be conversations at all—all of these made it so that I had to get out. Teaching in person became too frustrating."

Leaving

"I think if I was as brave as I wanted to be," Will declared, "I would have stayed and fought to the bitter end. But for my own well being, I had to leave. I was in a terrible, hopeless place. I literally could not function outside of teaching. I had only enough energy to get myself into the classroom to do what I needed to do. And after school, I collapsed. I sank into a bitter, ugly darkness.

"I couldn't have a life. It was getting worse as the year progressed. During that year, I told myself that if I ever felt that hopeless again, I would leave. And I wouldn't regret it.

"In December of the following school year, 2022–2023, I again felt a terrible hopelessness. I was not able to look forward to the rest of my life. I knew that this was impacting my presence in the classroom. I could feel that the ugly bitterness inside me was bleeding out into the space I loved so much.

In place of ideas and curiosity and the beautiful blooming of young people discovering life, I felt as though I was dying in front of them.

"At the end of that school year, I didn't sign my contract for the following year. I let my coworkers know in January that I would be leaving so that they would have enough time to hire someone to replace me.

"Even though I had to leave, it was a hard decision to make. I felt a lot like I was fighting a war and that I was leaving my fellow troops in the lurch. I was saying to them, 'Sorry. I'm out.' That was a heartbreaking thing to do.

"But if I had stayed, I would not have known who I was anymore. I think I would have become a husk of a human.

"When I went into teaching, I thought I was going to keep teaching until retirement. Now I don't know where I'm going.

"I think about getting back into teaching all the time. I wonder whether I would have the strength to do it the way I know it needs to be done, no matter the cost. I don't know whether I would.

"Still, books and words, reading and writing, are the loves of my life."

Bibliography

Burma Link. "Refugee Camps." https://www.burmalink.org/background/thailand-burma-border/displaced-in-thailand/refugee-camps/.

Burton, Robert A. *On Being Certain: Believing You Are Right Even When You're Not* (New York: St. Martin's Griffin, 2009). https://www.rburton.com/_i_on_being_certain_i___believing_you_are_right_even_when_you_re_not_63166.htm#:.

Centers for Disease Control National Center for Health Statistics. Cerebrovascular Disease or Stroke. https://www.cdc.gov/nchs/fastats/stroke.htm.

Cleveland Clinic. "Kyphoplasty is a minimally invasive procedure to treat compression fractures in your spine." Kyphoplasty. https://my.clevelandclinic.org/health/procedures/kyphoplasty.

———. "Stockholm syndrome." https://my.clevelandclinic.org/health/diseases/22387-stockholm-syndrome.

Du Bois, W. E. B. *The Souls of Black Folk*. New York: Dover, 1994. First published by A. C. McClurg and Co., Chicago, in 1903.

Hanna, Jason, and Tina Burnside. "Sandra Bland recorded her own arrest in 2015. The video was just published." CNN, May 8, 2019. https://www.cnn.com/2019/05/07/us/sandra-bland-cell-phone-video/index.html.

Kerrigan, John J. "Ronald Fisher, sentenced October 4, 1966, for the killing of a 15-year old girl in Springfield." "11 in N.E. Death Rows But None Executed Since 1960." The North Adams Transcript, 12/04/1967. https://www.newspapers.com/article/the-north-adams-transcript-john-j-kerrig/6542393/.

"Massachusetts Correctional Institution—Cedar Junction." https://en.wikipedia.org/wiki/Massachusetts_Correctional_Institution_%E2%80%93_Cedar_Junction.

Mayo Clinic. "Trigeminal Neuralgia: Symptoms and Causes." https://www.mayoclinic.org/diseases-conditions/trigeminal-neuralgia/symptoms-causes/syc-20353344#.

Moeder, Nicole. "Number of trans homicides doubled over 4 years, with gun killings fueling increase: Advocates." abcNews, October 12, 2022. https://abcnews.go.com/US/homicide-rate-trans-people-doubled-gun-killings-fueling/story?id=91348274.

National Coalition Against Domestic Violence (NCADV). "Why Do Victims Stay?" https://ncadv.org/why-do-victims-stay.

BIBLIOGRAPHY

National Drug Intelligence Center. "OxyContin Diversion and Abuse." January, 2001. https://www.justice.gov/archive/ndic/pubs/651/abuse.htm.

National Institute of Health. National Library of Medicine. "Anosognosia." https://www.ncbi.nlm.nih.gov/books/NBK513361/.

National Institute of Mental Health. Mental Health Information. "Attention-Deficit/Hyperactivity Disorder." https://www.nimh.nih.gov/health/topics/attention-deficit-hyperactivity-disorder-adhd.

National Institute of Neurological Disorders and Stoke (NINDS). "Tissue Plasminogen Activator for Acute Ischemic Stroke." https://www.ninds.nih.gov/about-ninds/what-we-do/impact/ninds-contributions-approved-therapies/tissue-plasminogen-activator-acute-ischemic-stroke-alteplase-activaser.

National Public Radio, June 1, 2020. "To Be in a Rage, Almost All the Time." https://www.npr.org/2020/06/01/867153918/-to-be-in-a-rage-almost-all-the-time.

Respond: Seeking to End Domestic Violence. "Domestic Violence Facts & Stats." https://www.respondinc.org/dv-facts-stats/.

UCLA School of Law. Williams Institute, March 23, 2021. "Transgender people over four times more likely than cisgender people to be victims of violent crime." https://williamsinstitute.law.ucla.edu/press/ncvs-trans-press-release/.

Van der Kolk, Bessel. *The Body Keeps Score: Mind, Brain, and Body in the Healing of Trauma.* New York: Penguin, 2015.

Wikipedia. "Karenic Languages." https://en.wikipedia.org/wiki/Karenic_languages.

———. "Mae La Refugee Camp." https://en.wikipedia.org/wiki/Mae_La_refugee_camp.

———. "Umpiem Mai Refugee Camp." https://en.wikipedia.org/wiki/Umpiem_Mai_Refugee_Camp.

Zinnia Health. "How Much Does Heroin Cost? (The Street Prices)." September 14, 2023. https://zinniahealth.com/substance-use/heroin/costs.

www.ingramcontent.com/pod-product-compliance
Lightning Source LLC
Chambersburg PA
CBHW050138170426
43197CB00011B/1879